Social Media and Politics

Social Media and Politics

A New Way to Participate in the Political Process

Volume 2
Redefining Politics: How Are Social Media
Changing the Political Game?

Glenn W. Richardson Jr., Editor

An Imprint of ABC-CLIO, LLC
Santa Barbara, California • Denver, Colorado

Library of Congress Cataloging-in-Publication Data

Names: Richardson, Glenn W., editor.
Title: Social media and politics : a new way to participate in the political process / Glenn W. Richardson Jr., editor.
Description: Santa Barbara, California : Praeger, 2017. | Includes bibliographical references and index.
Identifiers: LCCN 2016016780 (print) | LCCN 2016029540 (ebook) | ISBN 9781440839504 (hardback) | ISBN 9781440846540 (v. 1) | ISBN 9781440846557 (v. 2) | ISBN 9781440839511 (ebook)
Subjects: LCSH: Communication in politics—Technological innovations—United States. | Political participation—Technological innovations—United States. | Social media—Political aspects—United States. | Internet in political campaigns—United States. | Online social networks—Political aspects—United States. | Communication in politics—Technological innovations. | Political participation—Technological innovations. | Social media—Political aspects. | Internet in political campaigns. | Online social networks—Political aspects.
Classification: LCC JA85.2.U6 S67 2016 (print) | LCC JA85.2.U6 (ebook) | DDC 320.97301/4—dc23
LC record available at https://lccn.loc.gov/2016016780

ISBN: 978–1–4408–3950–4 (Set)
ISBN: 978–1–4408–4654–0 (Volume 1)
ISBN: 978–1–4408–4655–7 (Volume 2)
EISBN: 978–1–4408–3951–1

21 20 19 18 17   1 2 3 4 5

This book is also available as an eBook.

Praeger
An Imprint of ABC-CLIO, LLC

ABC-CLIO, LLC
130 Cremona Drive, P.O. Box 1911
Santa Barbara, California 93116-1911
www.abc-clio.com

This book is printed on acid-free paper (∞)

Manufactured in the United States of America

Contents

Introduction

The rise of social media has fundamentally altered political communication and the research programs of scholars who study it. This set offers readers a window into a wide range of academic studies of social media and politics that reflect this exciting moment.

Volume 1 is focused on candidates' and campaigns' use of social media and how that affects voters. The chapters in this volume address the use of social media in the United States and elsewhere, with a particular emphasis on U.S. campaigns for the House, Senate, and presidency. The contributing scholars focus on questions such as how information flows differ across social media and traditional media, how information flows to individuals, gender differences in Twitter-style among candidates, the role of social media in political polarization, and what campaigns become as social media becomes the infrastructure of political communication.

Volume 2 extends beyond the realm of strictly electoral politics to explore how social movements and others have engaged social media. Contributors explore how groups from Greenpeace to the Tea Party as well as more diverse social movements such as feminism and resistance journalism have flourished in an age of social media. Among the key issues raised are important questions of power, authenticity, and identity.

Almost every chapter in the set was strengthened by a double-blind peer-review process. Almost all of the contributors agreed to participate as reviewers, and their dedication to this task is evident in the quality of the chapters included. Additionally, a handful of additional reviewers were involved, with both Andi McClanahan and Tom Shevory serving as editorial advisors to the set.

The editor would also like to thank Alicia Merritt, Anthony Chiffolo, Barbara Patterson, Steve Catalano, and the folks at ABC-CLIO for the patient and generous assistance with this project.

Chapter 1

Structures of Dissent: Social Media, Resistance Journalism, and the Mobilization of Poverty Activism

Cindy S. Vincent and Sara Straub

5 generations of Poor/indigenous women & children colonized, criminalized displaced, removed & gentriFUKed in Amerikkka ends here wit a Poor People-led Solution we call Homefulness -cuz change wont come from a savior -a pimp or an institution -Change will only come from a poor peo[p]le led solution

— #2homefulnessinBlackAugust
(Tiny, POOR Magazine)

This status update was posted on the Facebook page of POOR Magazine's[1] director, Tiny Lisa Gray-Garcia, the day after POOR Magazine launched their Homefulness project in Oakland, California. The post, while just a snapshot of a moment in time, is representative of a much larger struggle occurring in the Bay Area and across the United States. Millions of people in the United States struggle with financial need and homelessness;[2] however, many dominant media outlets[3] often ignore the lived experiences of those living in extreme poverty or frame them in

denigrating stereotypes.[4] This [mis]representation evokes poverty myths
and reinforces dominant ideologies about what it means to live in poverty,
in turn, reinforcing and worsening social stratification. One way in which
individuals and communities living in poverty and homelessness have
responded to the dissemination and internalization of this representation
is through the creation of their own media such as newspapers, radio stations, blogs, and social media. This chapter examines the "resistance journalism" of people living in poverty and homelessness. Resistance
journalism is a type of citizen journalism that can be used to create a platform for marginalized voices to expose and dissent structures of oppression, disseminate experiential knowledges of poverty, and mobilize
activism as a way to "invert the 'hierarchy of access' "[5] and subvert the
political power structure of dominant narratives. This chapter examines
the use of social media as a citizen journalism platform to accomplish
these goals by media organizations engaged in the creation of media by
people in poverty and homelessness.

This study seeks to answer the question of how social media platforms
create a space for dissension, allowing the negotiation of political power
and cultivating a richer understanding of the power and potential of
digital media technologies for democratization and an engaged citizenry.
Dissent is a necessary constructive part of the democratic process. Scholars have long argued that societies should strive for consensus in order
to achieve democracy,[6] but this chapter argues that consensus should not
be viewed as an end goal and dissent should not be taken as a means to
an end. Instead, the two form a dynamic symbiotic relationship in which,
even when consensus is reached, a democratic people should still examine its results for contradictions and question whether that consensus
was reached at the expense of someone else's freedom. As Kendall
Phillips[7] points out, "Even when viewed as productive (i.e., heuristic or
corrective), dissent is relegated to a secondary position behind the push
toward consensus." However, dissent is an integral part of this equation,
constantly searching for contradictions, eternally questioning the status
quo. This study contributes to our knowledge of dissent, specifically as a
strategy of resistance journalism that creates possibilities for negotiating
political power between dominant narratives and subaltern counterhege-
monic voices.

Social media are able to provide a platform for spaces of dissension,
where marginalized perspectives can be expressed and seen as authentic
representations of experiential poverty knowledge. The literature for
this study looks at the research surrounding dissent, citizen journalism,
and social media activism to provide a framework with which to better
understand social media structures of dissent. To examine this phenomenon, this study conducts a dialogic analysis of social media posts

(Facebook, Twitter, YouTube) by media organizations focused on the dissemination of poverty perspectives. The findings for this study reveal that social media can be used to galvanize dissent and collectively mobilize around the social construction of poverty and what it means to live in poverty in contemporary U.S. society.

THE CITIZEN AS JOURNALIST

To examine the dissemination of experiential poverty knowledge, we focus on the use of citizen journalism specifically as a communicative strategy that empowers everyday citizens to construct and distribute their unique voices and perspectives. Citizen journalism is a way for marginalized groups to raise awareness on poverty issues and express dissent through the more distinct form of resistance journalism. Citizen journalism grew in popularity in the early to mid-1990s, as an opportunity to redesign the historical gatekeeper role of the mass media. Everyday citizens could engage in agenda setting and news dissemination on topics that were important to them and their communities. In this era, citizens seized the opportunity to "invert the 'hierarchy of access' to the news by explicitly foregrounding the viewpoints of . . . citizens whose visibility in the mainstream media tend to be obscured by the presence of elite groups and individuals."[8] Through their presence and action, citizen journalists question established media roles of journalists and raise publicity for everyday citizens as alternative experts and creators of reality.

Since its emergence, citizen journalism as a form of journalism has accelerated not only in quantity but also in credibility, as it has enticed amateur and professional journalists to engage. As Chris Greer and Eugene McLaughlin point out, citizen journalists are not inherently credible news sources the way traditional journalists are, but gain credibility "because of where they are and what they have."[9] Their research found that "when citizen journalism challenges the 'official truth,' as portrayed by those powerful institutional sources who have traditionally maintained a relatively uncontested position at the top of the 'hierarchy of credibility', that it becomes most potent as a news resource."[10] In addition to an increased level of perceived credibility, citizen journalists are also able to provide more diverse content and perspectives than corporate mainstream media typically provide. The organizations and individuals examined in this study were chosen because they use citizen journalism as a way to disseminate the knowledge and perspective of people living in homelessness and poverty to reconstruct media access points and subvert political power structures, as will be shown in the analysis section.

DISSENT AS RESPONSE

To frame the role of dissent in facilitating the possibilities for democratic engagement and social change, this literature review looks at how dissent has been defined and applied by communication scholars. According to Phillips,[11] communication scholars have placed too much emphasis on the role of communication to resolve dissent and move toward consensus. He argues that dissent is "the site of struggle between, and transformation of, multiple consensual communities. Ignoring these multiplicities and artificially imposing a rationality on these transformations does little to enable critical understanding or practical resistance."[12] Robert Ivie extends this argument by stating, "The problem is that dissent conceptualized as either oppositional or subservient to consensus does not allow a democratically adequate accounting for difference and diversity."[13] Erik Doxtader[14] places emphasis on the potentially symbiotic relationship of dissent and consensus to be interdependent of one another in a way that bridges difference and brings diversity to the forefront. Another function of dissent is that it makes space for democratic revision by allowing alternative perspectives. According to Ivie, "It is a minority voice raised in a rhetorical act of limited nonconformity.... It is a transgression that aims to destabilize a prevailing mindset more or less to allow for some degree of revision sooner or later."[15]

When dissent is expressed, it uses the discursive rules of the dominant culture to assert arguments seen as logical and to point out the inconsistencies and arbitrariness of those rules. By speaking in accordance with the dominant discursive rules, dissenters are forced to speak within the "oppressor's language" to hold the dominant culture accountable, while being viewed as credible and legitimate arguments of representation. When looking at the power of dissent and protest together (i.e., rhetorical and physical acts of resistance), we find the possibility for both to intentionally disrupt social norms and discursive formations and be adversarial to "unmask divisions of interest and forcefully challenge structural inequalities."[16] With these definitions and conceptualizations in mind, this study views dissent as an opportunity for positive democratic social change that relies on the power of contestation and contradiction to identify disjunctures in the dominant culture where systemic oppression can be challenged.

SOCIAL MEDIA AND ACTIVISM

The last section of this literature review looks at the scholarship on social media and activism to explore the ways in which people are using social media to mobilize activism and engage citizens. While some proponents hail digital media as the savior of contemporary activism,[17] others warn against so much enthusiasm around digital technologies.[18] Critics of digital media disregard the arguments of moderates, who state that digital media are but one tool/component/facet of contemporary activism, playing a role along with agents, resources, and events that make social change happen. Due to the inherent difference in the nature of historical activism when compared to contemporary forms of activism that use digital technologies, we should not hold contemporary activism to a paradigmatic standard of what "real" activism looks and feels like. This study will navigate the aperture between these two extremes and look at the role of social media as communicative channels for marginalized groups to mobilize participation.

Sandra González-Bailón[19] has argued that digital technologies increase the effectiveness of social movements by providing structural support via social networks that allow people to collectively coordinate actions and disseminate specified messages directly to target audiences with the possibility of reaching and involving more people. Her research has found that online networks assist in the self-organization of individuals through the provisions of and reliance on the connectivity of the network. She is quick to point out, however, that online networks use the same mechanisms for effective communication as offline networks, they are just able to do so more quickly and reach larger audiences. Sebastián Valenzuela's research argues that social media can be useful as a way for users to gather mobilizing information, based on Lemert's categories of mobilizing information: "(a) identificational (names and contact information that people or groups of citizens need to know to engage in political action), (b) locational (time and place of a political or protest activity), and (c) tactical (explicit and implicit instructions for how citizens can get involved)."[20] He asserts that in comparison to other types of media, like mainstream media whose ideological focus is on "neutrality," social media "are free from norms of objectivity and were built around personal connections."[21] The analysis section of this chapter looks at how social media are used by groups in poverty whose messages dissent dominant narratives and how their narrative frame may impact their ability to mobilize users around their perspectives on poverty issues.

DIALOGIC ANALYSIS OF SOCIAL MEDIA

This study uses dialogic analysis to examine the ways in which marginalized groups negotiate power and create contradictions within hegemonic discourses of oppression. Dialogic analysis stems from Bakhtin's theory of dialogism and looks at the interplay of social meanings and semiotic contexts to better understand the relations between people in communication. In this regard, this study specifically looks at the power relations that are constructed and negotiated between dominant narratives and the groups and individuals that are the primary subjects of those discourses. Dialogic analysis argues that contention dwells within dominant genres, which in turn leads to the emergence of new rhetorical genres through resistance. According to Marc Steinberg, "As challengers seek to transform existing meanings in discursive practices to articulate senses of injustice, make claims, and establish alternative visions, they also remain bounded by the field and the genres within which they struggle."[22] In this way, dialogic analysis focuses on "the ways in which challengers seek to delegitimate hegemonic genres within a field while appropriating pieces to inflect it with their own subversive meanings."[23]

To examine the ways in which this is done by poverty organizations, we analyzed posts that appeared on Facebook, Twitter, and YouTube. Posts consisted of text, photographs, videos, and hyperlinks to external websites. The analysis also included website pages and articles created by the organizations and linked to their social media accounts. Facebook, Twitter, and YouTube were chosen because of the intersection between the current popularity of the sites[24] and the availability of the organizations on a popular social media platform (although some YouTube accounts had not been posted to in over two years). Posts were categorized under three primary themes for this study: (1) dissent toward dominant narratives ("dissent"), (2) the dissemination of experiential knowledges of poverty ("dissemination"), and (3) calls to action as expressions of mobilization ("mobilization"). The analysis included axial coding and a constant comparison of code categories, which resulted in the final development of 6 subthemes under dissent, 7 subthemes under dissemination, and 10 subthemes under mobilization, where themes either originated from the literature or organically stemmed from the data. Of the 478 total posts analyzed, only 13 posts were determined to fall outside the scope of this study as being irrelevant. To account for intercoder agreement, 10 percent of the data were coded collaboratively by two coders. As codes were developed and data were analyzed, coders created a conscious and collaborative coding process to more closely align individual perspectives.

The organizations chosen for this analysis met the following criteria: (1) community media organizations whose primary mission focused on the creation of media by community members, (2) organizations that primarily focused on local or regional issues of poverty, and (3) organizations where all media were created by people living in poverty and homelessness, not an advocate on their behalf.[25] To examine an array of organizations across the country, at least one community media organization was chosen per continental geographic region based on the U.S. Census's construction of geographic areas.[26] Organization target audiences were determined to be people living in poverty or homelessness or allies/advocates of people living in poverty or homelessness.[27] The organizations analyzed that fit these criteria were Making Connections News (Appalachia), Media Mobilizing Project (Philadelphia), Picture the Homeless (New York City), POOR Magazine (San Francisco), and Project South (southern United States).

The data collection time frame was August 9–September 9, 2014. This time frame was chosen to coincide with larger national conversations addressing inequality, race, and class that were occurring at the time as a result of the murder of a young African American male in Ferguson, Missouri, and the rising of the Black Lives Matter social movement that may have made issues of poverty more prevalent to a larger target audience. The following section discusses the findings for this analysis.

NEGOTIATING POLITICAL POWER

This section discusses the findings of the analysis and the ways in which poverty media organizations used social media to negotiate political power via dissenting structures of oppression, disseminating experiential knowledges of poverty, and mobilizing activism.

Dissent

The findings for this study showed that poverty media organizations expressed dissent in a number of ways to engage with dominant discourses. Posts identified as adversarial—that is, hostile or confrontational—were written in a way to challenge "the official truth" of the issue at hand.[28] For example, Media Mobilizing Project confronted the idea of the American Dream and the real impact of minimum wage on people living in poverty in their YouTube video titled, "Where's My American Dream? I Need $15 an Hour Now." In this video, a mother in poverty speaks through tears at a protest in Philadelphia and describes how increasing the minimum wage to $15 per hour would help end her dependency on Temporary Assistance for Needy Families (TANF).

> I have several degrees but I can't find a job in my field making good money so I have to downgrade . . . it's not fair that I can't get a living wage to support my children. I'm working 40-something hours a week but I'm still on public assistance. I'm working 40-something hours a week and I'm still in a bad neighborhood. I'm working 40 hours a week and I still can't get what's mine. It's my right as an American, as a human, to be free and to live free, and I can't live free without $15 an hour.

Voices like hers and media like this, shared through social media platforms, help poverty media organizations confront "official truths" like

the *Washington Post*'s article on why raising the minimum wage to
$15 per hour would be negative for society.[29]

In confronting these official truths, this form of dissent provides a platform for alternative perspectives to make space for democratic revision.[30]
According to Ivie,[31] minority voices provide an alternative perspective
that aims to destabilize the status quo to allow for the creation of revision.
The dissemination of the "minority voice" or alternative perspective was
seen throughout social media posts as a way to challenge dominant discourses and propagate poverty perspectives:

> Homeless men pen op-ed piece: law enforcement is not the solution
> to homelessness! @NYDailyNews ... http://www.nydailynews.com/
> new-york/stop-treating-homeless-criminals-article-1.1905517 ...
> (Picture the Homeless)

In this example, the dissenter confronts the current trend in the criminalization of homelessness through the perspective of a man living in homelessness. His perspective adds an element of humanity to the debate to
counterbalance the absence of this voice in mainstream media depictions.
Through the dissemination of alternative perspectives, dissenters rupture
the status quo of mainstream media by highlighting these points of difference as instances of contradiction within the dominant discourse.

In turn, these points of difference disrupt social norms by breaking
rules of social conformity to emphasize incoherencies within the larger
discursive formation. As one of the media organizations located most
closely to the protests occurring in Ferguson at the time (both geopoliti-
cally and geographically), Project South used social media as a tool to rhetorically disrupt social norms by asking target audiences to directly
address the element of race in their policy considerations:

> During the Unite to Fight-On the Road to SMA4 road trip we learned
> about the FADE Coalition's policy recommendations! Check this out
> to see their response to the Durham City Manager's Report:
> "You cannot have a race neutral solution to a race-based problem."
> #Unite2Fight #OntheRoad #SMA4 #OrganizetheSouth

In addition, social media posts that supplemented offline activities, such
as protests, amplified the power of dissent to intentionally disrupt social
norms by directly targeting blatant structural inequalities, both in class
and race divisions. Social media platforms were used not only as a way
to rhetorically confront social conformity through tactical mobilizing
information but also as a way to supplement acts of activism to promote
their activities and convey physical acts of dissent within the public
sphere. This in turn created a digital representation of the intersection of

dissenters with the public and their adversaries. It brought the two realms together in a space of convergence that allowed target audiences to see what the organization's act of dissent looked like offline as well as provided target audiences a space to engage, reflect, or comment on the act online. According to Ivie,[32] this point of intersection is important as a way to avoid sheer antagonism and alienation and afford dissenters the opportunity to articulate linkages and commonalities between supporters and adversaries.

Poverty media organizations used dissent on social media as a way to revise the dominant discourse. According to John Lucaites and Celeste Condit, "To argue for change therefore requires a rhetor to speak against the dominant ideology, but from within its own vocabulary."[33] Of the five poverty media organizations analyzed for this study, one stood out from the rest in an active effort to appropriate, negotiate, and revise dominant discourse:

> While the violent War On Poor, Black & Brown peoples continue with the state-sponsored militia who call themselves Po'Lice, protecting property and "commerce" like it was gold- the GentriFUKation Wars increase on our communities of color - to make room for more 20-something, child-less, (eye-less) tech workers who march into our rooted communities of color like they have evey [sp] right to displace, destroy & remove anything in their wake, becuz they know that the same killer Po'Lice who murdered #MikeBrown & #EricGarner & so many more protect & serve them Always - pls come out tomorro, Wed, aug 20th @ 12:00p to 26th & treat in the GentriFUKed mission dist to stand up against more of these land-stealers and real estate snakkkes. (Tiny, POOR Magazine)

Within the context of race and class struggles in contemporary U.S. society, POOR Magazine and its director, Tiny, walk the fine line between antagonism and dissent to "denature and trouble repressive political orthodoxies."[34] In this example, we see a recalcitrant revision of dominant terms associated with oppression and racial/class struggle like *GentriFU-Kation* (in reference to the negative effects of gentrification and the displacement of low-income residents), *Po'Lice* (as a reference to police as an infestation in low-income communities), and *Amerikkka* (in reference to the systemic and historical racism prevalent throughout the United States). These terms are appropriated in an antagonistic fashion to unsettle target audiences who may be complacent in the roles of these institutions throughout society.

While this adversarial form of dissent could be seen by some scholars as potentially alienating,[35] this type of rhetorical invention facilitates the ability for dissenters to explore the range of possibilities to use oppositional language in a way that galvanizes potentially apathetic audiences and creates a sense of solidarity with other marginalized groups. For example, Tiny shared the video "Cops Abuse Homeless Man on Irving Street at 20th, San Francisco" with the caption:

> This is the way the police abuse the homeless in the City of St. Francis. I can't even imagine how much worse this will get now that we, despite the sound and rational arguments not to from reputable sources, implement Laura's Law. (And thanks so much David Campos for selling us out on this! frown emoticon)

The caption serves to provide context for viewers on the current state of homeless laws and policies in San Francisco; however, it is the video that works to galvanize audiences. Watching an incoherent man, who is presumed to be homeless, face down on the ground with two police officers on top of him provides an audio–visual catalyst for homeless advocates to galvanize an apathetic audience. The presumption of an apathetic society is supported when we see passersby in the video continue on with their daily lives while the man yells and pleads. Shocking or emotional videos, photos, and descriptions like this help to create a rhetorical space for dissenters by jarring the perceptions of homelessness and counterbalancing mainstream media depictions.

Dissemination

Social media is an essential tool for social movements to raise awareness of issues and disseminate information to supporters. The spread of information for the organizations in this study served several purposes: real-time information, awareness of resources, and promotion. Greer and McLaughlin[36] argue that citizen journalism adds value to the media landscape through the provision of important information in real time. Posts like this one from Picture the Homeless

> 2 MINUTE ACTION ALERT! Call DHS Commissioner, demand justice for shelter residents: http://picturethehomeless.org/blog/node/479

disseminate messages in up-to-the-minute updates to engage followers in real time as well as bridge online and offline realms for collective action. The use of real-time information was primarily seen as organizations rallied to garner support and action from followers/friends to supplement offline actions. Organizations also disseminated information to raise awareness of resources they could provide that would help followers living in poverty and homelessness as a way to grow and extend their network. For example, Making Connections News posted this tweet to followers in rural Appalachia who may need economic assistance in establishing a business:

> Need help for your small business? Got a great idea for a new one? KY Innovation Network now has a Pikeville office ready to assist you. Learn more from this Making Connections News/WMMT story

The dissemination of information allowed these organizations to set the agenda of what news and information would be important to them and their communities. These organizations also disseminated information that served a promotional function of their movement. Many of the organizations used social media to update followers on statuses concerning outreach efforts that simultaneously worked to promote their cause, organization, and/or programs. For example, Picture the Homeless posted this tweet after a campaign to prevent shelter residents from eviction:

> We won! With your help! But little victories only make sense in a bigger war—for housing, for everyone. http://picturethehomeless.org/blog/node/480

This campaign consisted of a protest on-site at the shelter with residents, phone calls, and e-mails to the director of the Department for Homeless Services in New York City, and dissemination of information via social media. In these types of promotional examples, organizations used social media to showcase their activist abilities to create social change.

Organizations also used social media to disseminate the experiential knowledge and perspective of people living in homelessness and poverty and framed them as poverty experts in comparison to dominant authorities. Through this dissemination, these organizations countered mainstream media content, provided real perspectives, and increased the participatory engagement of historically disenfranchised people. For example, Picture the Homeless's YouTube video documents the eviction of shelter residents and provides space for the residents to distribute their side of the eviction story:

> I understand we're in our shelter situation. I understand, that, you know ... for them in society, we're the lowest people on the totem pole—I get it! I really do get it. And we need to work as a people to get up, and I get that too. But in the same token, it is where we are. We do have human rights that ... affect us, whether we're at the bottom or the top or the middle. You understand? We do have human rights. And the way that they're treating us right now is un-human.

This example shows that the motivating force behind these media organizations is not only to transpose the hierarchy of access and subvert media power structures by creating space for poverty experts, but that they themselves are the best experts on poverty via citizen journalism. These organizations used journalism strategies and techniques (e.g., research, interviews, media creation) to set their own news agenda and disseminate the perspectives of citizens marked by marginalization and invisibility in the mainstream media.[37] They constructed rhetorical space online for everyday citizens in poverty to be perceived as experts and creators of reality with the credibility primarily reserved for professional journalists. They gain credibility by "where they are and what they have."[38] This was seen when organizations reported from the front lines: not only as members of protests but also as citizen journalists reporting on the protests, interviewing protestors, and documenting protest activities. For example, PNN TV (POOR Magazine's "POOR News Network Television" YouTube channel) "rep-ported" and "sup-ported" protest activities at Ferguson solidarity marches across the Bay Area as a way to carve out digital space for poverty experts on the front lines of the movement.

Lastly, poverty media organizations utilized the effectiveness of social media platforms by sharing messages across platforms internally as well as sharing and distributing messages of networked alliances. As Goode argues, the "democratic appeal of citizen journalism . . . lies in the prospect of citizens themselves participating in the agenda-setting process. This occurs not merely through passive bespoke consumption . . . but through active engagement: blogging, re-posting, commenting, recommending, rating, tagging and the like."[39] Organizations internally shared messages across their social media platforms—for example, from Facebook to Twitter, YouTube to Facebook, or their own website across their social media accounts. In some cases this was seen to be redundant when organizations like POOR Magazine simply shared posts verbatim from one platform to the next or linked their social media platforms to repost identical content (e.g., Facebook to Twitter). However, in other cases, cross-platform sharing was seen to create additional spaces for discourse by propagating multimedia messages like YouTube videos across social media, in turn building a complex multimodal media environment. The sharing and distributing of networked alliance material will be discussed further in the next section as we address the ability to create solidarity on social media.

Mobilization

The final section of our analysis focuses on how organizations used social media to mobilize followers. Of all the social media techniques and strategies the organizations used to create a space for dissension, solidarity was found to be used the most. For organizations, solidarity took several forms, to include group connections, network support, and resource sharing with networked alliances. Similarly to Lazaro Bacallou-Pino's research findings on social media activism and group connection, this study also found that social media made it possible for individuals to connect through "the miracle of solidarity and the power of the many."[40] Online group connections worked to reinforce existing offline relationships through strong ties, in which individuals shared inside jokes/Internet memes, photos, or videos that referenced their existing relationship. An example of this can be seen in Tiny's post about one of the POOR Magazine members:

> After years of houselessness, poverty, more racism ablism & profiling & poverty pimping than any human shud endure but who walks softly always on mama earth - & one of the few peoples my po mama Dee ever trusted in her deepest broken heart, POOR Magazines Uncle Joe is now comfortably resting in his luxury SRO at Homefulness -never in danger of GentriFUKation or Homelessness again #poorpeopleledrevolution
>
> [—with Al and 8 others].

Group connection was seen to be an essential component to core group member allegiances because it served to reinforce existing relationships and maintain strong ties, while also promoting the organization and its mission.

In addition to group connection, social media also worked to create a network infrastructure of support for group members/followers as well as networked affiliates. As organizations shared content across media platforms between individuals and groups, they created a "variegated interactive network that connects the movement with itself, connects social actors with society at large, and acts on the entire realm of cultural manifestations."[41] For these organizations, network support worked to construct bridges for followers to traverse resources, information, and mobilization efforts to ensure they received the most recent information on the organization/movement. According to González-Bailón, "Online networks help people self-organize by activating a number of mechanisms that rely on the connectivity of the network, and on the properties of that structure."[42] Core group members sought support and participation from their social media network as they reached out to their followers to promote or solicit feedback on programs/projects/resources.

> Writing a Krip-Hop library resource section for the end of the Krip-Hop book entitled Black Blind Blues to Krip-Hip-Hop: Resource List of Books, CDs & DVDs ect. [sp] This is a growing list not complete!

One more time, does anybody have ideals on what I should title the book? Lisa Tiny Gray-Garcia I like yours. Can you tell me again your suggestion? I can see the finish line! (Leroy, POOR Magazine)

In addition to building bridges for internal members to the organization/ movement, social media was also used to share resources with networked affiliates across organizations/movements. Resource sharing created access to information and an open information flow for networked affiliates by sharing/distributing relevant messages, in turn creating solidarity across social movements. Hubert Janos Kiss and Alfonso Rosa-García[43] found the sharing of these types of resources to increase the probability of success for protests and revolutions. For example, Making Connections News shared the resources of their network and platform to retweet National Rural Assembly:

RT Rural Assembly @RuralAssembly
"Keep the politics out and focus on values." Building consensus and #ruralideas

In this example, Making Connections expands their network outreach by engaging with Rural Assembly as well as by disseminating relevant information for members of their network. Resource sharing was also used as a way to create a sense of solidarity with affiliates in similar organizations/movements with complementary goals or missions.

Organizations also used social media as a way to engage in collective coordination. To this end, social media provided platforms for organizations to collectively and flexibly organize actions, self-organize in a decentralized way, and disseminate mobilizing information that served to supplement offline actions and create a "global space of flow" instead of a fragmented space of places.[44] Collective and decentralized organization was seen as organizations distributing tactical information and calls to action online for followers to mobilize offline or take action offline in real time. For example, in solidarity with a fast-food worker's strike, Media Mobilizing Project posted tweets throughout the day intended to rally support and provide real-time information about the event:

"Get up, sit down! #Philly is a union town!"—fast food strikers #15AndAUnion #StrikeFastFood
   @mediamobilizing: "We can't survive on 7.25!" #15AndAUnion #StrikeFastFood #FightFor15 #Philly

Dozens blocking the street at broad and arch for #15andaunion #StrikeFastFood Social media posts served to not only distribute mobilizing information but also loosely provide the opportunity for followers to self-organize around existing collective actions. When analyzing the distinct types of mobilizing information that was distributed through social media, we found the majority were tactical (instructions for involvement/calls to action), followed by locational (time and place of event), and then identificational (organization/individual name and/or contact information). Many of the organizations posted original or shared content that addressed at least two pieces of mobilizing information. For example, in preparation for the fourth annual Southern Movement Assembly (SMA), Project South shared the SMA's Facebook post to distribute identificational, locational, and tactical information:

> We are so excited to be co-hosting #SMA4 and want to see your face in the place! Join us! #organizethesouth #unite2fight
>
> [shared Southern Movement Assembly's post] TODAY is the day!! The fourth Southern Movement Assembly in Atlanta this weekend will converge over 250 community members and organizers while escalating attacks continue on our communities. Project South and the Georgia Citizens Coalition on Hunger will anchor the space, and movement leaders from across the US South will facilitate Frontline Assemblies to collectively develop analysis, strategy, and plans of action! #unite2fight #organizethesouth #SMA4

Posts like these show social media's capability to connect communities and organizations across space and time to collectively organize and mobilize for social change. In this sense, "the space of the new social movements of the digital age is not a virtual space, it is a composite of the space of flows and of the space of places."[45] It provides opportunities for individuals and organizations to engage with one another and push an agenda forward that meets the needs of their communities and people.

CONCLUSION

In conclusion, this study has shown that social media can be used to galvanize dissent and collectively mobilize around the social negotiation and construction of poverty in contemporary U.S. society. Dissenters relied on videos of crying mothers on welfare; photos of poor youth of color who had been murdered; multimodal communications to intertwine images, videos, and words; and most of all words, feelings, and pathos to describe their pain, struggle, and experiential knowledge that make them the true experts of the movement. In the ultimate form of dissent, these organizations sought to confront and deconstruct the very idea of expert knowledge and credibility by asserting that their perspective, which stems from lived experiences and experiential knowledge, is the most accurate perspective of poverty and homelessness.

I aint gonna lie- im trying really hard to walk into posiitivity [sp], but
after my insanely unstable, poverty/eviction/ trauma -filled life im
terrified of not being afraid..#theviolenceofpovertyleavesdeep-
wounds. (Tiny, POOR Magazine)

Through resistance journalism, poverty media organizations negotiated
the social construction of poverty and what it means to live in poverty in
contemporary U.S. society by sharing the experiential knowledge of poverty experts and resistance journalists.

While the direct target audiences for each of these organizations may
be limited to self-selecting followers/friends, the impact is much larger
than that when we look at the whole picture. Social media supplement
offline activities. Each of these organizations used social media to show
supporters how they protest and dissent face to face with their adversaries and how they collectively gather through community meetings and
social gatherings. While these organizations' adversaries may not be following their digital conversation, they are very much engaged when that
conversation is taken offline to the streets and mobilized into action.
This digital conversation is about more than expressing dissent directly
at structures of oppression (although it was used for that too), but about
collectively gathering those who will support the movement, both
present and future.

Some argue that the democratic potential of social media is limited to
armchair activism or the perception of engagement without commitment;[46] however, we should not forget to look at the bigger picture of
how social media fit within the larger framework of democracy. Social
media are but a few pieces of a larger democratic mosaic that serve to galvanize dissent through the sharing and distribution of emotionally strong
and disturbing images, videos, and words. They work to mobilize the solidarity of social justice issues and spread of necessary identificational,
locational, and tactical information members need to put their body on
the line for the movement. Lastly, social media help bridge the digital divide by disseminating the experiential knowledge of poverty experts,
those who live the experience of poverty in the United States on a daily
basis, to highlight contradictions in dominant poverty discourse, and
challenge systemic oppression. Through the dissemination of these voices,
our media sphere is that much richer and more complete.

NOTES

1. POOR Magazine is a poor people/indigenous people-led grassroots, nonprofit arts organization dedicated to providing revolutionary media access, education, arts, and advocacy to youth, adults, and elders in poverty.

2. Emmanuel Saez, "Striking It Richer: The Evolution of Top Incomes in the United States (Updated with 2009 and 2010 Estimates)," March 2, 2012, http://eml.berkeley.edu/~saez/saez-UStopincomes-2010.pdf.

3. Although many dominant media outlets ignore or denigrate populations in homelessness and poverty, not all do this. At this point in time, mainstream media are more fragmented and heterogeneous than ever before and some outlets do provide compelling reporting on poverty and homeless issues.

4. Diana Elizabeth Kendall, *Framing Class: Media Representations of Wealth and Poverty in America* (Lanham, MD: Rowman & Littlefield Publishers, 2011).

5. Chris Atton, *An Alternative Internet: Radical Media, Politics and Creativity* (Edinburgh, Scotland: Edinburgh University Press, 2004).

6. G. Thomas Goodnight, "Public Discourse," *Critical Studies in Mass Communication* 4, no. 4 (December 1987): 428–432, doi:10.1080/15295038709360154; Jürgen Habermas, *The Structural Transformation of the Public Sphere: An Inquiry into a Category of Bourgeois Society,* trans. T. Burger (Cambridge, MA: MIT Press, 1991, originally published 1962).

7. Kendall Phillips, "The Spaces of Public Dissension: Reconsidering the Public Sphere," *Communication Monographs* 63 (1996): 243.

8. Atton, *An Alternative Internet,* 40.

9. Chris Greer and Eugene McLaughlin, "We Predict a Riot?: Public Order Policing, New Media Environments and the Rise of the Citizen Journalist," *British Journal of Criminology* 50, no. 6 (November 2010): 1055, doi:10.1093/bjc/azq039.

10. Ibid., 1056.

11. Phillips, "The Spaces of Public Dissension: Reconsidering the Public Sphere."

12. Ibid., 243.

13. Robert L. Ivie, "Enabling Democratic Dissent," *Quarterly Journal of Speech* 101, no. 1 (February 2015): 49.

14. Erik Doxtader, "Characters in the Middle of Public Life: Consensus, Dissent, and Ethos," *Philosophy and Rhetoric* 33, no. 4 (2000): 336–369.

15. Ivie, "Enabling Democratic Dissent," 50.

16. Ibid., 53.

17. Clay Shirky, *Here Comes Everybody: The Power of Organizing without Organizations* (New York: Penguin Press, 2008).

18. Malcolm Gladwell, "Why the Revolution Will Not Be Tweeted," *The New Yorker,* October 4, 2010, http://www.newyorker.com/magazine/2010/10/04/small-change-malcolm-gladwell; Evgeny Morozov, "Foreign Policy: Brave New World of Slacktivism," *NPR.org,* May 19, 2009, http://www.npr.org/templates/story/story.php?storyId=104302141.

19. Sandra González-Bailón, "Online Social Networks and Bottom-up Politics," April 8, 2013, http://papers.ssrn.com/sol3/papers.cfm?abstract_id=2246663.

20. Sebastián Valenzuela, "Unpacking the Use of Social Media for Protest Behavior: The Roles of Information, Opinion Expression, and Activism," *American Behavioral Scientist* 57, no. 7 (July 2013): 925, doi:10.1177/0002764213479375.

21. Ibid.

22. Marc W. Steinberg, "Toward a More Dialogic Analysis of Social Movement Culture," in *Social Movements: Identity, Culture, and the State,* ed. David S. Meyer,

Nancy Whittier, and Belinda Robnett (New York: Oxford University Press, 2002), 213.

23. Marc W. Steinberg, "The Talk and Back Talk of Collective Action: A Dialogic Analysis of Repertoires of Discourse among Nineteenth-Century English Cotton Spinners," *American Journal of Sociology* 105, no. 3 (1999): 751.

24. Maeve Duggan, Nicole B. Ellison, Cliff Lampe, Amanda Lenhart, and Mary Madden, "Social Media Update 2014," *Pew Research Center: Internet, Science & Tech,* January 9, 2015, http://www.pewinternet.org/2015/01/09/social-media-update -2014/.

25. One partial exception was Picture the Homeless, which used a team of media experts paired with community members living in poverty and homelessness to create each piece of media.

26. One exception to this was the omission of a community media organization that met all of the criteria in the Midwest because one could not be identified after thorough research. In its place, an Appalachian community media organization was chosen.

27. While the digital divide is still very much a concern in contemporary U.S. society, because these organizations served as community media organizations, they provided access to digital technologies and the Internet to target audience members who might fall within the digital divide.

28. Greer and McLaughlin, "We Predict a Riot?," 1056.

29. Dylan Matthews, "A $15 Minimum Wage Is a Terrible Idea," *Washington Post,* June 22, 2013, http://www.washingtonpost.com/blogs/wonkblog/wp/2013/06/22/a-15-minimum-wage-is-a-terrible-idea/.

30. Ivie, "Enabling Democratic Dissent," 50.

31. Ibid.

32. Ibid.

33. John Louis Lucaites and Celeste Michelle Condit, "Reconstructing: Culturetypal and Counter-cultural Rhetorics in the Martyred Black Vision," *Communications Monographs* 57, no. 1 (1990): 18.

34. Ivie, "Enabling Democratic Dissent," 52.

35. Karen Tracy, *Challenges of Ordinary Democracy: A Case Study in Deliberation and Dissent* (University Park, PA: Penn State University Press, 2011).

36. Greer and McLaughlin, "We Predict a Riot?"

37. Saqib Riaz and Saadia Anwar Pasha, "Role of Citizen Journalism in Strengthening Societies," *FWU Journal of Social Sciences* 5, no. 1 (June 2011): 88–103.

38. Greer and McLaughlin, "We Predict a Riot?," 1055.

39. Luke Goode, "Social News, Citizen Journalism and Democracy," *New Media & Society,* November 24, 2009, http://nms.sagepub.com/content/early/2009/11/24/1461444809341393, 7.

40. Lazaro Bacallao-Pino, "Social Media Mobilisations: Articulating Processes or Visibilizing Dissent," *Cyberpsychology: Journal of Psychosocial Research on Cyberspace* 8, no. 3 (October 2014), doi:10.5817/CP2014-3-3.

41. Manuel Castells, "Communication, Power and Counter-power in the Network Society," *International Journal of Communication* 1, no. 1 (2007): 250.

42. González-Bailón, "Online Social Networks and Bottom-up Politics," 2.

43. Hubert Janos Kiss and Alfonso Rosa-García, "Why Do Facebook and Twitter Facilitate Revolutions More Than TV and Radio?," *Munich Personal RePEc Archive*, September 19, 2011, http://mpra.ub.uni-muenchen.de/33496/.

44. Castells, "Communication, Power and Counter-power in the Network Society," 250.

45. Ibid.

46. Morozov, "Foreign Policy"; Gladwell, "Why the Revolution Will Not Be Tweeted."

Chapter 2

Platforms with Purpose: Clicktivism and Crowdfunding Campaigns in the Era of *Citizens United*

Laura Williams

When in 1787, a small group of privileged, highly educated, politically sophisticated minds met in the Pennsylvania State House to transform a moment of revolution into a bold experiment in self-governance, they envisioned an American voting populace and an electoral system quite different from the one that will take up their challenge in November 2016. *The Federalist Papers* and *Common Sense* were written for, and were largely understood by, a comparatively narrow public sphere: long-form prose consumed by white men of some education, leisure time, and property, who comprised the entire electorate. Expansions of the voting franchise in the centuries since, as well as growth in public literacy, have combined to abundantly increase the number of Americans able to sustain the founders' vision of a well-informed populace. Our methods of participating in civic discourse and interacting with interested publics have also transformed dramatically, now enabled by international, interactive, instant networks.

From the beginning, the American ideal understood the public interest be best served by broad access to information about the governance process. The Acts of the First Session of the First Congress in 1789 required that all bills, orders, resolutions, and congressional votes be published in at least three publicly available newspapers.[1] When introduced to the political and civic process in the early 1920s, radio exploded the proximal restrictions on aural communication past those of the largest newspaper, and Warren G. Harding's voice was heard across the American continent.[2] For the first time, Americans began to expect to hear their elected representatives and campaign platforms delivered for their home consumption, rather than at train-stop stump speeches. To subsidize the cost of this personalized transfer of knowledge, Americans accepted that political discourse would arrive in advertiser-supported form, rather than in public gathering spaces.[3] By the 1950s, television networks granted access to the broadcast spectrum (and to the newly opened White House Press Room) were expected to provide a few hours of civic and publicly relevant programming in the form of advertiser-supported evening news, and by 1960, the first televised presidential debate reached voters already interspersed with nationally aired campaign ads featuring each candidate.[4,5]

As the influence of a few nationally available channels of communication grew, community and local organization took a backseat to nationalized campaigns capable of generating network coverage. Political discourse was increasingly packaged into consumable, uncontroversial sound bites to be sandwiched between lucrative national advertisements, leading to candidate outreach strategies commoditized both in their content and their consumption. The recent fracture of national and geographically bounded information networks, increased personalization of news consumption, and the universal access to and easy remediation of content present unique challenges to the political system, including the potential to destroy or to reimagine informed representation. Traditional political campaign coverage and interaction are mono-directional rather than interactive, are defined by artificial scarcity, and are heavily skewed by the advertising and the accompanying corporate agendas. The resulting commoditization and shallowing of the national discourse represents a serious threat to the ideals of self-governance.

The horizons of voter-campaign interactions for 2016 are perhaps as far removed from those of the national radio broadcasts as the first radio broadcasts were from whistle-stop campaigns and congressional proceedings printed in newspapers. Highly priced 15-second political ads remain the preferred way to reach voters, though neither these ads nor the events staged to capture media time ("earned media" press conferences and balloon-dropping arena announcements, symbolic stunts, and outrageous statements) are an effective way of communicating or evaluating a representative's platform. A majority of governing hours are spent raising money to purchase or attract favorable mentions in increasingly irrelevant print and broadcast media.[6] Television networks embrace campaigns as sideshows or production partners, rather than advocating for the people as an adversarial fourth estate, and have become dependent on periodic influxes of highly profitable televised events and ads in advance of each election.[7] Again, the model of false scarcity distorts political discourse: major networks compete to provide comfortable, uncontroversial, commoditized coverage to encourage high viewership and demand commensurate ad rates. Cable news channels find a niche audience for increasingly polarized personalities and viewpoints, and give up the pretense of objectivity in search of popularity. Still, the relative scarcity of national network airtime and column inches to reach one's preferred audience perpetuates a highly priced competition for influence and voter information during American primaries and election cycles.

The material scarcities on which these assumptions are based have been shaken, if not yet shattered, by the wildcard of the Internet, as near-infinite sources of information proliferate and interactivity alters voters' expectations of the political landscape. Virtually no marginal cost need be incurred in producing new information, duplicating, or disseminating it (though traditional labor costs of reporting and fact checking remain despite the difficulty of monetizing content—a topic broadly explored in other scholarship). Undeniably, political speech can become even further commoditized in online environments, as ad-supported models encourage reader-baiting to promote "clicks" and attract attention, rather than to sustain an informed public discourse, much as ad dependency threatened networks' roles. With communication nearly free, only attention is for sale: voter attention, consumer attention, national agenda attention, each representative's attention. As active producer–consumers in the attention market of this sensationalized infotainment, we have joined a bidding war for our own influence.

Clicktivism, and the clicktivist generation, are characterized by use of the Internet, particularly social media and networking sites, as a primary mode of engagement and participation in political discourse and social causes. This chapter will examine the well-founded criticisms of clicktivist engagement, including commoditization of discourse, reduced social engagement, and strained economies of attention in online environments. A brief timeline of American electoral communications demonstrates that none of these concerns is unique or new to the Internet, but may in fact be uniquely addressed by the Internet. As interactions between individuals, and between individuals and content, change shape, so do our methods of engagement with political campaigns and consequently, with political activism.

During roughly the same period as we have witnessed this growth in the Internet-enabled public sphere, the Supreme Court ruling on *Citizens United v. FEC* has redrawn the boundaries between campaign contributions and political speech, between the dollar and the word, between the economic entity and the individual.[8] This trend further commoditizes political representation from the demand side and allows representatives to command enormous private contributions subsidizes the inflated costs of traditional national media campaigns. The collision of these revolutionary factors brings us to a new precipice of democratic representation and political activism: the low barriers to social organization, immediacy, and post-geographic alliances, enabled by the Internet, coupled with relaxed restrictions on political contributions, and a further enshrined equivalency between unrestricted campaign contributions and freedom of political speech, prepare us for the first truly democratic political activism.

Clicktivist and crowdfunding communities challenge (and hold the potential to reverse) these worrisome trends in new-media-enabled public sphere discourse. We will examine two born-digital tools, both crowdfunding platforms in the model of Kickstarter, debuting in the 2016 election season that have tackled these concerns in innovative ways. Together, each site's interface characteristics and community activities increase political engagement by aggregating donations, empowering small donors to rival the influence of major banks and corporations. By earmarking campaign funds to the rhetorical constructions of issues rather than to potential representatives, the sites also more tightly tie funds with speech, and each proposes accountability measures for sustaining two-way interaction between donors and representatives.

NEW MEDIA AND POLITICAL PARTICIPATION

The rising cohort of the American electorate, currently 18–30 years old, is primed for this new avenue of interaction. Much maligned as overindulged, socially lazy, and politically disengaged, millennials have engineered an entirely new relationship with media, and as a result, with political discourse and activism. Rather than regional newspapers or local television stations, people born after 1980 rely primarily on social media "narrowcast news" comprised of (among a constantly evolving list) Facebook groups and newsfeeds, microblogs, Twitter communities, blogs, comment boards, news/commentary communities, conversation groups, podcasts, vlogs, and other peer-to-peer content platforms and participatory networks.[9] Accelerating this disconnection of speech communities and the public square from geography, and thus, geographic representation, is the accelerating shift toward personalized, prescreened, and algorithm filtered content. We negotiate our identities in self-constructed publics and interact with content mostly of our own choosing, not determined by regional readership or the strength of a broadcast antenna. Next-door neighbors might live in entirely alternate content universes, engaged in public and political discourses with a thousand self-selected strangers. This increase in Internet-enabled organization coincides with a disengagement from traditional social institutions and community groups: less than a third of those born after 1980 reporting a strong affiliation with one political party, and fully half are registered as independents, according to Pew Social Trends.[10] Just 49 percent of the same group would describe themselves as "patriotic" and 29 percent say they are religiously unaffiliated. By comparison, 81 percent are on Facebook. We are in some ways more connected than ever before, and in some ways more isolated and more fractured. But studies indicate millennials are seeking authentic opportunities to engage with public discourse and are using the Internet to engage in new conversations.[11]

Instant interactive networks dismantle many of the communication barriers those Philadelphia founders designed our representative system to address, for both better and worse. By moving public discourses online, thus lowering the barriers to entry and the costs of producing and distributing content, we are unlocking a post-geographic information sharing and activism potential that is largely untapped in the political realm. Individuals may gain international notoriety in hours. Words written in the morning can be uploaded, instantly translated and remediated, bounced from multiple satellites to reach a reader in every country on earth before evening reaches the author. Alliances and movements are organized along lines far more personally significant geographic location or national origin. Enormous amounts of money are raised for causes, individuals, and organizations, from millions of scattered strangers and small donors who find a momentary empathetic or strategic alliance.

With a technorealist's eye to emergent consumption habits and optimism about social media's political potential in general, a diligent and ethical study must be made of crowdfunding platforms specifically designed to enact policy change in newly legalized ways. By further blurring the line between "online" activity and quantifiable rhetorical-performative impact, such platforms challenge academics' fears of ineffective "clicktivism" and move our public sphere closer to full digital citizenship. We now possess both legal frameworks and technological tools to reimagine political participation, organization, representation, and accountability in ways not conceivable in previous decades, or possible in previous elections. By expanding the "donor class" and adapting to the commodification of representative-constituent messaging, we can aggregate issues and funds via our newfound voluntary associations and networks surrounding political messaging. The 2016 election presents the perfect opportunity to engage these tools and empower citizen collectives and crowdfunders to compete with major individual and corporate donors. Simultaneously, these technologies offer a unique opportunity for complex issues, platforms, and interest groups to supersede geography and political party as the primary determiners of political representation.

THE HIGH PRICE OF "FREE" SPEECH

For decades, scholars have lamented the commoditization of political discourse, the rise of contribution-based "speech," and the counterproductive results of these skewed incentives. The system of making, changing, and enforcing policy is, as Lawrence Lessig and others have detailed, a seemingly hopeless gridlock, a labyrinth of money and interests.[12] Only around half of eligible voters turn out to polls for any election, leaving some 900 million who do not seem to believe their vote matters, and even those who give financially see the limited impact amidst the expanding scope of high-donor giving. Adding to this sense of disenfranchisement and discontent are high rates of incumbency, the astronomical cost of entering an election, and gerrymandering practices that secure "safe" districts to be divided between parties currently in power.

In the 2012 election cycle, 1.2 million people, or about 0.4 percent of the population, gave $200 or more to a federal candidate, a party, or a political action committee.[13] Much larger percentages contribute, often without conscious intent, through compulsory means and coercive associations including taxes, compulsory union dues, professional boards, licensing fees, or governing bodies claiming to represent their interests, and still more unwittingly subsidize corporate giving, which the customer might strongly oppose. In addition to the easily tracked, Federal Election Commission-documented direct donations, high-donor giving already takes place in communicative networks of mailing lists, newsletters, and increasingly web-based campaigns. Issue-based donations can be funneled to candidates through an ever-increasing network of public affairs firms, think tanks, lobby shops, and others whose close relationships with representatives raise questions about quid pro quo bribery as serious as those posed by billionaires and top corporate executives.[14] Recent Supreme Court rulings, which further legitimized this flirtation with outright bribery, will seemingly not be revisited before the 2016 election.

The 2010 Supreme Court ruling in *Citizens United v. Federal Election Commission (FEC)* lifted many restrictions on political giving. The use of large amounts of loosely tracked money to control and persuade candidates and officeholders was thus validated by the courts as a function of free speech. Chief Justice Roberts's opinion on the 2014 clarifying case *McCutcheon v. FEC* narrows the concept of bribery or corruption to a direct money-for-vote, quid pro quo arrangement, while "[spending large sums of money in connection with elections, but not in connection with an effort to control the exercise of an office holder's official duties, does not give rise to such *quid pro quo* corruption . . . Nor does the possibility that an individual who spends large sums may garner 'influence over or access to' elected officials or political parties."[15] What many citizens view as rampant corruption was billed by our highest jurist as a feature of the system, not a flaw. The court's majority opinion even defers to the Internet's increasing of effective transparency as a defense of average citizens against major donors: "Reports and databases are available on the FEC's Web site almost immediately after they are filed, supplemented by private entities such as OpenSecrets.org and FollowTheMoney.org."[16]

Direct-to-candidate and third-party donations are classified as "speech," and thus as a legitimate way to exert influence over legislators' positions. This is best demonstrated by the largest corporations, who distinguish their attempts to secure influence over officeholders, rather than to advocate for particular views or policies, by donating to several or all candidates for a particular office, ensuring sway with the eventual winner. Since *McCutcheon v. Federal Election Commission* in April 2014 removed the previous cap of $48,600 in individual donations every two years, such unrestricted giving is no longer limited to the Super PAC structures designed to absorb such overages.[17]

Corporations treated as individuals attempt to curry favor for favorable tax policies or lucrative government contracts, such that campaign contributions function as a necessary business investment. The uneven distribution of payoffs, as well as available contributions, is in itself a potential threat: one corporation might have a multimillion dollar incentive to create a software, for example, that shaves away a little privacy and a few civil liberties, while the many who experience this erosion, if they even notice it, have much less incentive and capacity to alter it. Issues that do not attract the attention of billionaire contributors, unions, or corporations rarely make appearances on the public stage. Those who stand to gain—or to lose—millions in government contracts, targeted tax breaks, policy tweaks, agency agendas, and artificially reduced competition are difficult for even a broad, well-organized citizens' movement to challenge.

The implicit control that the interests of large donors have over the votes of Congresspersons who will need their donations in the next election cycle is intuitively obvious and reasonably well documented. Princeton researchers Martin Gilens and Benjamin I. Page conducted a metasurvey of nearly 1,800 policy initiatives from 1981 to 2002, determining that the interests of the 90th percentile of income earners are represented almost exclusively: "[t]he central point that emerges from our research is that economic elites and organized groups representing business interests have substantial independent impacts on U.S. government policy," they write, "while mass-based interest groups and average citizens have little or no independent influence."[18] The organizational capacities of Internet communities to aggregate donations and amplify accompanying messages are a promising step toward addressing this imbalance.

Activist scholar Lawrence Lessig makes a poignant call for civic intervention in his indispensable *Republic, Lost*.[19] After a piercing look at
Congressional corruption, incompetence, and ineptitude, Lessig offers
individual lawmakers a systemic scapegoat: "One of the least understood
explanations," Lessig quotes Grim and Carter, "is also one of the simplest:
[Washington] is too busy refereeing disputes between major corporate
interest groups." Grim and Carter quote one anonymous moderate
Democratic senator:

> I'm surprised at how much of our time is spent trying to divide up the
> spoils between various economic interests. I had no idea. I thought
> we'd be focused on civil liberties, on education policy, energy policy
> and so on. . . . I doubt there is a single member of the House or Senate
> who thought, "I'm going to go to Congress so I can divide up the
> spoils between various economic interests."

The introduction of new funding methods holds the potential to give
civil liberties, education, and energy policy a chance to be represented
by significant economic influences legitimized by Supreme Court
provisions.

The ideal of small donations spread over a large network gained some
traction in the year preceding the 2012 election, though with a (perhaps
inevitable) partisan split. The campaign to reelect President Obama raised
a total of $118.8 million online, but this was considered an "alternative
mode" of giving and represented less than a fifth of his total raised.[20]
Of the total crowdfunded, about half was in donations of $200 or less.
From a digital crowdfunding perspective, Republican candidate Mitt
Romney either represents interests of a generally higher-donating and
higher-earning demographic or failed to appeal much to the broader base:
only 9 percent gave small donations of $200 or less, and 82 percent of
donors gave $1,000 or more. It is also worth noting that while the ratio of
small donations and online donations to total fund-raising is similar for
President Obama (57 percent in small donations total, 48 percent of online
donations), former governor Romney's nearly tripled. Republican campaign
donors likely to make those small contributions seem less likely to do it online, perhaps representing disparities in age, access, or regular use of the
Internet among party contributors. Crowdfunding, especially from small
donors, remains a small portion of direct-to-candidate contributions.

The 2016 election is predicted to be a $5 billion race, with up to $1 billion
contributed by the Koch brothers and their shadow network of individual
donors, PACs, foundations, and organizations.[21] The premise of a merito-
cratic one-man-one-vote representation has effectively been undermined.
Immense reservoirs of campaign cash must be expended to reach voters
along traditional single-direction communication networks via the

production and dissemination of physical texts: newspapers, newsletters, targeted mailing, ghostwritten hardcover books (a near prerequisite to successful candidacy), mentions and attention on national network and cable news channels, commercial spots with high-production costs and price-per-second airtime. But all these constructs for speech and influence are artifacts of other ages, other ways of communicating, contingent on an information and attention market attempt to get attention and pedal influence with a dwindling number of voters who rely on these traditional formats for political decision making. Political campaigning in an economy of artificial media scarcity involves a tremendous amount of unnecessary travel, event space rentals, motorcades, endorsements, in-person appearances, and door-to-door canvassers. While they make up the backbone of the modern political party machine, these techniques are massively inefficient at producing ballot-box returns on such staggering investments, much less at executing the public interest.

With heavy use of e-mail and online marketing, and several weeks of $1,000-per-plate fund-raising dinners with hundreds of donors vying for his attention, Ted Cruz raised $10 million in individual donations for his campaign in the three months before August 1, 2015.[22] That total was matched and bested by the $11 million check cut by Robert Mercer, a New York hedge-fund manager, at the conclusion of that July 2015 junket.[23] Rarely has the problem been seen so explicitly: even politically active, fairly generous citizens, in their hundreds of thousands, are overshadowed by a single individual with an immovable agenda and a personal fortune. While it might be easy to conceive of this "matching donation" as an advancement and endorsement of the goals of all the smaller individuals to elect a president, the inequity of their representation—including time and attention from the candidate, backing of favorable legislation, and greasing of committee members—once he takes office is not difficult to anticipate.

Top individual donors to each candidate gave between $5 and $15 million directly in 2012, and nearly half of all Super PAC donors were of a million dollars or more, according to The Campaign Finance Institute.[24] Even when individuals donate freely, they cannot do enough individually to change the prospects of the election, and thus the level of their giving limits its relevance and influence as "speech." Thousand-dollar-a-plate fund-raising dinners and golf outings are where platform and policy inquiries can be made and be taken seriously. Jessica McKenzie of TechPresident summarizes the disconnection felt by many who did make a small donation to a candidate: "that in no way means that the candidate you back knows why you contributed or what you hope they will do once in office. Money talks, but only if you have enough to get a phone call or an invite to a fundraising event. Everything else is just chatter."[25] Part of the promise of clicktivist and crowdfunding political campaigning is the ability to tie even small contributions to meaningful issue articulation and compound that message by aggregation with others.

CRITIQUES OF CLICKTIVISM

Between the 2012 and 2016 election cycles, significant progress has been made in online organizing and fund-raising for political and social causes, and criticisms of these approaches mirror fears about the dumbing down and commercializing of discourses in general. Some argue that this so-called clicktivism or slacktivism cannot be true civic engagement, or at least that it serves only as a prelude to feet-on-the-ground activism. The assumption of techno-pessimists has been that born-digital campaigns are less valid, less effective, less sustainable, efficacious, or engaging than "real-world" actions.

Malcolm Gladwell fears the kind of loose ties we form on social media won't support radical social change, claiming, "social networks are effective at increasing participation—by lessening the level of motivation that participation requires."[26] The low cost of online advocacy results in the assumption that born-digital campaigns are less valid, less effective, less sustainable, efficacious, or engaging than "real-world" actions.

Chris Csikszentmihályi of the Massachusetts Institute of Technology's Center for Future Civic Media described to the *Washington Post* a "worst case scenario" for what he calls "click-through activism."[27] When the anger, guilt, or enthusiasm kindled by a post can be assuaged instantly, much in the manner of indulgences given by the Catholic Church, "to what extent are you removing just enough pressure that they're not going to carry on the spark?" The *Washington Post* reporter summarized the next section of Csikszentmihályi's comments, so I repeat the (no doubt impoverished) paraphrase, "A better scenario for Internet activism, Csikszentmihályi says, would be if causes could break down their needs into discrete tasks, and then farm those tasks out to qualified and willing individuals connected by the power of the Internet."

Consciousness/awareness raising, public education, and similar "change within the brain," activism might find success online, but there is still the perception (among Gladwell and others) that such advocacy must be moved offline to find practical effect in the physical world. Scholars often dismiss "clicktivist" rhetoric as merely symbolic; mere feel-good self-congratulatory noise. Others fret about a substitution effect, where the opportunity to assuage guilt via a public display of support creating a perverse incentive for more substantial activism (i.e., signers of a petition were less likely to give money to a particular charity than nonsigners).

Jodi Dean, in her incisive *Communicative Capitalism*, agrees with Gladwell that currently available fora for online debate are antithetical to critical cognitive discussion: "Post-politics thus begins from the premise of consensus and cooperation. Real antagonism or dissent is foreclosed. Matters previously thought to require debate and struggle are now addressed as personal issues or technical concerns."[28] She claims that there is a "strange merging of democracy and capitalism in networked communications, fetishizing technology, the fantasy of choice, and the simultaneous easing and worsening of affective anxieties in the user." Her concern about the intertwining of money and politics online, as well as the concern that the "message" as the unit of communication has been replaced with the "contribution," belies a total disconnection from the realities of the existing systems. Washington, DC, K Street, the Hill, and most federal agencies are already governed by capitalist and statist intentions, and already hugely unresponsive to an individual not prepared to make a substantial cronyist "contribution." What's more, the consensus and cooperation characterizing Dean's post-political age is exactly the kind of potential that could alleviate the need to condense complex problems into sound bites, because those who sought out that small corner of the collaborative tool would be well equipped to handle such complexity in that specific area (the Wikipedia model) as Csikszentmihályi suggests.

These skewed incentives discourage honest discourse, without which the public sphere does not function. The public sphere has become increasingly about "culture consumption," as preeminent public sphere theorist Jürgen Habermas calls it, and "less about a public sphere in the world of letters itself."[29] That is, when private citizens are grouped into publics by their patterns of consumption of literate texts, "the laws of the market governing the sphere of commodity exchange and of social labor also pervaded the sphere reserved for private people as a public, rational-critical debate."[30] In seventeenth-century Europe, Habermas reflects, culture-consumption has become less critical as it has become less private as it is more social, and thus less up to the task of dialectical self-criticism that had characterized the world of Mills and Marx: "Convivial discussion among individuals gave way to more or less noncommittal group activities . . . no public was formed around 'group activities.' "[31] Branded panel discussions, choreographed public debates, joint press conferences, and other consumer-oriented spectacle experiences replace "the rational debate of private people" with "a salable package read for the box office; it assumes commodity form."[32]

The consumption model of public rhetoric, now presented as a commodity and intended to generate donations and support, is expected by the electorate to be comfortable and enjoyable, which does much to undermine its functional value of advancing complex issues. Habermas continues,

Discussion, now a "business," becomes formalized; the presentation of positions and counter positions is bound to certain prearranged rules of the game; consensus about the subject matter is made largely superfluous by that concerning form. What can be posed as a problem is defined as a question of etiquette; conflicts, once fought out in public polemics, are demoted to the level of personal incompatibilities. Critical debate arranged in this manner certainly fulfills important social-psychological functions, especially that of a tranquilizing substitute for action; however, it increasingly loses its publicist function.[33]

This shift has accelerated concomitantly with a more public-facing, campaign-focused rhetoric that policy promises must stand up to sound bite scrutiny and fuel fund-raising appeals. Habermas: "The speeches made in the plenary sessions of the parliament are no longer meant to convince delegates whose opinions differ, but are directed instead—at least as regards, the basic issues that dominate political life—directly to the active citizenry. . . ." The performance of politics for the voter, and the sensationalist nature of the media coverage we consume of it, does not promote critical analysis of the information presented.

The public's indifference or hostility to complex rhetoric is seen in the decreasing length of presidential candidate's sound bites: It fell from 42.3 seconds in 1968 to 9.8 seconds in 1988 and is now just over 7 seconds.[34] Susan Jacoby's *Age of American Unreason* details the rise of unabashed antirationalism and "faux-populist" rhetoric.[35] This aversion to complexity is exacerbated by short attention spans and meme-ification of discourse, and could be especially troubling if an anti-intellectual counter public mobilized in clicktivist fashion.

Eli Pariser, former executive director and current board member of MoveOn.org and author of *The Filter Bubble*, has expressed discouragement about the ability of current online networks to improve the quality of debate.[36] Still, he has not lost faith in the ability of the Internet to produce platforms that serve higher public purposes. Pariser told NPR before a live audience in 2012:

> Internet technologies amplify so much of what we already are and what we already want. And the fact is, we're pretty provincial animals. So add the Internet to it, we just double down. We get more provincial. Platforms matter, defaults matter, and policies matter. . . .
>
> There is nothing about the nature of the Internet that prevents us from being political, richly political. We just haven't built those platforms. But we do know that the Internet by itself does not topple dictators, does not undermine newspapers. It's just not that simple. If we recognized the biases inherent in many of the platforms of our media systems, we can correct, we can adjust, we can invest, we can invent, we can resist, persist, and thrive.[37]

Fetishized social media can function as an echo chamber, according to Dean and Pariser, and its role in placating the masses rivals the Marxian characterization of religion as "an opiate of the masses," a mirage of satisfaction whose destruction is required for real happiness. But this interpretation fails to adequately appreciate—as many have before—the context of that quote. Rather than simply subduing the populace with a placebo-like platform in which they can enact the motions of change without effect, we overthrow the illusion with real impact "not so he may wear his chain without consolations, but so that he shall throw off the chain, and cull the living flower."[38] Technologies can be employed to stultify, marginalize, or polarize, and may even temporarily compete with real progress, and some of that substitution and sedation effect may delay social action. With the ability to connect across continents and centuries, though, advocates for political change are empowered, not impeded, by social media. By taking both the power of interactive platforms and the *Citizens United* ruling into account, we can choose to see this era as an opportunity to make the political system more responsive and transparent. If we can tolerate temporarily the unsettling realities of bribery and of consumerized, meme-ified, socially networked political messaging, we can use them to enact reform on the crest of the 2016 election season. Leveraging crowdfunding techniques to bridge the temporal and proximal gaps, the aggregated funds represent a tangible social act, representing a valuable and largely unexplored contribution to the democratic public sphere. For the first time we will glimpse the potential of these tools aimed at direct democratic action. The volume of political interactions that have at least one interactive social media component is ever growing. Mobile technologies provide unprecedented scope and reach, including the ability to act or donate from anywhere. What's more, online activity is generating real change in new ways, many of which assuage Csikszentmihályi and Gladwell's fears. Not all online acts are lost-cost or low-risk, and they are certainly not low-impact.

The enormous, well-coordinated response to the 2012 Stop Online Piracy Act (SOPA) and the Protect Intellectual Property Act (PIPA) resulted in a reported 13 million citizen-to-Congress contacts, including 8 million people who looked up their representative on Wikipedia on the day of the first SOPA hearing.[39] If each of those 13 million people had given a few dollars—the proverbial cost of a cup of coffee—to a cause or platform intended to challenge a particular bill, suddenly an organized citizenry would have become political player to rival the paid lobbying influence of Hollywood and Silicon Valley in shaping that legislation. The network of large-scale donors capable of weighing in on candidate selection and the tenets of platforms, especially in the pre-primary stages, has been expanded.

If money is to be, as the Supreme Court seems to favor, the primary method of having one's policies and positions considered, the models suggested to us by crowdfunding sites excite possibilities to alter this discrepancy of attention and money. When individual donors (be they unions, political action committees, corporations, or persons) are relied on for funding, officeholders are beholden to narrow political agendas and easily manipulated. If instead, small donations from a much larger scope of persons were the primary method of seeking funding, an officeholder is likely to become beholden to an issue-oriented constituency, which may or may not be geographically connected to the office he or she occupies.

Opening the political system to unlimited funding was a questionable ruling for the Court, but it creates opportunities for crowdfunding that might not previously have been possible. Nationalized politics disempowers individuals, dividing us into political factions and lobbying groups, think tanks, and competing corporations, which give money to candidates with whom we might not agree, to buy airtime and influence on genres of media few voters will be consuming in a few years. The campaign financing and platform development processes are largely secret, restricted to a small cohort of major donors and party insiders. We certainly should not expect representatives to welcome this change in their job description, nor corporations and unions to take kindly a threat to their power and influence over the political process. Revolutions always have some casualties, some creative destruction. In the early spring of 2015, while national news networks were gearing up "will she or won't she," campaign coverage an absurd 20 months before an election, two issue-based campaign crowdfunding websites were quietly coming online.

PLATFORMS WITH PURPOSE: PIONEERS IN CAMPAIGN CROWDFUNDING

if.then.fund and ShiftSpark.com, both launched in February 2015, promise not just a new method of crowdfunding campaigns but a revolution in the way constituents and representatives interact.[40,41] Rather than donating to a party or an individual candidate, these platforms encourage users to tie their money to issue statements. if.then.fund makes visible a particular action a congressperson can take (like a particular bill introduction or vote), briefly explains the position, and asks for a contribution. When a bill or action comes up for a vote, collected funds are distributed evenly among the officeholders who took the donor's desired stance. Donations are designed to fund reelection committees, which might make the if.then.fund model incompatible with strategically similar efforts aimed at reducing incumbencies. The focus on Congress is particularly notable due to the gerrymandering of districts, and binary representation currently in practice mean many people are never in agreement with the views of their representative but have no other way to influence national policy under which they will live.

if.then.fund's cofounder Jonathan Zucker told TechPresident the platform gives to citizens the advantage of a professional lobbyist like those employed by corporations and unions. By carefully monitoring the bills that impact them, we can tell them, "Here is who is working in your favor and here is who is not; donate accordingly. We're giving people the ability to make that same kind of calculus as that lobbyist did."[42] Unlike a lobbyist, though if.then.fund and ShiftSpark.com also offer accountability for officeholders in the form of "protested donations" if politicians do not follow through on the conditions of the donation.

In the "Theory of Change" portion of its website, if.then.fund explains the four functions it hopes the platform will serve. One is accountability: "Instead of making an aspirational donation to a candidate, campaign contributions made here on if.then.fund are based on what legislators actually do, not what they say they will do. if.then.fund routes your contributions to members of Congress who vote the way you want and to the opponents of those who do not. By being targeted, your contributions will be more effective at supporting candidates with similar views to your own."[43]

ShiftSpark shares the issue-over-individual method of funding candidates, but uses an accountability model of pledges. The actual contribution is withheld until the action is taken (a vote, a motion), essentially as a reward for the lawmaker's acting in accordance with the donor's views. The donor decides if and when to release the donation (which is visible to all) to reward the officeholder and help fund his reelection. If the action is not taken, the pledge is not collected, or may be collected to be donated to an opponent. While its intentions are good, this model dances perilously close to Chief Justice Roberts's explicit explanation of the exception to giving protected by *Citizens United*—that is, the quid pro quo of exchanging a particular vote for a particular sum of money. Interestingly, this exchange is reflected more accurately in the title of rival, "if.then." The platform is even more promising, though, for its user-generated legislation and petitions, to which pledges can also be attached. As of July 2015, ShiftSpark.com's homepage read: "Big money is the problem. You are the solution." The platform's billing of its accountability feature was equally concise: "Make political donations with confidence. If your politician doesn't perform, you get your money back." The ability to attach both positive and negative consequences to a donation speech act provides a new avenue of dialogue for donors.

MapLight.org analysis of data from the Federal Elections Commission illustrates exactly what Congress people must do with their time. Average spending indicates a newly minted senator would need to raise over $14,000 every day until his or her next election to win. House members are inexpensive by comparison: just $2,315.[44] Fifty-two voting senators are worth $10.5 million each, seven times as much as a $1.7 million house seat; this ratio is exactly what power ratios would predict for a free market model of purchased influence.[45]

A few years ago these sums seemed insurmountable to average citizens, no matter how well organized, who lacked the fund-raising machinery of a major political party. But the Ice Bucket Challenge raised $8 million in four days, and while amyotrophic lateral sclerosis (sometimes called ALS or Lou Gehrig's disease) impacts a relatively small number of families each year, the born-digital, viral campaign raised more in *one day* than libertarian candidate Gary Johnson raised for his 2012 presidential run.[46,47] Since the last nonincumbent election, the stakes of online organizing and giving have changed, as has the most common way of associating and communicating.

Twitter has for years aspired to prominence among platforms hosting political debate. The real-time, character-limited interface style promotes interaction with real-time events, including debates and political speeches. The ease of searching and tagging identities results in a radically egalitarian access and influence by allowing, for example, President Obama to instantly, publicly, and directly reach out to high school Ahmed Mohamed with an invitation to the White House after the high school engineering student was arrested for bringing to school a clock project his teacher allegedly mistook for a bomb.[48] Twitter also granted a platform to Democrat Bernie Sanders to "live tweet" his critiques of the Republican debates of September 2015, using the hashtag #DebateWithBernie in place of a mainstream media microphone.[49]

Just days later, Twitter made a major leap from narrowcasting news to crowdfunding candidates with the introduction of Federal Election Commission compliant method for "tailored digital fundraising, in real time."[50] Through a partnership with Twitter cofounder Jack Dorsey's mobile payment platform Square Cash, the cash.me command and a campaign's legally registered $Cashtag permit donation via tweet. While Twitter's introductory commentary promotes the tool as issue- and cause-focused, the interface emphasizes direct-to-candidate contributions because $cashtags have largely been established by individual campaigns.

With these campaign-compliant technologies at hand, the potential for clicktivist impact is tremendously amplified. Born-digital campaigns relying on digital action is becoming tremendously successful: when comedian and commentator John Oliver issued a call to action on a subscriber-only HBO network, the 15-minute comedy-news-program diatribe made issues around net neutrality so accessible and so persuasive that it gained YouTube 5.5 million views in only a few days. Just five days after the segment aired, the Federal Communication Commission's public comment website, the URL for which Oliver had displayed, had received

46,000 citizens' comments (a record) before the comment page crashed.[51] While the ultimate wisdom of the policy enacted is yet to be determined (the final language of so-called Net Neutrality regulations was passed without public review) the case was a powerful demonstration of clicktivism's potential. Most importantly for the discussion of identifying crowdfunding's possibilities, John Oliver's campaign invited primarily Web 2.0 viewers to take a Web 2.0 action, without requiring offline action. While critics of "clicktivism" are likely to see this as a mere lowering of the amount of effort required to participate, this underestimates the potential of performative action to correspond to real-world action, and be aggregated on the Internet's scale to magnify.

Each of these born-digital campaigns demonstrates a distinctly technorealist understanding of the emergent norms of actual, not idealized, behavior of both voter and statesman. GovTrack and Thomas.gov have given us the ability to view the voting schedules and texts of bills for several years, but legislation is time-consuming to track and read and most voters have other priorities. The position that the literacy skills and tastes of Internet users have irrevocably turned toward more consumable, reader-rewarding material can seem distasteful or fatalistic to those who idealize a democracy forged by Lincoln–Douglas debates and the Federalist papers. Recall, however, that these methods of communication and deliberation of political ideas were consumed by only a tiny fraction of the population, who had similar backgrounds, educations, and ideas about how to profitably invest one's citizenly energies. Those priorities are not shared by the twenty-first century's literate and enfranchised many, and lawmakers would be wise to make the composition and deliberation of laws under which we live accessible in these new media environments. Internet-enabled political discussion, because it is self-navigated, broadens the potential for learning through engaged social activism.

CONCLUSION

Crowdfunding platforms offer a relatively new opportunity to combine digital funds collection with a closely linked rhetorical platform advancing issues and platform planks, rather than candidates. The difference between this and a PAC is perilously—or promisingly, depending on one's viewpoint—narrow. Since all congressional votes are of roughly equal value (and many cabinet positions or committee seats might be of significantly higher value) it is no longer essential that geography bound our support for candidates or for ideas. We do not need them to return to the home district to meet in town halls or fund-raising dinners—to do so, in fact, encourages only the kind of high-value-donor courting that is the signature lifestyle of some politicians. Since gerrymandering has relegated the geographically distributed voting system to near uselessness, it is just as sensible for a potential voter to seek out the candidate who most closely adheres to his or her positions, regardless of the representatives' geographic area of original election. Since money can be freely given to candidates across state lines, the stakes of single-district fund-raising are reduced, as is the high-donor impact on money and power distribution. If the distribution of viewpoints were across a spectrum of possibilities at Internet-enabled scale, (hundreds, rather than two or three) citizens' groups could apply targeted and cumulative pressure and spending in a single district, rivaling major donor expenditures. This type of arrangement is better suited to the senate, which deals primarily with national matters and laws under which the whole country might live. Less true to the federalist model is any arrangement that would allow out-of-state national officeholders pass laws for individual communities, based on the opinions of persons living and voting outside of those localities.

Given the scope, channels, networks, and currencies of our post-Internet, post–*Citizens United* sphere, a new era of political activism is dawning. Born-digital social interest groups advance interests at least as effectively as national-party-appointed "local" representatives juggling competing large-donor interests, and committed but disparate interest groups can raise campaign funds as effectively as professionally coordinated hierarchical campaigns. The tools for a populist, third- or nonparty candidate (indeed, for direct democracy) exist, if we can select platforms and defaults to encourage sound civic debate and the development of new forms of social-civic action, online and off.

NOTES

1. United States, *Acts Passed at a Congress of the United States of America: Begun and Held at the City of New York, on Wednesday the Fourth of March, in the Year M.DCC.LXXXIX. And of the Independence of the United States, the Thirteenth. Being the Acts Passed at the First Session of the First Congress of the United States.* New York: Printed by Hodge, Allen and Campbell, and sold at their respective bookstores; also, by T. Lloyd, 1789.

2. Samuel L. Becker, "Presidential Power: The Influence of Broadcasting," *Quarterly Journal of Speech* 47, no. 1 (1961): 10–18.

3. Allan Brown, "Economics, Public Service Broadcasting, and Social Values," *Journal of Media Economics* 9, no. 1 (1996): 3–15.

4. William L. Benoit and Allison Harthcock, "Functions of the great debates: Acclaims, attacks, and defenses in the 1960 presidential debates," *Communication Monographs* (1999): 341–357.

5. Gladys Engel Lang and Kurt Lang, *Politics and Television Re-viewed* (Beverly Hills, CA: Sage Publications, Inc., 1984).

6. Opensecrets.org., "2012 Outside Spending, By Race," *Center for Responsive Politics* (2015), https://www.opensecrets.org/outsidespending/summ.php?disp=R.

7. Andrew Vanacore, "Political Ads Called 'Gigantic Band-Aid' For TV Stations' Bottom Lines," *Associated Press Dispatch*, October 29, 2010, http://www.cnsnews.com/news/article/political-ads-called-gigantic-band-aid-tv-stations-bottom-lines.

8. *Citizens United v. Federal Election Commission.* No. 08-205 52, United States Supreme Court (January 21, 2010). *LII*, Cornell University Law School (January 22, 2010).

9. Media Insight Project, "How Millennials Get News," *American Press Institute*, March 16, 2015, https://www.americanpressinstitute.org/publications/reports/survey-research/millennials-news/.

10. Pew Research Center Social & Demographic Trends, *Millennials in Adulthood (The Next America)* (Washington, DC, 2015).

11. Abby Kiesa, Alexander Orlowski, Peter Levine, Deborah Both, Emily Kirby, Mark Hugo Lopez, and Karlo Barrios, "Millennials Talk Politics: A Study of College Student Political Engagement," *Center for Information and Research on Civic Learning and Engagement*, 2015, http://www.civicyouth.org/PopUps/CSTP.pdf.

12. Lawrence Lessig, *Republic, Lost: How Money Corrupts Congress—And a Plan to Stop It* (New York: Twelve, 2011).

13. Opensecrets.org., "Donor Demographics," *Center for Responsive Politics* (2015), https://www.opensecrets.org/overview/DonorDemographics.php.

14. Paul Abowd, "Donors Use Charity to Push Free-Market Policies in States," *Center for Public Integrity*, February 14, 2013, https://www.publicintegrity.org/2013/02/14/12181/donors-use-charity-push-free-market-policies-states.

15. SCOTUSblog, "*Mccutcheon v. Federal Election Commission*," 2015, http://www.scotusblog.com/case-files/cases/mccutcheon-v-federal-election-commission/.

16. Ibid.

17. Adam Liptak, "Supreme Court Strikes Down Overall Political Donation Cap," *The New York Times*, April 3, 2014, A1.

18. Martin Gilens and Benjamin I. Page, "Testing Theories of American Politics: Elites, Interest Groups, and Average Citizens," *Perspectives on Politics* 12, no. 3 (2014): 564–581.

19. Lawrence Lessig, *Republic, Lost*.

20. Michael Beckel, "Small-Dollar Donors Propel Barack Obama, Non-Romney Republicans," *Opensecrets.org*, February 1, 2012, http://www.opensecrets.org/news/2012/02/small-dollar-donors-propel-obama/.

21. Aime Parnes and Kevin Cirilli, "The $5 Billion Presidential Campaign?" *The Hill*, January 21, 2015.

22. Rebecca Ballhaus, "GOP Presidential Candidate Ted Cruz Raises $10 Million in Second Quarter," *The Wall Street Journal*, July 5, 2015, http://www.wsj.com/articles/gop-presidential-candidate-ted-cruz-raises-10-million-in-second-quarter-1436119549.

23. Theodore Schleifer, "The Big Money Behind the Super Pacs," *Cnnpolitics.Com* July 30, 2015, http://www.cnn.com/2015/07/30/politics/super-pac-fundraising-filing-fec/.

24. Opensecrets.org., "Top Individual Contributors: All Federal Contributions," (2015), https://www.opensecrets.org/overview/topindivs.php.

25. Jessica McKenzie, "Next-Generation Political Crowdfunding Platforms Reimagine Small Dollar Giving," *Techpresident*, March 13, 2015, http://tech

president.com/news/25482/next-generation-political-crowdfunding-platforms
-reimagine-small-dollar-giving.

26. Malcolm Gladwell, "Small Change: Why the Revolution Will Not Be Tweeted," *The New Yorker*, October 4, 2010.

27. Monica Hesse, "Facebook Activism: Lots of Clicks, But Little Sticks," *The Washington Post*, July 2, 2009.

28. Jodi Dean, "Communicative Capitalism: Circulation and the Foreclosure of Politics," *Cultural Politics: An International Journal* 1, no. 1 (2005): 51–73.

29. Jürgen Habermas, *The Structural Transformation of the Public Sphere: An Inquiry into a Category of Bourgeois Society* (Cambridge, MA: MIT Press, 1989).

30. Ibid., p. 163.

31. Ibid., p. 163.

32. Ibid., p. 164.

33. Ibid., p. 164.

34. Mark Mattern, *Putting Ideas to Work: A Practical Introduction to Political Thought* (Lanham, MD: Rowman & Littlefield, 2006).

35. Susan Jacoby, *The Age of American Unreason* (New York: Pantheon Books, 2008).

36. Eli Pariser, *The Filter Bubble: What the Internet Is Hiding from You* (New York: Penguin Press, 2011).

37. National Public Radio, "Is the Internet Closing Our Minds Politically?" *Intelligence Squared US*, podcast, April 23, 2012, http://www.npr.org/2012/04/23/151037080/is-the-internet-closing-our-minds-politically.

38. Karl Marx, Annette Jolin, Joseph O'Malley, and Georg Wilhelm Friedrich Hegel. [Kritik Des Hegelschen Staatsrechts.] *Critique of Hegels' "Philosophy of Right,"* edited with an Introduction and Notes by Joseph O'Malley (Cambridge University Press, 1970).

39. Timothy Lee, "SOPA Protest by the Numbers: 162M Pageviews, 7 Million Signatures," *Ars Technica*, January 20, 2012, http://arstechnica.com/tech-policy/2012/01/sopa-protest-by-the-numbers-162m-pageviews-7-million-signatures/.

40. ShiftSpark.com, "Shiftspark" (2015), https://www.shiftspark.com.

41. If.then.fund.com, "If.Then.Fund" (2015), https://if.then.fund.

42. McKenzie, "Next-Generation Political Crowdfunding Platforms."

43. If.then.fund.com.

44. Jay Costa, "What's the Cost of a Seat in Congress? | Maplight—Money and Politics," *Maplight.Org.*, March, 10, 2013, http://maplight.org/content/73190.

45. Ibid.

46. The ALS Association, *Ice Bucket Challenge Donations Reach $22.9 Million to the ALS Association*, August 19, 2014, http://www.alsa.org/news/media/press-releases/ice-bucket-challenge-081914.html.

47. Opensecrets.org., "Gary Johnson Candidate Summary, 2012 Cycle," *Center for Responsive Politics* (2015).

48. Shafik Mandhai, "Muslim Boy Arrested over Clock Invited to White House," *Aljazeera,* September 17, 2015, http://www.aljazeera.com/news/2015/09/muslim-boy-arrest-clock-sparks-outrage-150916143739052.html.

49. "Bernie Sanders Live Tweets GOP Debate, Gets Bored, Goes Home Early," *It's All Politics NPR.org*, last modified September 17, 2015, http://www.npr.org/

sections/itsallpolitics/2015/09/17/441004967/bernie-sanders-live-tweets-gop
-debate-gets-bored-goes-home-early.

50. "Political Donations, Now through a Tweet," Twitter Blog, last modified
September 15, 2015, https://blog.twitter.com/2015/political-donations-now
-through-a-tweet.

51. Amanda Holpuch, "John Oliver's Cheeky Net Neutrality Plea Crashes
FCC Website," *The Guardian*, June 3, 2014, https://www.theguardian.com/
technology/2014/jun/03/john-oliver-fcc-website-net-neutrality.

Chapter 3

Caught between Televisual and Digital Presence: Greenpeace's Foray into the Twittersphere

Thomas Breideband

INTRODUCTION

Audacious, bold, altruistic. Over the course of the preceding decades, these and similar attributes have been mainstays of professional reporting to describe and interpret the protest activities conducted by members of the environmental group Greenpeace—and for good reason. What better way to disseminate information about the group's high-profile actions such as lowering protest banners from spiraling heights, physically obstructing oil-drilling activities, chaining activists to trees to prevent logging operations, or actively maneuvering tiny rubber boats into the crosshairs of formidable whaling harpoons, than through the prism of drama and spectacle. Since the founding of the group in the 1970s, the protest activities of Greenpeace and the corresponding news footage of activists offered exciting and newsworthy content. Bob Hunter, one of the cofounders of Greenpeace, defined the group's particular style of dramatic interventions and provocations as "mindbombs," designed to not merely to bring environmental issues to public attention but also to attract the attention of news outlets for the purposes of information dissemination.[1] Merely *informing* the public about environmental issues that are usually both complex in scope and, as Anders Hansen explains, "often shrouded in scientific uncertainty and in a language of probability and likelihoods" was allegedly not enough to foster a sense of urgency.[2] Environmental groups such as Greenpeace understood, very quickly, how a dramaturgy of audacity and a "critique through spectacle" would aid the group's public communication strategies to exert pressure on both private and political sectors.[3] Tailored to a "one-to-many" media ecology, in which public life was largely configured by televisions functioning as institutional centers,[4] disseminated images and protest footage consistently featured Greenpeace activists engaged in risky stunts to protect and defend nature from the encroachment of corporate and governmental players. By focusing on activists, commonly clad in specialized attire, and their bodies engaged in practices of disruption and intervention, Greenpeace routinely utilized what we might call embodied rhetorics as inventional resources to crystallize "more complex political positions into a [set of] visual signifier[s]."[5] Such a conceptualization of protest practice lines up with the concept of the "image event," originally coined by Kevin DeLuca in 1999, an often-used analytical framework for the description and interpretation of the inventional rhetorics of environmental groups. As "staged acts of protest designed for media dissemination," image events are grounded in a postmodern understanding of argumentation, whereby activists aim "to deliver images as argumentative fragments that serve as inventional resources for public deliberation."[6] Delicath and DeLuca situated the concept within "public communication [that] takes place in a context dominated by mass communication technology and charged by the prominence of dramatic visual imagery."[7] In the public eye, Greenpeace activists came to be seen and recognized as a small group of exemplary and brave citizens who would risk their personal well-being to expose the moral wrongdoings of powerful adversaries. For many years this has been quite a "win-win" situation not only for the environmental group, interested in public exposure, but also for television, radio, and print news outlets interested in attracting audiences to increase profit.

Corporate actions of containment, in turn, solidified the now common and ubiquitous narrative of the "brave few Davids" fighting to protect the environment against powerful corporate and/or political "Goliaths," who would operate the sites where Greenpeace protests would often unfold such as oil-drilling platforms, whaling ships, or nuclear testing grounds. Headlines in the news such as "Duel on the High Seas" or "Greenpeace vs. [Insert adversary's name here]" commonly perpetuated the melodramatic appeal of activists putting their lives on the line, which often resulted in sustained coverage on the news. At least, this has been the case for Greenpeace campaigns up until the end of the twentieth century, as up to this point the organization routinely managed to monopolize media attention over the course of weeks at a time.[8] As a result, the "brave few" metaphor became a controlling element of Greenpeace's protest communication strategy.

Since Greenpeace's activism has operated according to DeLuca's work on the "image event" and Scannell's theorization of television as the institutional center of information dissemination, we can see how the organization routinely worked through elite media intermediaries. However, changes wrought by the deregulation of traditional media and the rise of social media that have promised "many-to-many" communication via social media currently threaten or promise to unsettle previous communication models grounded in the mass communication era. Here, the underlying media ecology of digitally mediated social networks has been explained thoroughly by Yochai Benkler.[9] He proposes that participation becomes self-motivating as personally expressive content is shared with and recognized by others who, in turn, repeat these networked activities of contributing and circulating content. When these interpersonal networks are enabled by technology platforms that may function as aggregators, the resulting actions can resemble collective action, yet without the same role played by formal organizations or transforming social identifications. In place of content that is distributed and relationships that are managed by hierarchical organizations, social media involve coproduction and co-distribution, revealing a different economic and psychological logic: coproduction and sharing based on personalized expression. As Jan-Hinrik Schmidt explains, social media have given rise to "personal publics" that need to be distinguished from mass-media publics. While mass-media publics were "based on a mode of publishing or broadcasting … [p]ersonal publics, on the other hand, are characterized by the communicative mode of 'conversation,' where the strict separation of sender and receiver is blurred."[10] Given Greenpeace's established perception in the public eye as an environmental organization whose identity is grounded in the notion that activists are frequently sent to remote and outlying locations to bring environmental issues to public attention via television, the question arises if and how the incorporation of social media into a protest activity influences Greenpeace's overall image. Commonly perceived as an ephemeral and fluid protest space that can facilitate the formation of so-called ad hoc issue publics[11] through the curating use of hashtags, Greenpeace's utilization of Twitter and its attempt to mobilize users online may have the effect of (re)negotiating established public perceptions of Greenpeace activists whose image seems to be tied to outlying geographical locations.

This so happened in 2012 when the organization staged its first official Twitter protest as part of its "Save the Arctic" campaign. Announced a few days in advance via their official Twitter account, Greenpeace asked

Twitter users to contribute protest messages to the hashtags #SavetheArc-
tic and #StopShell. The actual protest happened on September 14, 2012,
and it coincided with a number of local, small-scale demonstrations in
front of various Shell gas stations in the United Kingdom, Germany, and
the Netherlands, where Greenpeace activists protested Shell's plans to
launch oil-drilling operations in the Arctic;[12] in fact, the tweets of online
protestors were prominently featured on large projection screens that
activists had set up close to the gas stations. In other words, the online
space of Twitter and the feed of protest messages from users across the
globe joined the protests in physical space as well as in real time. That
being said, the goal of this chapter will be to investigate whether the inclusion of Twitter as "space" in general and protest hashtags as "places" in
particular affect the prominent and established perception of Greenpeace
as a specialized group of the "brave few." In addition, I ask if and how
the tweeting activities of Twitter users—now potential message shapers
not after but during a protest event—influenced the shape and direction
of the online protest.

Twitter can be understood as an awareness system that facilitates
immediate, fast, and widespread dissemination of information.[13] The service originally began as an "urban lifestyle tool for friends to provide each
other with updates of their whereabouts and activities" through a sophisticated system of following.[14] Twitter really entered the news media ecology at the end of 2009, when the service changed its tagline from "What
are you doing?" to "What's happening?," which paved the way for the
platform to become a more complex information space that would offer
users multiple ways to share a plethora of information from all kinds of
sources and engage in conversation.

Twitter has become a multifaceted and ambient news experience, and
over time its affordances have become quite attractive to professional entities such as media outlets, political offices, corporations, and last but not
least, nonprofit organizations such as Greenpeace.[15] For movements outside the establishment such as Greenpeace, the rise of digital technology
promised access to larger audiences as well as the potential to activate
sympathetic citizens to their cause. However, the advantages that accrue
to a few dedicated activists situated on a television screen do not necessarily transfer to the multiplicity of social media screens. Thus, it becomes
incumbent for researchers to investigate how structural changes from a
rather centralized media ecology to a more laterally arranged and destabilized social media information ecology might affect Greenpeace's
organizational strategies, especially as they saw particular success in a
mass-communication paradigm.

Following the "visual turn" in communication and media studies,
researchers have assessed the way visuals may influence our perception
of social, political, and identity issues.[16] Most studies are grounded in

what sociologist Andrew Szasz recognizes as the necessity to craft "political icons rather than symbols, iconography rather than rhetoric ... [as a means] to break through the indifference of the intended audience."[17] More recently, however, and informed by blurring of established sender–receiver transmission principles through social media, communication scholars have begun to investigate rhetorical performances outside the embodied orator paradigm, including the study of place and space.[18] Scholars of the so-called spatial turn in communication and media studies have taken issue with DeLuca's concept of the "image event" not only because of its heavy focus on the verbal and physical actions of protestors but also because the concept requires an intermediary for information dissemination—that is, the televisual screen dominated by major news outlets. "Research on social movements," as Endres and Senda-Cook explain, "has been focused on the actions of protesters through their words or use of bodies ... [while neglecting that] embodied rhetorics of protest are always situated in particular places."[19] Following the "spatial turn" in communication studies and as my point of departure in this chapter, I posit that the prevalent public perception of Greenpeace activists as the "brave few" not only stemmed from an embodied aesthetics of protest but that the protest identities of environmental activists were also fundamentally conditioned by the symbolic qualities of the particular "places" they appropriated and occupied.

Places have an objective, geographic dimension. Yet, any conquered place for protest also gains an additional semantic dimension as a scenic backdrop that can allow activist groups to craft symbolic messages to stimulate larger public responses. In their work on spatial rhetorics, Danielle Endres and Samantha Senda-Cook distinguish between "space," which refers to the ways "society and social practice are regulated ... by spatial thinking," and "place," which refers to "particular locations ... that are semi-bounded, a combination of material and symbolic qualities, and embodied."[20] They continue to explain that both concepts are connected in a perpetual cycle that activates processes of meaning-making.[21] In this sense, their work echoes Jessica Enoch's assessment that "[r]hetorics of space have the potential to make a space either powerful or diffused by giving value to the activities that happen inside that space and by suggesting or prescribing the kinds of occupants that should (and should not) move into and out of that space."[22] Building on their work, I argue that public perceptions of Greenpeace's protest identities are not only conditioned by physical actions but also negotiated by the "rhetoricity of places themselves."[23] Thus, situating a protest activity in a particularly meaningful place enables activists to "create temporary fissures" as a means to highlight problems and garner public support.[24] Through the rhetorical practices and performances of protestors, places are "made, maintained and contested."[25] Endres and Senda-Cook argue that "places have rhetorical import, such as the choice of a place," can "disrupt a dominant meaning of a particular place."[26] Recent protest events such as the revolution in Egypt or the Occupy Wall Street movement in New York City cannot be understood without also taking into consideration the symbolic qualities of the places that protestors occupied. Tahrir Square in Downtown Cairo, for example, is historically significant as a place that celebrates political liberation while Zuccotti Park in Downtown Manhattan is symbolically situated in the heart of American financial capitalism.

Moreover, and disregarding for a moment the currently prominent debate about the issue whether social media can affect change,[27] these two aforementioned protest events did rely heavily on the use of online networking platforms such as Facebook, Twitter, and YouTube—now common tools for activist purposes—in terms of both allowing participants to coordinate efforts on the ground and providing avenues for individuals to express sympathy and solidarity.[28] In this sense, social media spaces and their particular rhetorical affordances have become enmeshed in the spatial fabric of physical protest activities. Therefore, "we need to think of space and spatial relations," as Raka Shome highlights, "not as inert backdrops against which struggles of identity occur. Rather, these relations themselves must be seen as active components in the unequal and heterogeneous production and distribution of identities, politics, and actions."[29] Endres and Senda-Cook use the example of the 19-month occupation of Alcatraz Island by the American Indian Movement as an example to illustrate how the temporary reconstruction of the former prison island functions as a rhetorical act in itself, allowing the protest group to express "their right to occupy and self-govern on their own land."[30] As a rhetorical performance, places become the sites where struggles over "pre-existing meaning, temporary reconstruction, and repeated reconstruction" play out.[31] As such, the choice of conducting a protest in a particular place is as much an element that informs protest messages, as are the actions of participating activists.

STUDY DESIGN AND METHODS

This chapter will identify prevalent activist identity frames from the Twitter protest of 2012 and compare them to established Greenpeace identity frames taken from a pre-social media environmental protest: the highly successful occupation of the derelict oil platform, Brent Spar, in 1995. The juxtaposition of these two events makes for a fruitful comparison because both protest events essentially involved the same stakeholders, except that the latter introduced Twitter as a protest space and social media users as active participants. As far as the Brent Spar occupation is concerned, I use the studies of Löfstedt, Renn, and Kruse, which provide great illustrations of the ways Greenpeace and traditional news framed the protest event. When it comes to analyzing the 2012 Twitter protest, I employ a mixed-methods approach. I use Endres and Senda-Cook's work on the rhetoricity of places as a heuristic for my assessment of Twitter as a space for protest whereby its particular communication conventions (use of hashtags, cross-linking, tweeting and retweeting) both foster the construction of dedicated protest "places" and negotiate protest identities. In addition, I employ network analysis as put forth by researchers from the Queensland University of Technology in Brisbane, Australia, to assess overall user activity over the course of the study period. The social media data collection service, *DiscoverText*, which allows researchers access to communications data and metadata via the Twitter Application Programming Interface,[32] was used to create a hashtag-based data set that contains the entire Twitter conversation for the two hashtags #SavetheArctic and #StopShell between September 14 and 16, 2012—that is, the day of the actual protest as well as two additional days to see if and how the conversation on Twitter continued. Hashtag-based research has become a suitable approach to assess how Twitter users respond almost immediately to issues of social and political concern.[33] For each message posted to the two hashtags under examination, the following data points become available for analysis: sender, recipient, timestamp, tweet type (original or retweets), hashtags, and URL links.[34] Tweets from subsequent days were not collected because initial search queries revealed that user activity after September 14 significantly decreased. Additionally, my goal in this chapter is to focus on user- and time-based dimensions for early contributors to the two hashtags in order to assess both their activities and types of contributions rather than extending the study period, which would potentially include tweets of users who joined the conversation only after having heard about the protest from news outlets outside of Twitter. As far as user-based activities are concerned, the metadata for each tweet allows researchers to "draw distinctions between users who take a largely annunciative approach (mainly original tweets), conversational approach (mainly @replies), or disseminative approach (mainly retweets)."[35] Moreover, the data set also provides information pertaining to the use and extent to which Twitter users aligned additional hashtags to the two main ones sponsored by Greenpeace. Hashtags may function as semantic markers, allowing protest participants on Twitter to actively bridge a given hashtag conversation with other conversations on the micro-blogging platform, which in turn may shape the thematic direction of the original conversation. To assess overall tweeting patterns, I use Tedjamulia's proposed distinction of the so-called 1/9/90 rule:[36] this division "groups the one per cent of lead users . . . separately from the next nine per cent of still highly active users, and separately in turn from the remaining 90% of least active users in the long tail of participants."[37] In total, 5,323 tweets were logged over the course of the study period. Finally, to get a sense of major protest themes that emerged on Twitter I employ framing analysis as developed by rhetorical scholar Jim A. Kuypers.[38] Framing analysis complements the quantitative analysis. Kuypers defines framing as "the process whereby communicators act—consciously or not—to construct a particular point of view that encourages the facts of a given situation to be viewed in a particular manner, which some facts made more or less noticeable (even ignored) than others."[39] Framing analysis has become a reliable approach for the critical examination of the configurations and structural features of communicative practices, finding its way into a number of related disciplines such as media research, political science, and sociology.[40] Frames are communication devices that diagnose, evaluate, and prescribe issues,[41] and we rely on them to make sense of what we read.[42] To give an example, the issue of abortion can be framed in the sense of killing unborn human life or it can be communicated from the perspective of free choice. Functioning as a means of interpretation that enables individuals to "locate, perceive, identify, and label" issues,[43] frames induce processes of meaning making, the organization of experience through language, and guide action, whether individual or collective.[44] As metaphors, frames encompass two related but different purposes: on the one hand, frames are a particular grammar, "a structure in which meaning is contained in and conveyed by the relationships among the elements."[45] On the other hand, similar to a window or a picture frame, they function as a "boundary that keeps some elements in view and others out of view."[46] Gamson and Modigliani identify "framing devices" (e.g., metaphors, examples, catchphrases) that condense information and offer a "media package" of an issue.[47] Kuypers suggests two steps to analyze frames: (1) finding main themes and (2) assessing the framing of themes by looking for keywords, concepts, labels, metaphors, and phrases that help contextualize remarks. Textual analysis of the top 1 percent of shared tweets in the data set will provide the basis for analysis here.

WHEN "DAVIDS" MET "GOLIATH"—THE OCCUPATION OF THE BRENT SPAR

Hardly any Greenpeace campaign has resonated more in the public sphere than the organization's occupation of the Brent Spar in 1995. With this campaign, Greenpeace called for the first time public attention to the role that oil companies had been playing in polluting the seas. The derelict, rust-ridden oil rig turned into a remarkably potent place for protest since it was the first decommissioned oil platform ready for disposal. The motivation for the occupation, which stands as one of the most representative examples of Greenpeace's distinct style of protest, arose from the UK government's approval of Shell's plans to sink the rig into the North Atlantic. Greenpeace had warned that such an action would create an impermissible precedent for future marine disposals of structures containing toxic materials as well as a danger to the environment.[48] With no compromise in sight, a nondescript freighter carrying 18 Greenpeace activists safely hidden in its cargo hold disembarked from Hamburg harbor, Germany, on the night of April 27, 1995, shortly before Shell would have commenced with the disposal. The occupation began on April 30, 1995, and the entire campaign lasted for almost two months.[49] In the course of the occupation, Shell readily embraced its adversarial role and attempted to evict the activists numerous times from the platform. For example, the company issued its servicing vessels, that were patrolling the Brent Spar, to use on-board water cannons not only to prevent activists from climbing onto the structure but also to make it difficult for helicopters to aid the occupants with supplies.[50] During the occupation, activists frequently conducted live TV interviews with news outlets all over Europe using satellite equipment, and some activists kept online diaries of the protest for later dissemination. The images of this large-scale protest operation caught significant and sustained attention from the media, particularly television, and over time more and more European governments turned away from Shell and demanded that the company should devise alternative disposal plans. On June 20, 1995, after close to two months of protest and growing political and public pressure, Shell finally abandoned its sea disposal plan for the oil rig and the company agreed to the more costly solution of dismantling the Brent Spar on land.[51] In the aftermath of Greenpeace's successful protest, European nations agreed to put a ban on sea disposals for offshore steel oil rigs during the 1998 Oslo and Paris Convention (OSPAR) in Sintra, Portugal.[52]

Not surprisingly, the driving metaphor of the occupation was the "David versus Goliath" narrative to which news outlets resorted to repeatedly. According to Endres and Senda-Cook, "place (re)constructions can function rhetorically to challenge dominant meanings and practices in a place."[53] And the major component of the occupation was the aesthetic and symbolic appeal of the derelict oil platform. Originally commissioned in 1976, the Brent Spar had already been in use for close to 20 years, thus showing significant wear and corrosion. While being the result of common natural processes at sea, the derelict condition of the installation itself enticed the public to perceive the activities of Shell as toxic and environmentally irresponsible. In addition, as a product of impressive technical engineering, the Brent Spar, weighing approximately 14,500 tons and peaking about 44 meters above sea level, created a formidable image of corporate control and exploitation of a peaceful, natural habitat. Moreover, given the inhospitable conditions on the platform and the constant water cannon bombardment, the Brent Spar as an occupied place also exerted rhetorical influence by solidifying public sympathy for the Greenpeace activists who were enduring the harsh conditions. In this sense, both the actions of activists and the material conditions of the occupied platform provided the basis for the public perception of Greenpeace activists as modern-day Davids, "concerned with the wellbeing of the environment and thus also with the wellbeing of humanity."[54] For her analysis, Kruse analyzed a sample of German and French newspaper articles published over the course of the occupation. She identifies the "David versus Goliath" metaphor in news content such as "[d]espite constant bombardment with water cannons, Greenpeace managed by helicopter to supply its two members ... with food, clothes, and blankets" from the German *Frankfurter Allgemeine Zeitung*[55] or the headline, "Unequal battle."[56] In this "dramatic warlike scenario," the majority of news outlets humanized Greenpeace as an "environmental protectionist organization" while dehumanizing the image of Shell as a "cool [and] calculating corporation."[57] The Brent Spar controversy "offered the media three ingredients it finds difficult to resist: conflict, event and personality."[58] The countermeasures employed by Shell, then, further helped to solidify the oil company's role as adversary. News stations framed the company as a greedy corporation, as an "insensitive, capitalist giant whose only interest was profit."[59] As a consequence of such framing, "conservative groups joined Green action groups in asking for consumer boycott of Shell gasoline stations."[60] The Brent Spar became a symbol for dominant industrial attitudes, which seemed to consider the world's oceans as convenient dumping places for toxic substances.

Its occupation in 1995 stands, therefore, as one of the most memorable Greenpeace campaigns, especially with regard to the level of political and public support that the protest was able to generate. By appropriating and reconfiguring this remote location as a central place for protest and casting the Brent Spar as a symbol of corporate greed, Greenpeace activists quickly turned the protest into a compelling narrative of the heroic few that braved the corporate super structure in the name of the environment. By attempting to drive activists violently away from the oil rig using water cannons, Shell UK failed to anticipate the impact that images of the occupation would have on public relations.[61] Major news outlets across Europe readily assembled the stream of images they received from Greenpeace into a striking narrative, frequently casting the protesters as romantically appealing "Guerrilla"-warriors, clad in characteristic jumpsuit uniforms, and Shell as the greedy and irresponsible environmental villain.[62] The occupation turned the derelict Brent Spar, then, into a driving spatial metaphor to mobilize publics. This provocative style of protest to invigorate public debate was perfectly tailored to a public sphere with television as the dominant channel for information dissemination. Through TV interviews, the lowering of banners, and the dissemination of diary entries, the occupiers were able to reduce a complex set of issues into straightforward, rhetorically powerful symbols that would invigorate publics to question controversial corporate and governmental practices. The principles of drama and spectacle were used to great effect to attract attention in the public sphere.

GREENPEACE'S FORAY INTO THE TWITTERSPHERE

As an ephemeral, ambient information environment, Twitter has the ability of (re)organizing communication mechanisms within specific protest ecologies. Not only does the platform foster the transmission of information, Twitter also provides the ability to constitute networked protest places as negotiated performances of individual and collective agency. These kinds of networks, comprised of individuals and groups and technological affordances, may certainly engage differently with regard to questions of message coherence and perpetuation. Endres and Senda-Cook argue that protest places are grounded in a "fluid tension between materiality and symbolism."[63] On Twitter, these tensions come into play as the service enables users not only to define places through the use of issue-specific hashtags but also to negotiate the direction of hashtag-based discourses by including hashtags in their tweets that may either refer to thematically similar or opposed conversations. Especially the inclusion of hashtags that do not directly refer to the issue can give researchers a sense of the extent to which "protesters may build on a pre-existing meaning of a place to help make their point."[64] In this sense, the utilization of additional hashtags becomes a rhetorical performance that can aid activists "in making and unmaking the possibilities of protest."[65] The #SavetheArctic and #StopShell hashtags, as stated, were launched by Greenpeace as part of a wider campaign to publicize their "Save the Arctic" campaign and to mobilize support. The total number of tweets sent to these two hashtags amounted to 5,323 between September 14, 2012, and September 16, 2012. As the data set shows, the hashtags involved a burst of activity around the day of the protest, but ceased shortly after. In terms of general user composition, both were multi-language hashtags consisting of tweets posted in languages including English, German, Dutch, Spanish, and Italian. Out of the total number of tweets under examination, 42.16 percent (2,245) were retweets and 57.84 percent were original tweets. Twitter protesters were more willing to participate with original content and messages of protest rather than merely relegating and amplifying already existing tweets through Twitter's retweet function. While the findings illustrate that the majority of Twitter users actively embraced their roles as active protest participants, the dynamic shifts when distributed user activity is concerned. In total, 1,864 unique user accounts contributed to the Twitter protest. The top 1 percent consisted of 19 users, 13 of which were—based on their respective Twitter handles—Greenpeace affiliated accounts. This most active group posted a total of 1,979 tweets (37.18%) to the hashtags and 1,542 (77.92%) were marked as retweets. The next group of still highly active users consisted of 144 unique users in total who posted 1,199 messages (22.52%), of which 504 (42.04%) were retweets. Finally, the least active group of hashtag contributors consisted of 1,701 accounts. This group posted 2,145 messages in total (40.3%), and they only retweeted 199 times (9.28%). This not only illustrates that the protest was largely moderated by a few Greenpeace affiliated accounts but also suggests that the most active users engaged more in information brokerage practices rather than supplying original content. The least active but at the same time least visible users supplied more original content to the hashtags.

In a media ecology in which the dissemination and circulation of information becomes a matter of active user participation, the use of links becomes an important tool for directing attention to specific media objects.[66] In the data set examined here, links appeared in 62.2 percent of the tweets. Of those links posted to the two hashtags, 210 unique links (73.18%) referred to websites and social media profile pages of various Greenpeace groups, which either featured additional campaign information or contained uploaded photos of the demonstrations in front of Shell gas stations. These links were shared a total of 2,656 times (80.22%). The remaining 77 unique links (26.82%) were shared 655 times (19.78%). These links led users to various online news outlets such as the *Guardian* or the *Huffington Post*, which provided further information regarding the potentially negative ramifications of conducting oil-drilling operations in the Arctic. This suggests that the ad hoc community that formed around the two hashtags strongly consisted of already environmentally conscious citizens. While earlier studies on Twitter and political protest have found that the platform can facilitate the integration of very different agents into a hashtag conversation,[67] the analysis of #SavetheArctic and #StopShell reveals a remarkable consistency in terms of shared opinions. Twitter streams have the potential of attracting diverse senders, from individuals to organization, supported by their respective networks of followers so that message contributors from afar may enter a hashtag conversation in the midst of a communicative action place. Yet, in terms of linking activity the analysis of the two hashtags illustrates a rather homogeneous group formation. There was a pronounced lack of debate regarding the issue of arctic drilling.

Unlike a Twitter profile feed, which a user has control over, hashtagged conversations can allow anyone to contribute. The practice of adding additional hashtags into a tweet has the potential of allowing the main hashtag conversation to cut across communicative places and, thus, both seep into other conversations across a variety of feeds and networks as well as shape the direction of the main hashtag conversation as well.[68]

Figure 3.1
Two Greenpeace Activists Roping Down from the Brent Spar Oil Rig

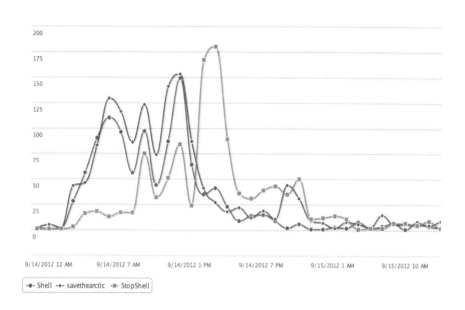

Used in such a way, Twitter users can engage in the "temporary reconstructions of places [to] create short-term fissures in the dominant meanings of [other, established] places in productive ways."[69] Earlier research on the #myNYPD Twitter scandal in 2014, an event that began as a social media branding campaign for the New York Police Department, illustrated how a community of Occupy Wall Street affiliated protesters managed to redirect the original hashtag conversation through the use of various, emotionally charged hashtags such as #FTP (referring to the expression "Fuck the Police") or #OWS (referring to the official hashtag of the Occupy movement) and turn #myNYPD into an online protest place surrounding the issue of police brutality in the United States.[70] As Endres and Senda-Cook explain, "[r]epeated temporary constructions of place may result in long-lasting additions to the meaning of a place."[71] The #myNYPD hashtag is now commonly regarded as a cautionary tale of social media campaigning due to the interventions of former Occupy Wall Street protesters. The analysis of #SavetheArctic and #StopShell, however, revealed a remarkable consistency as far as hashtag use is concerned. The former was shared a total of 3,060 times, while the latter was posted 3,669 times. The most widely used hashtags outside of the two official ones were predominantly translations of the two main ones into other languages, the most prominent being the German hashtag #StoppShell, which was shared a total of only 187 times. The only other two widely posted hashtags in the data set were #Shell (104 times) and #Arctic (49 times). There is no indication that Twitter users actively engaged in crosscutting discourses by tapping into other hashtag conversations. The discrepancy in total numbers, again, suggests that the Greenpeace Twitter protest remained rather exclusive for the duration of the protest event. Moreover, as Figure 3.1 highlights, hashtag activity was very much synched to mentioning the official Shell Twitter account in tweeted messages as well. This shows that rather than extending the protest place onto the Twittersphere, the entire online protest was negotiated between Greenpeace, environmentally conscious Twitter users, and the Shell Corporation. As a side note, the official Twitter account of Shell did not post a single message to the hashtag conversation.

Quantitative analysis of the most shared tweets reveals that the top 10, most retweeted messages on their own amounted to 35.25 percent of the total number of retweets. Thematically, all of these 10 tweets engage in practices of mobilization. The most shared tweet in the data set, "We have to work together to help #SavetheArctic! Sign and share: http://t.co/qCC4JA1h #StopShell," posted by the official Greenpeace Twitter account, was the only one out of the top 10 that attempted to establish a solidarity and community frame for the protest through the use of the first person plural pronoun. A sample of other, less visible tweets on the hashtag illustrates the way Twitter users participated in the framing of Arctic drilling as an issue. Following are a couple of representative tweets out of this set: "RT @Camz99: The Arctic is not Shell's property, it belongs to all the creatures of this planet. #stopshell;" "RT @ClaudiaFCaicedo: #stopshell #shellexecutives what would you say to your kids about this? #SHAMEONYOU;" or "RT @Sokolowicz: what do you want for your kids, some money or a planet? #stopshell." These tweets show how Twitter users employed a "taking responsibility for future generations"-frame to criticize the plans of Shell to begin drilling operations in the Arctic. This frame corresponds with official and established Greenpeace communication that often resorts to "commensurability" and "social responsibility" frames to garner public support.

Overall, the analysis suggests that #SavetheArctic and #StopShell were used rather strategically by Greenpeace to personalize and mobilize protest participants. While Greenpeace's strategy of personalizing their public communication through the use of Twitter meant running the risk of losing control over their message and brand, the two hashtags under observations were surprisingly conformist and orderly. Protest participants commonly addressed each other rather than a general public. In this sense, they formed what Davis has called an "online elite discourse network."[72] In this sense, the organization retained its image of the few, albeit slightly increased in total numbers. #SavetheArctic and #StopShell reflected a rather organization-centered and centrally managed protest place. Given that the hashtag feeds were also prominently featured on large projection screens in front of various Shell gas stations, the analysis suggests that Greenpeace instrumentalized the Twitter space as a stylistic and aesthetic device for its protest purposes designed to highlight allegedly global dissatisfaction with Shell's oil-drilling plans. Yet, a global outcry failed to appear.

CAUGHT BETWEEN TELEVISUAL AND DIGITAL PRESENCE

This chapter has argued that the critical examination of the relation between the transformation from a centralized media ecology to a more destabilized social media information ecology on the one hand and its potential ramifications for collective action practices on the other demand the recognition of the ways in which digital technologies in general and social media spaces in particular infuse protest ecologies. The incorporation of social media into the communication practices of environmental groups, such as Greenpeace, invites attention to the ways established protest practices play out under social media circumstances. While Twitter as a digital mechanism of aggregation through hashtags can involve loss of message control while at the same time promising that grievances may become viral very quickly, in the end the direction, scope, and willingness to let go of authorial control is also situational and becomes a matter of choice. Given the active role that Greenpeace played on #SavetheArctic and #StopShell, activists could have used Twitter's communication conventions to crosscut into other hashtag conversations. Yet, the analysis showed that this did not happen. This means that Greenpeace, as an organization that originated in the mass-communication era, is still very much in tune with established principles of the "image event." The Brent Spar oil rig was framed as a peripheral place that accentuated the notion that environmental issues need to be moved to the center of public discourse via televisual media channels. And in order to accomplish that, Greenpeace arranged the protest to be cast as a dramatic standoff between the heroic few and a formidable corporate stakeholder. While the Twitter protest could have offered Greenpeace the opportunity to relinquish authorial control and allow citizens across the globe to raise their voice, the analysis has shown that the protest hashtags remained very much in isolation on the Twittersphere. Based on these results, the large projection screens that featured the tweets from Twitter users on September 14, 2012, can be regarded more in terms of the formidable and imposing aesthetic of the derelict Brent Spar. From a stylistic perspective, Greenpeace's communication strategy was geared toward making Twitter as a global network visible and prominent within the framework of DeLuca's image event.

Still, the opportunities and challenges of social media for citizens to access and participate in protest are important strands of discussion within academic debates surrounding the nature of political participation and social connectivity.[73] Especially those protest groups that were born in the mass-communication era, as this chapter has shown continue to be significant objects for analysis for researchers to investigate the ways they adapt to shifting media landscapes. Current work on spatial rhetorics can help in these assessments not only with regard to the spatial dynamics that are at play in social media but also to distinguish between "place-based arguments and place-as-rhetoric."[74] Finally a note of caution is necessary. It needs to be emphasized that focusing on social media in the context of protest in isolation can yield only tentative answers rather than full descriptions. Whenever Twitter has been used for protest, it has always been a part in the bigger, spatial fabric of a given protest event. Further, in many cases of direct online action, Twitter hashtags are just one of many social media communication conventions to bring people together in more or less concerted ways.

NOTES

1. Greenpeace International, "Bob Hunter 1941–2005: Greenpeace Founding Member Dead at 63," *Greenpeace.org*, May 2, 2005, http://www.greenpeace.org/international/en/news/features/bob-hunter/.

2. Kevin M. DeLuca and Jennifer Peeples, "From Public Sphere to Public Screen: Democracy, Activism, and the 'Violence' of Seattle," *Critical Studies in Media Communication* 19, 2002: 134; Anders Hansen, "Claims-Making and Framing in British Newspaper Coverage of the 'Brent Spar' Controversy," in *Environmental Risks and Media*, eds. Stuart Allan, Barbara Adam, and Cynthia Carter (London: Routledge, 2000): 56.

3. DeLuca and Peeples, "From Public Sphere to Public Screen," 134.

4. Paddy Scannell, "The Centrality of Televisions of the Center in Today's Globalized World," In *Communication and Power in the Global Era*, eds. Marwan M. Kraidy (London: Routledge, 2013), 118–119.

5. John W. Delicath and Kevin M. DeLuca, "Image Events, the Public Sphere, and Argumentative Practice: The Case of Radical Environmental Groups," *Argumentation* 17, 2003: 326.

6. Ibid., pp. 315, 322.

7. Ibid., p. 319.

8. One such action, which this chapter will discuss more in depth, was the successful occupation of Shell's derelict oil platform, Brent Spar, by Greenpeace activists in 1995 after the oil company had announced its plans to dump the platform into the North Atlantic seabed.

9. Yochai Benkler, *The Wealth of Networks: How Social Production Transforms Markets and Freedom* (New Haven, CT: Yale University Press, 2006).

10. Jan-Hinrik Schmidt, "Twitter and the Rise of Personal Publics," In *Twitter and Society*, eds. Katrin Weller, Axel Bruns, Jean Burgess, Merja Mahrt, and Cornelius Puschmann (New York: Peter Lang, 2014), 8.

11. Axel Bruns and Jean Burgess, "The Use of Twitter Hashtags in the Formation of Ad Hoc Publics," Paper presented at the European Consortium of Political Research Conference (Reykjavík, 26 August 2011).

12. "Shell Sues Greenpeace to Curb Arctic Protests," *Telegraph.co.uk*, September 21, 2012, http://www.telegraph.co.uk/finance/newsbysector/energy/oilandgas/9558482/Shell-sues-Greenpeace-to-curb-Arctic-protests.html.

13. Haewoon Kwak, Changhyun Lee, Hosung Park, and Sue Moon, "What Is Twitter, a Social Network or a News Medai?," In *WWW'10: Proceedings of the 19th International Conference on World Wide Web* (New York: ACM, 2010), 591–600.

14. Cuneyt G. Akcora and Murat Ali Bayir, "Seems Stupid Until You Try It: Press Coverage of Twitter, 2006–2009," *New Media & Society* 12, no. 8 (2010): 1262–1279.

15. Alfred Hermida, "Twittering the News: The Emergence of Ambient Journalism," *Journalism Practice* 4, no. 3 (2010): 297–308.

16. Margaret R. LaWare, "Encountering Visions of Aztlan: Arguments for Ethnic Pride, Community Activism, and Cultural Revitalization in Chicano Murals," *Argumentation and Advocacy* 34 (1998): 140–153; DeLuca and Peeples, "From Public Sphere to Public Screen," 125–151; Catherine H. Palczewski, "The Male Madonna and the Feminine Uncle Sam: Visual Argument, Icons, and Ideographs in 1909 Anti-Woman Suffrage Postcards," *Quarterly Journal of Speech* 91 (2005): 365–394; Robert Hariman and John L. Lucaites, *No Caption Needed: Iconic Photographs, Public Culture, and Liberal Democracy* (Chicago, IL: University of Chicago Press, 2007).

17. Andrew Szaz, *EcoPopulism: Toxic Waste and the Movement for Environmental Justice* (Minneapolis, MN: University of Minnesota Press, 1994), 62–63.

18. Greg Dickinson, Brian L. Ortt, and Eric Aoki, "Memory and Myth at the Buffalo Bill Museum," *Western Journal of Communication* 69, no. 2 (2005): 85–108; William V. Balthrop, Carol Blair, and N. Michael, "The Presence of the Present: Hijacking 'The Good War'?," *Western Journal of Communication* 74, no. 2 (2010): 170–207; Danielle Endres and Samantha Senda-Cook, "Location Matters: The Rhetoric of Place in Protest," *Quarterly Journal of Speech* 97, no. 3 (2011): 257–282.

19. Endres and Senda-Cook, "Location Matters," 258.

20. Ibid., pp. 289–260.

21. Ibid., p. 260.

22. Jessica Enoch, "A Woman's Place Is in the School: Rhetorics of Gendered Space in Nineteenth-Century America," *College English* 70, no. 3 (2008): 276.

23. Endres and Senda-Cook, "Location Matters," 257.

24. Ibid.

25. Tim Cresswell, *Place: A Short Introduction* (Malden, MA: Blackwell Publishing, 2004), 5.

26. Endres and Senda-Cook, "Location Matters," 277.

27. In this chapter I am less concerned with questions whether Twitter triggers revolutions, and whether twittered uprisings are effective. In the wake of protest events such as Occupy Wall Street or the Arab Spring, prominent social media skeptics like Malcolm Gladwell or Evgeny Morozov problematized the effectiveness of achieving social change when set next to the engagement of protestors in physical settings. Yet, Internet scholars like Clay Shirky or Howard Rheingold have argued that social media platforms offer means to organize and collaborate that may lead to effective action as well. While this is an important debate as far as the role of social media in politics is concerned, my goal in this chapter is rather

to examine how Twitter as a protest space might affect established perceptions of Greenpeace activists and the depiction of corresponding environmental issues.

28. Kevin M. DeLuca, Sean Lawson, and Ye Sun, "Occupy Wall Street on the Public Screens of Social Media: The Many Framings of the Birth of a Protest Movement: OWS on the Public Screens of Social Media," *Communication, Culture & Critique* 5, no. 4 (2012): 483–509; A. Velasquez, "Social Media and Online Political Discussion: The Effect of Cues and Informational Cascades on Participation in Online Political Communities," *New Media & Society* 14, no. 8 (2012): 1286–1303; Zizi Papacharissi and Maria de Fatima Oliveira, "Affective News and Networked Publics: The Rhythms of News Storytelling on #Egypt," *Journal of Communication* 62, no. 2 (2012): 266–282; Gilad Lotan, Erhardt Graeff, Mike Ananny, Devin Gaffney, Ian Pearce, and Danah Boyd, "The Revolutions Were Tweeted: Information Flows During the 2011 Tunisian and Egyptian Revolutions," *International Journal of Communication* 5 (2011): 1375–1405.

29. Raka Shome, "Space Matters: The Power and Practice of Space," *Communication Theory* 13, no. 1 (2003): 43.

30. Endres and Senda-Cook, "Location Matters," 269.

31. Ibid., p. 272.

32. For more information on Twitter data, see Cornelius Puschmann and Jean Burgess, "The Politics of Twitter Data," In *Twitter and Society*, eds. Katrin Weller, Axel Bruns, Jean Burgess, Merja Mahrt, and Cornelius Puschmann (New York: Peter Lang, 2014), 43–54.

33. Devin Gaffney, "#iranElection: Quantifying Online Activism," *Proceedings of the WebSci10: Extending the Frontiers of Society On-Line* (Raleigh, NC, April 26–27, 2010); Lotan, Graeff, Ananny, Gaffney, Pearce, and Boyd, "The Revolutions Were Tweeted," 1375–1405; Emma Tonkin, Heather D. Pfeiffer, and Greg Tourte, "Twitter, Information Sharing and the London Riots?," *Bulletin of the American Society for Information Science and Technology* 38, no. 2 (2012): 49–57.

34. Axel Bruns and Stefan Stieglitz, "Metrics for Understanding Communication on Twitter," In *Twitter and Society*, eds. Katrin Weller, Axel Bruns, Jean Burgess, Merja Mahrt, and Cornelius Puschmann (New York: Peter Lang, 2014), 70.

35. Ibid., pp. 72–73.

36. S. J. J. Tedjamulia, D. L. Dean, D. R. Olsen, and C. C. Albrecht, "Motivating Content Contributions to Online Communities: Toward a More Comprehensive Theory," *Proceedings of the 38th Annual Hawaii International Conference on System Sciences* (Washington, DC, 2005), 193.

37. Bruns and Stieglitz, "Metrics for Understanding Communication on Twitter," 74.

38. Jim A. Kuypers, "Framing Analysis," In *Rhetorical Criticism: Perspectives in Action*, ed. Jim A. Kuypers (Lanham, MD: Lexington Books, 2009), 181–203.

39. Ibid., p. 182.

40. Shanto Iyengar and Donald R. Kinder, *News That Matters: Television and American Opinion* (Chicago, IL: University of Chicago Press, 1987); Shanto Iyengar, *Is Anyone Responsible? How Television Frames Political Issues* (Chicago, IL: University of Chicago Press, 1991); T. Michael Maher, "Framing: An Emerging Paradigm or a Phase of Agenda Setting," In *Framing Public Life: Perspectives on Media and our Understanding of the Social World*, eds. Stephen D. Reese, Oscar H. Gandy, and August E. Gran (Mahwah, NJ: Lawrence Erlbaum Associates, 2001).

41. Robert M. Entman, "Framing: Toward Clarification of a Fractured Paradigm," *Journal of Communication* 43, no. 4 (1993): 51–58.

42. William A. Gamson and Andre Modigliani, "Media Discourse and Public Opinion on Nuclear Power: A Constructionist Approach," *American Journal of Sociology* 95, no. 1 (1989): 1–37; Erving Goffman, *Frame Analysis: An Essay on the Organization of Experience* (New York: Harper & Row, 1974).

43. Goffman, *Frame Analysis*, 21.

44. David A. Snow, Burke Rochford, Jr., Steven K. Worden, and Robert D. Benford, "Frame Alignment Processes, Micromobilization, and Movement Participation," *American Sociological Review* 51 (1986): 464–481.

45. Rhys H. Williams and Robert D. Benford, "Two Faces of Collective Action Frames: A Theoretical Consideration," *Current Perspectives in Social Theory* 20 (2000): 129.

46. Ibid., pp. 129–131.

47. Gamson and Modigliani, "Media Discourse and Public Opinion on Nuclear Power," 1–37.

48. Nathaniel C. Nash, "Oil Companies Face Boycott Over Sinking of Rig," *NYTimes.com*, June 17, 1995, http://www.nytimes.com/1995/06/17/world/oil-companies-face-boycott-over-sinking-of-rig.html.

49. Svenja Koch, Christian Krüger, Jochen Lohmann, Matthias Müller-Henning, Manfred Redelfs, and Karsten Smid, "Brent Spar und die Folgen: Zehn Jahre Danach," *Greenpeace.de*, 2005, 16–24, https://www.greenpeace.de/sites/www.greenpeace.de/files/Brent_Spar_und_die_Folgen_1.pdf.

50. Julia Kruse, "Fantasy Themes and Rhetorical Visions in the *Brent Spar* Crisis: A Comparative Analysis of German and French Newspaper Coverage," *Argumentation* 15 (2001): 439–456.

51. Ragnar E. Löfstedt and Ortwin Renn, "The Brent Spar Controversy: An Example of Risk Communication Gone Wrong," *Risk Analysis* 17, no. 2 (1997): 131–136.

52. Koch, Krüger, Lohmann, Müller-Henning, Redelfs, and Smid, "Brent Spar und die Folgen," 16–24.

53. Endres and Senda-Cook, "Location Matters," 258.

54. Kruse, "Fantasy Themes and Rhetorical Visions in the *Brent Spar* Crisis," 442.

55. Ibid., p. 445.

56. Ibid., p. 445.

57. Ibid., pp. 442–443.

58. Joe Smith, "After the Brent Spar: Business, the Media and the New Environmental Politics," In *The Daily Globe: Environmental Change, the Public and the Media*, ed. Joe Smith (London: Earthscan Publications, 2000), 168.

59. Kruse, "Fantasy Themes and Rhetorical Visions in the *Brent Spar* Crisis," 442.

60. Löfstedt and Renn, "The Brent Spar Controversy," 132.

61. Kevin M. DeLuca, *Image Politics: The New Rhetoric of Environmental Activism* (New York: Guilford Press, 1999).

62. Marlise Simons, "For Greenpeace Guerrillas, Environmentalism Is Again a Growth Industry," *NYTimes.com*, July 8, 1995, http://www.nytimes.com/1995/07/08/world/for-greenpeace-guerrillas-environmentalism-is-again-a-growth-industry.html.

63. Endres and Senda-Cook, "Location Matters," 262.

64. Ibid., p. 259.

65. Ibid., p. 258.

66. Henry Jenkins, *Convergence Culture: Where Old and New Media Collide* (Cambridge, MA: MIT Press, 2006), 4.

67. A. Maireder and C. Schwarzenegger, "A Movement of Connected Individuals: Social Media in the Austrian Student Protests 2009," *Information, Communication & Society* 15, no. 2 (2012), 171–195.

68. D. Boyd, S. Golder, and G. Lotan, "Tweet Tweet Retweet: Conversational Aspects of Retweeting on Twitter," *Proceedings of HICSS-43* (Kauai, HI, January 2010); C. Honeycutt and S. Herring, "Beyond Microblogging: Conversation and Collaboration Via Twitter," *Proceedings of the 42nd Hawai'i International Conference on System Sciences* (Los Alamitos, CA, 2009).

69. Endres and Senda-Cook, "Location Matters," 259.

70. Thomas Breideband, "Ecologies of Subversion and Inspiration on Twitter: The Hijacking of #myNYPD," Paper presented at Internet Research 16, Phoenix, AZ, October 21–24, 2015.

71. Endres and Senda-Cook, "Location Matters," 270.

72. A. Davis, "New Media and Fat Democracy: The Paradox of Online Participation," *New Media & Society* 12, no. 5 (2010): 745–761.

73. For a review see H. Farrell, "The Consequences of the Internet for Politics," *Annual Review of Political Science* 15, no. 1 (2012): 35–52.

74. Endres and Senda-Cook, "Location Matters," 258.

Chapter 4

Big Data Goes to Washington: How Protesters Navigate Aggregated Social Media Content

Candice Lanius

Big data have arrived on the scene in American politics. Unlike Mr. Smith's presence in the fictional film *Mr. Smith Goes to Washington*, however, it is unclear whether the effects of big data technologies will, as a whole, be largely positive or negative for the political landscape. Political participation in America is perpetually in crisis, with limited numbers participating in elections or interacting directly with their elected representatives. Big data analysis is a potential solution for better understanding the American public: it utilizes available data streams to quickly provide a holistic picture of Americans' opinions and sentiments about current and pressing issues. As a result, big data technologies for political participation are set to accomplish two major goals: (1) expand the number of individuals represented in politics by ambiently collecting their preferences on key public issues, and (2) reaching currently underrepresented populations to understand their perspectives, integrating them into the political process. While these goals are commendable, it is important to be cautious in relying on new technologies for something as important as political representation. Good intentions can pave a dangerous road, and this chapter looks at the uses of big social data to represent a section of the public during two political protests to understand how protestors navigate big social data as a representative technology.

Political protests are an attractive tool for the American public to interact with and lobby the government. For protests to be effective, they must articulate a clear message, transmit that message to a broader audience with the intention of persuading the public to their point of view, and preserve their message over time. A consistent message is necessary since political change requires a sustained effort and palatable image. To use big data as a representative technology, the analytics must be able to distill a clear message that maintains the core intention of the protesters, be legible to a broad audience, and preserve the message and content over time to allow for a sustained record of political discourse. These three attributes are key to the function of protests in broader political discourse, and on face, big data analysis appears to fulfill these requirements quite well.

BIG SOCIAL DATA: THE OMNISCIENT VIEW

Big data is a term used to describe data sets that are too large or complex for common computer platforms and software solutions to handle. With big data, new techniques have been engineered to support data collection, storage, and the analytical capacity to generate insight from data resources. These insights tend to reveal correlational relationships where one variable of interest changes in some way as another variable changes. As a result, the goal of many big data projects is to continuously predict future behaviors rather than explain the underlying causes for past behavior. Big data analytics that are used to investigate political questions often rely upon data from social media platforms and networked communication technologies to generate an image of how the populace is feeling at a given moment in time. Examples include coverage of the Green Revolution in Iran and the Egyptian Revolution of 2011, where the vast majority of news reports were mediated through Twitter and Facebook.[1]

Social media data are one of the most challenging types of big data to process due to volume; there were more than 2 billion social media users worldwide by early 2015. Social media data also offer a great deal of variety, with text, audio, video, and all the corresponding metadata that are necessary to make data exchange work across a dispersed network, such as the timestamp, location marker, and file type. Social media data are also distinct because they offer a constant stream of digital content; there is no way for analysts to bracket the flow of information. Social media companies process their users' data using internal resources and generally make a portion of that data available through an API (application programming interface) for use by other companies and researchers. Social media data resources are compiled and analyzed in social listening labs that are spaces dedicated to seeking out certain types of valuable insight. Social listening labs are very common in marketing or for-profit contexts to collect information passively from consumers to target them with better advertisements.

An early example of a big social data project is Google's *Flu Trends*, a program made available to the public in 2008. *Flu Trends* is instructive for how insight is generated from social media data, but it also illuminates potential problems with big social data practice.[2] In 2008, Google claimed its search engine results could predict flu outbreaks before even the Centers for Disease Control (CDC) was able to identify trends from public records. Three years later, Google admitted that *Flu Trends* was inaccurate a large portion of the time due to its reliance on search history data alone. This inaccuracy was from a lack of intentionality or temporal connection between the individuals searching for information about the flu and their own health. Google assumed that individuals searching for flu symptoms must be experiencing symptoms at that precise moment in time and at that specific IP address. To improve the programs' accuracy, Google began combining search data with traditional CDC data. As an example of found resources, social media data are a risky resource for sociological projects looking at discourse online. The data are readily available, but they are radically decontextualized from their origin, which means they could be addressing any number of alternative situations.[3]

Beyond problems with intentionality that emerge from the use of found social media data, other scholars, such as danah boyd and Kate Crawford (2012), have discussed the limitations of using these technologies for research.[4] boyd and Crawford argue that these new tools change research outcomes in unpredictable ways, that big data are not always better or more accurate, and that the use of big data in certain situations is not ethical. Some media scholars, such as Clay Shirky, welcome this change with excitement, while others, like Nicholas Carr, see social media for meaningful political engagement as an empty promise.[5] The volume *Twitter and Society* discusses the methodology and politics of using Twitter data in great detail, providing a history of how the platform has been studied and used since 2006.[6] Another potential problem with the use of big social data is what political scientists and communication scholars describe as the bandwagon effect. This effect involves an individual changing his or her belief to bring it closer to what the larger community believes.[7] With big social data applied to political discourse, a similar feedback effect is possible. The stakes for a representative democracy are high and require that citizens have their voice represented fully and fairly; this should temper enthusiasm for the use of big data as a mechanism to generate public opinion figures. Despite the known methodological limitations and ethical concerns, big social data technologies continue to be used as a way to represent modern publics. As a result, it is important to study how individuals understand and adapt to big social data.

Big social data are used by a diverse set of actors in humanitarian, security, and commercial applications, but they are also used for political gain. Two known instances for this occur in political campaigns and news coverage. Andrejevic's book *iSpy* explores examples of data mining in political spaces as early as 2006.[8] As he explains, political campaigning is now achieved using massive databases filled with dossiers on prospective voters that are compiled using data mining techniques on users' online activities. This campaigning method "target[s] individuals and groups based on key motivating issues—to provide not a generalized, blurry portrait of the candidate, but a customized, high-resolution perspectival portrait that can be modified to meet the interests and concerns of specific audiences."[9] With a keen understanding of the issues that are most likely to invigorate their base, political candidates are able to find new, active voters using social media for customized campaigning.[10]

The other primary user of big social data in politics is data journalists, professionals who are a growing sector of American news coverage. Starting in 2008 with Nate Silver's site *FiveThirtyEight*, the use of traditional data sets (e.g., census and economic data from government agencies) has been coupled with social media data resources to answer important contemporary questions. *FiveThirtyEight* focuses on political and sports forecasting, while the *UpShot*, the *New York Times* data journalism blog, covers sports, American politics, and current events; Ezra Cline's *Vox Media* also uses social media data to cover current issues. The competitive marketplace of online journalism brings these various media outlets into competition, and the competition is most visible in the representation of the *Black Lives Matter* protest.

In relation to the *Black Lives Matter* protest, *Vox Media* has explored and contextualized the physical protests using the virtual hashtag on Twitter, painting a sympathetic picture of the protesters' demands and their grievances. Conservative editorial sites, on the other hand, have used available Twitter data to argue a contradicting narrative: they claim that *Black Lives Matter* intentionally targets white individuals and police officers and that their protest activities have led to an increase in violence across the country.[11] The conservative narrative, well captured by the *Daily Caller*, links *Black Lives Matter* to the "fyf911" hashtag. This hashtag was propagated from a group that aggressively opposes the United States' military interventions overseas and held rallies to burn the American flag on September 11, 2015.[12] The competing narratives from *Vox* and the *Daily Caller* are supported and contested using existing institutional statistics on policing and racial violence and with social media analytics. Big social data tools are becoming important representative technologies in America's political and cultural wars. A great deal of interpretation goes into how Twitter data are analyzed, however, in these news accounts, the results are presented as objective truth and as an omniscient view from above. The aura of objectivity makes these transformed social media messages and updates into "statistical evidence" for use by data journalists, and that has important ramifications for how protesters interact with the larger community.

Big social data analytics used to capture public opinions exist in a lineage of older analytic tools. The French sociologist and cultural theorist Jean Baudrillard discussed the future of hypermedia and opinion polls on the public in the 1980s.[13] He describes hypermedia as an example of the hyperreal, where a digital simulation of something becomes indistinguishable from the real substance it is mimicking. Opinion polls are one case of the hyperreal simulation of political discourse; polls are third-order simulacrum because they mirror a manipulation of an actual social process, so they are a copy of a copy, and that imitation leads to a loss of specificity. When opinion polls are collected, the questions will drift toward a homogenous scale, losing the complex detail that is traditionally included in political discourse. Furthermore, public opinion polls also become devoid of meaning because the social exchange between the respondent and the pollster has been reduced to simply "obtaining an answer," not reaching a consensus or using persuasion to discuss potential policy options.[14] Rather than measuring opinions, polls measure the process that has been created to control and create opinions, and as a result, polls reinforce that system rather than reveal actual "social production."[15] Another way of stating this idea is that opinion polls are medium as message. Baudrillard's concerns are potent warnings that speak to the uses of big social data analytics to generate simulations of political discourse. Rather than collect surveys directly from respondents, big social data systems ambiently process social media records for potential insights into the public's mind. One danger that Baudrillard discusses is the ability of inferential models to produce the outcome desired by the analyst. This can easily occur with social media data when the analyst follows a rigorous and scientific approach with consistent internal logic, yet due to the massive quantity of available data, it is possible to find contradictory answers within the same data set. Political scientist Luca Simeone and his team have experience with gauging public opinion using ambient social media content to determine sentiments.[16] While social media data have been used for several years behind the closed doors of private corporations such as Facebook and Google, new tools are being created that allow anyone to synthesize and analyze networked communications to find insights and potential points for intervention. Simeone worked on the *Urban Sensing* platform that collects social media data with the intention of relating it to urban planning. For example, the platform might record and analyze utterances related to the desire for a new public library, and that information could be used to support new public works projects and modify existing policies. Despite these honorable goals, Simeone argues that the platform is agnostic about the type of content it collects, so it relies on a broad mixture of private and public, humorous and serious data, with no clear connection to the topics of interest by urban planners. Simeone describes this as a lack of "clear intentionality" between user data and "actions to influence urban planning and management processes."[17] A lack of intentionality could have implications for social media data and political speech; taken as a whole, social media data may not be directed with the force necessary for use as political discourse. However, social media data that are *explicitly* tagged as part of a protest may provide the necessary force to be useful and representative.

STUDY: THE PROTESTER'S VIEW

Big social data have entered the fray of political contest and discourse in America. This chapter discusses the implications of big data technologies for political speech by looking at how protesters, individuals highly invested in a specific political outcome, respond to the changing dynamic of social media and big social data for their protest efforts. This conversation is necessary as scholars and the public react to and guide the deployment of social media and big data technology use in the future. The study employed ethnographic approaches during the *Rally to Restore Sanity and/ or Fear* in 2010 and the 2014 *Justice for All March*, including attendance at events, active participation, conversation with protesters, and semi-structured interviews. The goal was to understand the complex socialization and discourse that emerge from contemporary political protests and social media. The project started with the overarching research question: How are social media technologies incorporated into protest activities, such as coordination of on- and offline activities and the presentation of the protester's message? By using grounded theoretical approaches, additional research questions arose that captured issues in the field over time. In particular, these questions uncovered patterns in the valuation and importance of social media to political speech and encompassed surprising secondary uses of social media data. By allowing the questions to evolve with dynamic sites and evolving technologies, a more practical and performative understanding of protesters' social media use emerged.

The interviews and conversational records were studied using critical discourse analysis (CDA). One of CDA's main research agendas is to "[analyze, understand and explain] new phenomena in Western political systems, which are due to the impact of (new) media . . . and related institutions."[18] Ruth Woodak and Michael Meyer, two experts in CDA, tell practitioners to focus on the context that texts are delivered in; by studying what is said, how it is said, and where it is said, a critical researcher can better understand the meaning that informs social interactions. This approach is valuable to understand how participants are negotiating the use of new media in their protest efforts. It remains an invaluable method in response to big data where the provenance of data records is frequently lost, and qualitative methods can provide auxiliary or supplemental data that enrich and contextualize social media data sets.

Media scholar Mark Andrejevic employed a similar study to understand what Australians know about privacy protections and data mining practices of their online activities. His study began with a large-scale telephone survey, then moved to focus groups and structured interviews with 27 individuals to uncover "public attitudes toward collection and use of personal information."[19] He found that the public was unable "to anticipate the potential uses of such data," and Andrejevic now works to mitigate the effects of the big data divide between practitioners and lay members of the public. The current study parallels Andrejevic's efforts by comparing the known affordances of social media platforms and big social data analytics used by political campaigns and data journalists to what individual protesters are prepared to handle as part of their activism.

Rally to Restore Sanity

The first case study was the *Rally to Restore Sanity and/or Fear* that occurred on October 30, 2010, and had approximately 215,000 attendees on the National Mall in Washington, DC. The 2010 rally, hosted by *Comedy Central* comedians Jon Stewart and Stephen Colbert, was partially a response to the emergence of the Tea Party in America. In September 2010, Glenn Beck hosted a *Rally to Restore Honor,* and Stewart and Colbert quickly lampooned the event on their nightly television shows. The *Rally to Restore Sanity and/or Fear,* because of its inspiration from political satire, required lots of discursive negotiation on the day of the event. Many participants arrived with serious political messages displayed on their signs: "Got PIISD? (Private Insurance Induced Stress Disorder) Get The Cure . . . Improved Medicare for All." Others, however, were there to simply have a fun time with messages such as "This sign is important" and "I stopped having tea parties when I was 9." During the hours preceding the event and during the speeches, I was able to walk slowly through each quadrant of the rally space (with the exception of the VIP section), listening to conversations, taking pictures of signs, and asking questions of participants about why they were there and how social media fed into their activities. Several patterns emerged in the discourse. First, there were a great deal of "meta" conversations about the protest itself. Each time someone met a new person, they asked why they were at the event and what they got from participating. This meant that the discussion was experience focused

rather than issue directed. The following sample of conversation illustrates this theme in relation to Facebook use:

D: Do you think this is something we're going to be telling our
     gran' kids about? Or maybe we'll forget it happened.

B: Maybe

C: Take photos! Put them on Facebook

D: I guess I'll remember then

B: rally for whatever . . . march . . . angriness not angry

C: [Are you angry?]

C: I guess that's the point right   ((laughter))

B: I'm not like (1) demonstration. We're demonstrating whatever

C: We're demonstrating that we're not emotionally unstable

B: there we go.   ((laughter))

This conversation is an exemplar, capturing the discussion of what the
event is for, showing the sense of humor most individuals had about
the event, and revealing the importance of social media (Facebook) for
the preservation of their memory of the event. A second common theme
was the importance of social media and cellular devices for coordinating
that day. Nearly every participant lost their cellular signal due to the high
density and demand for service in the small national park space. It was
very common to see participants holding their devices high in the air,
looking for signal, and expressing anxiety about being disconnected from
their social networks. The lack of signal meant that the majority of posts
and additions to social media occurred afterward, in moments of reflection, rather than immediately as part of the protest.

   As I walked through the crowds, I found that several participants
reminded those around them to be polite and pick up any trash, since
these were two common criticisms of Glenn Beck's rally earlier in the year.
These individuals wanted to ensure the rally's image was respectful and
superior to tea party members. To better understand the role of social
media in the protesters' activities, I was able to perform 18 in-depth interviews with participants. For the individuals who agreed to be inter-
viewed, I began by asking if they used social media, and if yes, if they
used it to discuss the protest. Sixteen of the 18 did use Facebook, but it
was used only in a handful of cases to organize "meet ups" for the protest.
Coordinating and planning was done using texting, calls, or e-mails.
Instead, Facebook was used to share anecdotes and stories after the event,
and participants discussed their use of Facebook to record the event as a
moment of closure—there was little added to the live experience, but

sharing their participation was useful for socializing and staying connected with friends and family. This use of Facebook is similar to what political scientist Nathan Teske described as identity construction.[20] Teske observed that people become involved in politics because it is fulfilling to the individual and to become the type of person they see as desirable. The use of social media as part of the *Rally to Restore Sanity* was markedly different from the 2014 *Justice for All March*.

Justice for All March

The *Justice for All March* was generally much more serious in tone, with approximately 10,000 attendees in Washington, DC, and a large number of participants marching simultaneously in other cities on December 13, 2014. Reverend Al Sharpton and the *National Action Network* organized marches to protest a lack of indictment for the police officers who killed two black men, Michael Brown and Eric Garner, in Missouri and New York, respectively, earlier in the year.[21] At *Millions March NYC*, social media was a fundamental part of the experience. It was not uncommon to hear individuals reminding their fellow protesters, "Don't forget to use the hashtag." This referred to the use of a set key word or phrase on Twitter to ensure that those public messages can be found and are part of the narrative. To organize for the march, participants all agreed that "social media was everything," allowing for dispersed yet simultaneous action.

I was able to perform three in-depth interviews with protesters about their use of social media to protest and how they felt about big social data analysis. One protester described the physical and digital as very important spaces for sharing the message but noted "this is a completely different space we are dealing with." According to the protester, certain digital channels, such as Facebook, were useful for communicating and coordinating with sympathetic audiences, but Twitter (one of the most common resources for creating maps of political discourse) is much more antagonistic in quality. As a result, it will provide a distinct and alternative narrative if it is the sole resource used to capture and describe the protest. Another respondent echoed this sentiment by stating that Twitter and the hashtags are important, but they cannot represent the whole protest. The respondent pointed me to community meetings, sit-ins, and other protest activities as important parts of sharing the movement's message. This is not to say that the respondents were creating a neat digital/physical divide for their actions, but they were dissatisfied with the idea that their political activism would be captured and analyzed using the physical or the digital exclusively. The experience and discourse were being produced in multiple channels, simultaneously, with an eye to the different and dispersed audiences for each textual flow. These discursive channels are consistent with what Alexandra Segerberg and Lance Bennett observed in their analysis of Twitter communication during the United Nation's 2009 Climate Summit.[22] The authors describe the protest situation as an ecology upon which Twitter streams connect various sides, and they describe Twitter as having "differing roles" throughout the event.[23] The various roles social media channels can play means it is important to understand Twitter data as specific and localized rather than general, especially when discussing political discourse where nuance and representation are a fundamental part of making a democratic government function.

My respondent's insight into the distinctive quality of social media versus on-the-ground speech provides another complication for the use of big data analysis to comprehend protest movements. One common technique is to run a sentiment analysis that cleans textual data down to root words before comparing these roots to a library of words associated with common moods. For example, the most basic sentiment analysis will cleave text into two categories, positive or negative mood, based on word association networks.[24] This can be expanded to include a variety of other dimensions, such as calm or angry, but the underlying logic is to create a holistic impression of the data set using a generic understanding of language. The results of a sentiment analysis, then, are fraught as protesters try to gain or maintain their political and cultural capital and be sympathetic to a broader audience. While most protesters seemed savvy to the layered, interpersonal uses of new and traditional media to share their message, most respondents were confused or unaware of the big data applications for understanding protest movements.

The most common response to questions about aggregated social media data is captured in one respondent's answer: "I don't really understand what you are talking about. Is it marketing stuff?" As a researcher, this created a complicated interview situation for me. Rather than eliciting opinions about a subject that the respondents could define in their own terms, I was on the spot for providing a definition for big data and its uses for capturing political discourse. Rather than attempt to define big social data from a "neutral" stance between utopian promises of greater democratic participation and cynical warnings about the all-seeing gaze of those in power, I took this confusion and lack of awareness as a meaningful result in its own right. Big social data are an unseen and unknown technology; its operations and functions are opaque to American protestors, hidden behind the better publicized use of big social data as a marketing tool.

DISCUSSION: THE MEDIATED VIEW

Over the course of four years, social media, as it is increasingly integrated into daily social life, has likewise become more important for political protests. There has been a major transition in how attentive protesters are to the importance and power of social media. In 2010, social media was used as a bracketing device, coordinating meetings before the event and sharing memories afterward. During 2014, however, social media played a role throughout the protests and enabled a dispersed community to simultaneously protest in different cities across the country. Interviewees raised important points about the different audiences they are directing their speech to across different platforms, and it is important to be cautious when using social media records in a large-scale analysis. Social media has changed political protests by making them widely accessible and visible. Interviewees felt this in the diversity of messages they can publish and in the speed of messages they sent. Yet, while social media has changed the texture of political protests, social media cannot tell the full story. This is especially true due to the lack of an outside boundary for many movements supported on new media. A great deal of the content is generated from people who are displaced from the geographical location of the protest, and new media, with all of its potential, has no way to prevent a large group from overshadowing the voices from a small protest. For example, for every affirmation on Twitter under the *Black Lives Matter* hashtag, there are other messages from individuals using "all lives matter" to argue about the validity of the protest. When the hashtag *Black Lives Matter* is collected to capture the essence of the protest movement, it is also capturing these antagonistic responses.

Protesting in an environment saturated with social media requires paying attention to not simply what is said on an individual, case-by-case basis, but rather how messages are collected and analyzed to construct a larger, totalizing narrative and argument. For interviewees, the use of big social data to understand political protests is an unseen and unknown practice in the midst of protests. Essentially, big data are an invisible complex of technologies. Frank Pasquale describes this as the "black box effect" in his discussion of the algorithms that run modern, networked social systems.[25] According to Pasquale, modern technologies are so complicated and embedded in the functions of our daily lives that individuals cannot comprehend the force they exert over us on a daily basis. Information communication technologies are used to measure and make decisions about individuals, and those processes are intentionally obscured to avoid scrutiny. The average protester has never considered the implications of big data on political representation. Currently, big data analytics are a technology used by a select few with the resources and knowledge to use them, and this advantage means that the interests of the larger community are not always considered in their deployment.

What is the solution to the blind spot surrounding big social data analysis? Omer Tene and Jules Polonetsky address the problem of opaque technologies from a legal standpoint, arguing that technological developments have "far outpaced the existing legal frameworks."[26] While the White House did update the Fair Information Practice Principles (FIPPS) to include accountability, focused collection, accuracy, and access in 2013, Tene and Polonetsky explain that big data challenge these basic rights. On one hand, big data are collected from a variety of sources, meaning that if data sets are combined, previously anonymized data can still be used to identify individuals due to the mosaic effect. The mosaic effect occurs when one data set has two attributes, say A and B, for the same person. When that data set is combined with another that shows B and C with a geographic location, it identifies individuals. This is important when considering political dissent. In many cases, political speech will not result in direct retaliatory action, but it can result in prejudicial action by governments and private businesses. Another regulatory problem is that policies for data minimization (that only necessary data are collected rather than all available resources) are rare. Finally, Tene and Polonetsky discuss the lack of individual consent and control over data after the initial collection. Once a user agrees to allow his or her data to be collected, he or she has no control or input into how his or her data are shared in perpetuity. These final two principles are very difficult to enact with the continued use of big data technologies, but as a result, there must be increased transparency, access, and accuracy surrounding the technology. Pasquale argues that this transparency will only occur as a result of increased regulation.

The *Rally to Restore Sanity and/or Fear* and the *Justice for All March* provide an interesting comparison for the role that social media and aggregated social media data play in participating, contextualizing, and remembering acts of political protest. Big social data analysis can be situated in a lineage of communication technologies, such as the pamphlet or iconic news photograph. Big data analytics are used to represent a cause and create an imagined community in modern political spaces; it is the semblance of a totality where the fragmentation of social media means iconic photographs are harder to produce. As discourse, data analysis can both facilitate and constrain certain types of political expression. Despite the implications for "big" social data, most individuals are still focusing on the "small," interpersonal uses. In order for big data to be a democratic tool, it must be transparent with equal means of access for the public. There are several ways to imagine big data used in the service of the populace. For one, big data have been leveraged by news organizations to educate the public on subjects that are relevant for an educated electorate. Relevant data sets are analyzed and then presented in interesting data visualizations that allow the viewer to explore a complex issue. One example is "The State of Gerrymandering," a project by *Silicon Valley Data Science* that shows redistricting practices by one political party to prevent the formation of a majority from another party in an electoral district.[27] Gerrymandering data visualizations are extensive, showing how districts change over time and offering some predictive capabilities for how redistricting can strategically control future changes in the population. These projects are important for making political maneuvers transparent to the public. Another example of a potentially empowering use of big data analysis is mapping and visualizing the number of days each congressional member is in Washington, DC, their home state or district, and in other parts of the country based on social media appearances. Such figures provide an important indicator of the representatives' continued relationship to their constituents, and, in the case of individuals running for higher office while still serving in an elected position, it monitors the amount of time they spend governing versus campaigning. These are two clear examples where democracy is supported by the use of big data analysis to clarify the activities of representatives and their relationship to the public.

Monitoring elected officials is a compelling civic use for big social data in the future, yet there are possible uses achievable today. Existing open-source tools and free analytics suites can be used to analyze and understand political protests; if used by the protesters, these tools can provide them with the ability to control their movement's narrative. For one, the Twitter analytics suite is fairly powerful, allowing the user to understand what topics are trending and how content is being shared. In the primary UI, the search bar facilitates navigating different content. These Twitter tools are limited temporally, however, since Twitter provides only a brief slice of time: the present and immediate past. To get a diachronic picture, other tools must be used that capture data from Twitter's API and store them remotely. iScience Maps is one program that focuses on changes over time.[28] Wasim Ahmed curates a list of other services that can do time series analysis, sentiment processing, and statistical hypothesis testing (with R).[29] These software suites remain an imperfect solution because the computational power is still asymmetrical compared to what is available to companies, but they do offer protesters the opportunity to participate in how they are depicted. The burden for engaging with social media data is not exclusively on protestors; community organizers, news media, and civic leaders must recognize the importance of tools for meaningful participation and use their resources to provide them.[30] A strong example is the open government data initiative that provides public data sets and toolkits for American citizens to explore.

The interviews and background research for this chapter serve as a foundation for future inquiry. There are some limitations for this study: since big data technologies are an unseen force in politics, it is difficult to elicit opinions about their use. However, this research does provide a pointer toward future longitudinal studies that seek participants' sentiments about the evolving use of social media in their protest activities and the effects of big social data analysis. By considering big data as a representational technology in addition to its function as an analytical tool, researchers can look at how big data insights are used as political arguments. Big data tools are currently used to extrapolate the number of participants present at an event and to determine the response of the nation to a protest movement, but there are many potential applications, such as efforts to determine the tone of an event or to correlate potential desires of the demographic in question. This information can be used to direct and control the message, and therefore, warrants heightened scrutiny as new technologies are deployed. It is still early in the deployment of big social data technologies, but by placing them in a succession of representative technologies, we can begin to see potential effects of their deployment. The early themes surrounding the role of social media for political protest caution against the mantel of objectivity that big data currently hold. Speech qua discourse, with its contradictions and complexities, may be a safer form to represent political protesters and negotiate outcomes. Direct speech provides protection against manipulation or asymmetrical power relationships inherent in complex technical systems.

CONCLUSION

With the scale of big social data comes an equally large need to theorize its effects on society. The use of social media data must be negotiated, especially as part of ethical practice, in the collection, processing, and dissemination of public opinion. This chapter discussed the user-protester as a complicated subjectivity. While the protester is politically active in one facet of his or her life, it is difficult to juggle his or her convictions within a social media environment. Social media technologies are persistent and saturated in many mundane aspects of daily life, and their use is normalized. While protesters may share content that is political in nature, the actual use of the technology is not politicized. To help with this contradiction between purpose and performance, protesters and users more generally should be aware of both their individual activities and the larger technical ecosystem, support the regulation and oversight of big data technologies, and take advantage of open-source tools for their own civic ends.

NOTES

1. Henry Jenkins, "Twitter Revolutions?" *Spreadable Media*, accessed October 12, 2015, spreadablemedia.org/essays/jenkins/#.VlY4CnarSUk.

2. Steve Lohr, "The New Thing in Google Flu Trends Is Traditional Data," *The New York Times*, October 31, 2014, http://bits.blogs.nytimes.com/2014/10/31/the-new-thing-in-google-flu-trends-is-traditional-data/.

3. Mark Andrejevic, "The Big Data Divide," *International Journal of Communication* 8 (2014): 1673–1689.

4. danah boyd and Kate Crawford, "Critical Questions for Big Data: Provocations for a Cultural, Technological, and Scholarly Phenomenon," *Information, Communication & Society* 15 (2012): 662–679.

5. Clay Shirky, "The Political Power of Social Media: Technology, the Public Sphere, and Political Change," *Foreign Affairs* 90 (2011): 28–41; Nicholas Carr, "How Social Media Is Ruining Politics," *Politico*, September 2, 2015, www.politico.com/magazine/story/2015/09/2016-election-social-media-ruining-politics-213104.

6. Katrin Weller, Axel Bruns, Jean Burgess, Merja Mahrt, and Cornelius Puschmann, eds., *Twitter and Society* (New York: Peter Lang, 2013).

7. Tom W. G. van der Meer, Armen Hakhverdian, and Loes Aaldering, "Off the Fence, onto the Bandwagon?" *International Journal of Public Opinion Research* 27 (2015): 1–27.

8. Mark Andrejevic, *iSpy: Surveillance and Power in the Interactive Era* (Lawrence, KS: University Press of Kansas, 2007).

9. Ibid., 193.

10. Ibid., 188.

11. Sarah Seltzer, "The Worrisome Media Narrative behind the False Post-Ferguson Crime Wave Story," *Flavorwire*, September 14, 2015, flavorwire.com/537132/the-media-narrative-behind-the-false-post-ferguson-crime-wave-story.

12. Dara Lind, "#FYF911: Why Conservative Media Thinks Black Lives Matter Is Planning 9/11 Attacks on Police," *Vox Media*, September 11, 2015, www.vox.com/2015/9/11/9312175/fyf911-fuk-yo-flag-black-attacks.

13. Jean Baudrillard, *Simulations*, trans. Paul Foss, Paul Patton, and Phillip Beitchman (Los Angeles, CA: Semiotext[e], 1983).

14. Ibid., 124.

15. Ibid., 125–126.

16. Luca Simeone, "Missing Intentionality: The Limitations of Social Media Analysis for Participatory Urban Design," in *Civic Media Project*, eds. Eric Gordon and Paul Mihailidis (Cambridge, MA: The MIT Press, 2015), civicmediaproject.org/works/civic-media-project/missingintentionalityparticipatoryurbandesign.

17. Ibid., 1.

18. Ruth Woodak and Michael Meyer, eds., *Methods of Critical Discourse Analysis* (London, UK: Sage, 2009), 11.

19. Andrejevic, "The Big Data Divide," 1673.

20. Nathan Teske, *Political Activists in America: The Identity Construction Model of Political Participation* (New York: Cambridge University Press, 1997).

21. Darryl Fears and Michael E. Ruane, "Thousands Join 'Justice for All' March," *The Washington Post*, December 13, 2014, www.washingtonpost.com/national/thousands-join-justice-for-all-march/2014/12/13/f217a4c8-82e8-11e4-b005-b260c9ec5217_story.html.

22. Alexandra Segerberg and Lance Bennett, "Social Media and the Organization of Collective Action: Using Twitter to Explore the Ecologies of Two Climate Change Protests," *The Communication Review* 14 (2011): 197–215.

23. Ibid., 198.

24. Weller, Bruns, Burgess, Mahrt, and Puschmann, *Twitter and Society*.

25. Frank Pasquale, *The Black Box Society: The Secret Algorithms That Control Money and Information* (Cambridge, MA: Harvard University Press, 2015).

26. Omer Tene and Jules Polentsky, "Big Data for All: Privacy and User Control in the Age of Analytics," *Northwestern Journal of Technology and Intellectual Property* 11 (2013): 239–273, 241.

27. Silicon Valley Data Science, "The State of Gerrymandering," accessed July 23, 2015, svds.com/gerrymandering.

28. Ulf-Dietrich Reips and Pablo Garaizar, Designers, *iScience Maps: Experimental Psychology & Internet Science* (Bilbao, Spain: Universidad de Deusto), maps .iscience.deusto.es.

29. Wasim Ahmed, "A List of Tools to Capture Twitter Data," January 30, 2015, wasimahmed1.wordpress.com/2015/01/30/a-list-of-tools-to-capture-twitter-data.

30. Candice Lanius, "Open NY: Civic Engagement through Open Data and Open Platforms," in *Civic Media Project*, eds. Eric Gordon and Paul Mihailidis (Cambridge, MA: The MIT Press, 2015), civicmediaproject.org/works/civic -media-project/openny-civic-engagement-throughopen-data-and-open-platforms.

Chapter 5

Hashtag Feminism, Digital Media, and New Dynamics of Social Change: A Case Study of #YesAllWomen

Bernadette Barker-Plummer and Dave Barker-Plummer

> It would be difficult to imagine how a development as world-changing as the emergence of the Internet could have taken place without having some impact upon the ways in which politics is expressed, conducted, depicted, and reflected upon.
>
> —Stephen Coleman and Deen Freelon,
> *Handbook of Digital Politics*, 2015

The emergence and widespread use of digital communication platforms—such as Facebook, Twitter, Instagram, YouTube, and Tumblr—are changing the face of political life in the United States and globally. These new forms of communication, open to individual citizens, activists, or politicians—in fact, to anyone with a net connection—are not only affecting traditional politics as people seek out political information and engage in conversation in a much wider range of places than they could previously, but they are also reshaping the dynamics of activism and social change.[1] In pre-digital eras, if citizens wanted to get together and advocate for social change, they could "get the word out" by creating public events such as protests, marches, and sit-ins to attract media and public attention. They could produce their own media such as newsletters or videos, or they could engage in strategic interactions with journalists to try and shape the way their issues and events were communicated to the public.[2] Now, though, engaged citizens and social change groups have access to communication platforms with the potential to reach large audiences directly. Instead of waiting for media coverage of events, for example, activists can now upload text and film about these events themselves through Twitter, YouTube, or Indymedia platforms. Digital media platforms, and the communication possibilities they provide, have shifted the architecture of the public sphere away from a centrifugal model—in which political actors targeted their communications at commercial media at the center—to one that is weblike, multi-nodal, and potentially much more participatory.[3] Of course, digital activists still have to carefully frame their messages, they still need to reach audiences, and they need to strategize around the constraints of different platforms, but in general digital platforms have significantly expanded access to public debate.[4]

A critical tool in this new digital sphere is Twitter, a media platform that allows users to communicate with, follow, and connect to potentially large publics, albeit in very short message (140 character) formats. Using shared hashtags (e.g., #YesAllWomen), participants link their comments to those of others, and when large numbers of people join a conversation, the hashtag *trends* and is highlighted by Twitter and often covered by journalists. Since its founding, Twitter has emerged as an especially popular platform for activists, journalists, elected officials, and others interested in social justice and social change, and identifiable clusters of speakers have emerged around particular social issues—for example, "Black Twitter," "Feminist Twitter," "Green Twitter," and so on.[5]

In this chapter, we examine and discuss a recent Twitter event that we think illustrates the potential for digital media platforms and their participants to play an important new role in social change—the 2014 hashtag campaign #YesAllWomen, a massive Twitter event that involved more than 2 million tweets around the issues of sexual harassment, male entitlement, and sexual violence. #YesAllWomen trended in May 2014 after Elliot Rodger, a self-identified misogynist, killed 6 people, injured 13, and then killed himself. The murders and Rodger's "manifesto" and YouTube videos, in which he argued that men had a right to sex with women and that women should be forced to service men, sparked general outrage. In response to the public outrage, a Twitter hashtag, #NotAllMen arose to argue that not all men were like Rodger. #YesAllWomen was a response to both the killer and to the #NotAllMen thread. As Soraya

Chemaly argued in an early #YesAllWomen tweet, "#notallmen practice violence against women but #YesAllWomen live with the threat of male violence. Every. Single. Day. All over the world."

Drawing on a large archive of #YesAllWomen tweets for the period May 24–June 24, 2014, that we obtained from Twitter, as well as on a sample of press and TV coverage of #YesAllWomen in the same period,[6] we ask: What was the #YesAllWomen hashtag about? What made it so compelling to participants and to the journalists who covered it? And, what role did this hashtag campaign, and hashtag campaigns more generally, play in social change politics?

We are interested, of course, in the content of #YesAllWomen and we carefully track the topics and themes of #YesAllWomen using both automatic and close textual strategies. But we are also interested in how hashtag campaigns like #YesAllWomen may be providing new possibilities and pathways for social change communication. Consequently, we also consider the ways in which #YesAllWomen was received and recirculated by mainstream media and how it was linked, by its users, to other online sites and platforms. Though mainstream media is less central to politics than in previous eras, it is still the case that media's attention to what is trending online can take a specific digital conversation and make it a national or international phenomenon—for example, #BlackLivesMatter quickly moved from a topic on Black Twitter to national discussion through mainstream media.

Though some observers have dismissed the effectiveness of hashtag campaigns, calling them "clicktivism," for example, and noting that hashtags do not always directly impact policy,[7] in this project we take a more dialogical approach to social change. A dialogical approach recognizes the importance of political *communication* in changing the cultural environment, in particular the communication of new discourses and frames for experience that social movements typically produce.[8] Though #YesAllWomen may not have immediately changed public policy around sexual violence, it produced a coherent and systematic (counter) narrative about the circumscribed lives of women that challenged claims that gender equality has already been achieved. Thousands of people, mostly women, took to the net to explain and critique how gendered violence and the threat of that violence impacted their day-to-day lives, stories that many commentators (especially men) were shocked to hear about. The importance of hashtag campaigns may not necessarily be in producing direct changes in policy, then, but in making the experiences and stories of oppressed groups visible and part of our national and global conversations. Traditional news media has often been criticized for its narrow range of sources and voices. Digital media-based campaigns are opening up more pathways for citizens into the democratic conversation.

SOCIAL MOVEMENTS, DIGITAL MEDIA, AND SOCIAL CHANGE

Research on how specific activists, protesters, or movements are using digital media platforms in their work is beginning to emerge. Bonila and Rosa,[9] for example, make a case for the critical importance of Twitter in Ferguson's race protests, not just in planning and discussions but as a space for black collective identity work and the creation of alternative narratives. They analyze #Ferguson and other related hashtags (such as #HandsUp-DontShoot, #WeAreTrayvonMartin, #HoodiesUp, and #TheyGunnedMe-Down, all of which focus on police violence against black men) and argue that these served not only as sources of early and local information on these killings but most importantly as sites for "creative reinterpretation" of these events, where people could articulate and share a more authentic, alternative, and resistant narrative about the value of black bodies.[10]

Studies of Twitter's role in the Occupy movement have also unpacked how Twitter was used in, and with, Occupy protests. Tremayne, for example, tracked early Occupy organizing on Twitter and found that there were some strategic and timely hashtag "brokership"—moments, when early Twitter activists linked up #OccupyWallStreet with other emergent antigovernment hashtags like #FuckYouWashington, #USDOR (US Day of Rage), and #Sept17, and thus critically expanded the audience and potential participants for #OWS ideas and events.[11]

Recent studies of Twitter in other protest mobilizations—such as the Indignados in Spain and the Aganaktismoi in Greece (protests against government austerity programs), the G20 protesters in Pittsburgh, and the Wisconsin government workers' protest against de-unionizing laws—have also identified key roles for Twitter as a resource in organizing, coordinating, and communicating about issues.[12]

There have been few studies of the role of Twitter in *gender politics*, though, and in this project we offer a case study of "Feminist Twitter." By investigating the contours and functions of #YesAllWomen, our goal is both to understand this specific communicative event and to think about what it may represent for feminist politics and for contemporary social movement communications more generally.

RESEARCH STRATEGIES AND METHODS

The project mobilized three main research strategies:

Content and Discourse Analysis of #YesAllWomen

The Twitter sample consists of 500,294 tweets and 1.48 million retweets from May 24 to June 24, 2014, retrieved from the hashtag #YesAll-Women. We obtained these tweets from GNIP, the Twitter-owned intermediary company that manages archival (older than three months) requests. This it constitutes the entire corpus of tweets for this hashtag for this period.

Using automatic (computer-based) analysis[13] of the tweets, we tracked the main *topics* (word frequency lists);[14] the *gender* of contributors (through comparison of tweeters to gendered name lists);[15] the ways people used the hashtag; and the page *links* made from each tweet. We also identified the most retweeted messages to identify repeated messages and memes.[16]

Though automatic analysis can sketch in the contours of a large corpus like this, we also used critical discourse analysis strategies on a random sample of the tweets (1% or 5,000 tweets)[17] to identify major linguistic patterns, themes, arguments, and other discursive structures in and across the tweets. Here, we were looking for how participants used the stream— what did they say, how did they say it, what were the shared issues, frames, and narrative structures.

Content and Discourse Analysis of News Stories

We also conducted content and discourse analysis of 122 press stories from LexisNexis and from 21 TV news stories from broadcast news sites. Using the search term #YesAllWomen for the time period May 24–June 24, 2014, this census sample of major U.S. and international English language press and TV stories was created.

Automated analysis was conducted on the LexisNexis file of 122 press stories to determine topic frequencies as well as closer discourse analysis of these and TV stories to determine themes, tone, arguments, and frames. We compared #YesAllWomen and media topic rankings to compare how the event was constructed.

Identify Possible Interactions between #YesAllWomen and Other Spheres

To sketch in how #YesAllWomen connected to media and to the larger public sphere, we tracked the ways in which participants used #YesAll-Women—for example, did they index often to other hashtags or attach their own media, or was the discourse mostly expressive (simple tweets)—and what kinds of links #YesAllWomen tweets used.

The Case Study

Because every single woman I know has a story about a man feeling entitled to access to her body. Every. Single. One.

—Emily Hughes, Twitter, May 24, 2014

I. #YesAllWomen Discourse

The #YesAllWomen conversation was dominated by women, with an approximately 3:1 ratio between tweeters that could be name-identified as women and men—237,026 women and 83,422 men.

As Table 5.1 shows, the main topics in this conversation were women, men, rape, feminism, fear, sex, and violence.

As these general topics indicate, a large proportion of the Twitter stream (and press coverage, which we talk about later) focused on gender and violence. Within these general topics, #YesAllWomen tweeters reported on the kinds of experiences they encountered day to day around sexuality and power and how oppressive these gender relations could be. From being asked to "smile," by strangers, to being made to change clothes at school by teachers, to being "catcalled" on the street, to being groped, flashed, or masturbated at on the subway, to threats, insults, and controlling behavior online and offline, to sexual assault, violent rape, and gang rape, the stream rang with the pain and resentment of women whose lives were constrained by the threat of male violence. Many of the tweeters thanked the hashtag's founders for creating a space and other tweeters for sharing their experiences and providing support. For some tweeters it was the first time they had publicly communicated their experience of rape or abuse, making the stream not just a public protest but also a public service and a *consciousness-raising* moment.

The visibility in the #YesAllWomen discourse of specific feminist analytical terms such as *misogyny* (14,963 mentions, see Table 5.1) and the centrality of the terms *feminist/feminisms* (18,780 mentions) show that this was an unusually feminist discourse as well.

In addition to reporting on instances of harassment, there was also a deeply ironic strain of commentary on the strategies women had developed to intercept, go around, or defuse the persistent threat of male

Table 5.1
Main Topics (Ranked) in #YesAllWomen and Traditional Press Sample

Topics Twitter	Topics Press
1. Women/Girls/Females (133,633)	1. Women/Girls/Females (1,258)
2. Men/Guys/Boys/Males (131,319)	2. Men/Boys/Males (578)
3. Rape (37,567)	3. Violence (238)
4. People(s) (20,048)	4. Rodger (232)
5. Feminism/Feminist(s) (18,780)	5. People(s) (195)
6. Fear/Afraid/Fearful (17,882)	6. Sex/Sexual (187)
7. Sex/Sexual (17,845)	7. Rights (181)
8. Misogyny/Misogynist(s) (14,963)	8. Misogyny/Misogynist(s) (163)
9. Love/Loved (12,486)	9. Rape/Rapist(s) (123)
10. Violence (11,622)	10. World(s) (121)

violence. For example, women tweeted that they made detailed plans each day about where to park (under a streetlight); that they kept their phone pre-dialed to 91- in case of a stalker; that they checked the backseat of their car before getting in; that they wore cycling shorts under their dresses to stop invasive groping in clubs; that they never left drinks unattended or never returned to unattended drinks; that they had various kinds of weapons (keys, knives, mace) and alert systems (whistles, phone apps) in place to feel safer. When approached by men they were not interested in, women shared how they had learned to give out wrong numbers or to invoke a fake boyfriend. A telling comment, repeated many times, was the advice women had been given to yell "fire" rather than "rape" to get help. These strategies, what we might call "survival strategies for living in a patriarchy," were often presented with irony and sarcasm and sometimes with gallows humor but always with resentment. For example, the fake boyfriend strategy was a highly retweeted idea (more than 9,000 times)—an example of which was produced by Cindy Da Silva:

> I have a BF is more effective than saying "I'm not interested" bc men respect other men more than my right to say no. #yesallwomen
> —Cindy Da Silva

DISCURSIVE FEATURES: LANGUAGE, FRAMES, AND GENDER PARALLELISMS

Though the #YesAllWomen Twitter conversation was not coordinated by any organization or moderator, it was a remarkably coherent and patterned discourse in both content and form. Many of the tweets shared common *assumptions* (that women lived under threat), and they shared similar *experiences* (e.g., of feeling unsafe after dark). The widespread use of complex and specific analytical vocabulary, such as misogyny, patriarchy, rape culture, and so on, also suggested that most participants shared *frames*, often feminist frames, for their experiences.

Critically, many #YesAllWomen participants also shared a form of discourse, a pattern of communication in which tweets typically focused on everyday events—for example, looking in the backseat of your car before getting in or looking behind you on the street—and then linked these to a larger critique. This linking of personal experiences to structural power (as articulated in the phrase, *the personal is political*) is a definitive feminist discursive formation that links micro-aggressions to macro-power structures, and in which everyday, taken-for-granted, gendered practices are shown to both enact and reproduce male supremacy. This linking was sometimes explicitly mentioned by the tweeter, in other cases, the link was more *implicit* and it was the inclusion of the tweet within the (already understood) feminist framework of the #YesAllWomen hashtag that filled in that part of the meaning. For example, when Sophia Bush tweeted about her fear of walking home at night, she was not saying she lived in an unsafe neighborhood, but that her life was circumscribed by the threat of male violence, though she does not say that directly:

> I shouldn't have to hold my car keys in hand like a weapon & check over my shoulder every few seconds when I walk at night #YesAll-Women—Sophia Bush

Bonila and Rosa call this process, in which hashtags function not only as search terms but also as macro-frames for a way of thinking, "index-ing," which they note is both a pragmatic and a semiotic linking practice produced by Twitter's design.[18]

A pattern of *parallelism* was also often visible across this discourse. This was a way of writing tweets in which men and women's experiences were compared or paralleled, always to the detriment of women. For example, some highly retweeted tweets called out the gender hypocrisies in school dress codes, such as this one, retweeted more than 6,000 times:

> Because a "cool story babe, now make me a sandwich" shirt doesn't break the school dress code. A girl's bra strap does. #YesAllWomen

Another highly popular example involved gendered approaches to refusal and consent:

> When a man says no in this culture, it's the end of the discussion. When a woman says no, it's the beginning of a negotiation. #YesAll-Women—Emily Thomas (retweeted more than 5,000 times)

Perhaps the most eloquent of these parallelisms is attributed to feminist author Margaret Atwood who imbues it with deep anger and pathos:

> Men are afraid that women will laugh at them. Women are afraid that men will kill them—Margaret Atwood. #YesAllWomen

Underlying these parallelisms, of course, is a deep sense of injustice and inequality. As Neil Gaiman tweeted, "The #yesallwomen hashtag is filled with hard, true, sad and angry things."

The most retweeted message of this sample—an idea retweeted more than 32,000 times—was one that related centrally to the double standard surrounding men and women's sexuality:

> #YesAllWomen because this film was made almost 29 years ago and this line is still relevant ... *If you don't you're a prude. If you do, you're a slut. It's a trap.*

(An embedded link goes to a gif of Ally Sheedy in *The Breakfast Club* with the statement printed on the image.)

Universalism and Its Limits in #YesAllWomen

#YesAllWomen's articulation of a shared female experience—that is, the idea that all women shared experiences of male violence and threat—was an effective frame, tying women together and mobilizing a coherent narrative. But it was also an extremely *universalizing* frame that often presumed similarities in women's lives that some critics saw as oppressive. For example, alongside #YesAllWomen there emerged another hashtag #YesAllWhiteWomen as a critique and alternative to what was perceived as white feminist generalizations. Even the founder of #YesAllWomen, a feminist of color, wrote about her dismay as the hashtag that she began became, in her view, much narrower and less intersectional than she intended as time went on.[19] Some queer and trans critics also pointed to the heteronormativity of much of the #YesAllWomen discourse, and these critics worked to expand the conversation to include transphobia, transmisogyny, and socially condoned harassment and violence against transwomen. Although all of these critics recognized the central problem of violence against women, they argued for the inclusion of other, intersecting forces such as racism, homophobia, and transphobia, in the discourse, forces which shape gendered violence in specific ways for different groups of women.

II. Representing #YesAllWomen in Mainstream Media

Though mainstream media has a very mixed history in mediating social movements, coverage of #YesAllWomen was mostly positive. Journalists sympathetically recirculated many of the hashtag's most compelling tweets and memes. There were some exceptions to this, of course, located mostly in conservative media environments (such as Fox News or the *Federalist*), but the majority of articles were supportive of the hashtag.[20]

Media writers (three-fourths of whom were women) approached the #YesAllWomen event with surprise (because it was so large) and recognition (many writers related it to their personal experiences), and most saw it as an important intervention into public debate, describing #YesAllWomen as a good use of hashtag politics. For example, Alexandra Petri of the *Washington Post* after declaring herself a skeptic about hashtags generally—"I know, I know. Not another hashtag. Didn't we just leave this party?" comes around to see #YesAllWomen as something exceptional:

Obviously hashtags have their limits. But this is a subject well suited to one. #YesAllWomen has turned into a forum for sharing stories, which strung together, one after another, form a vivid picture. . . . The sheer number of 140 character accounts also makes them powerful and unsettling.[21]

Journalists recirculated tweets that they thought were important or representative, including some of the most retweeted messages described earlier in the chapter. But they also focused disproportionately on tweets by celebrities, so, for example, tweets by Lena Dunham or Kerry Washington were commonly reprinted:

> "Just gotta say, on the almost-summer's day, I love you my brave web friends #YesAllWomen." Lena Dunham
> " . . . Just now reading the #YesAllWomen tweets. Powerful. Very Powerful." Kerry Washington

However, the overall contours of press coverage followed #YesAllWomen discourse quite closely—see Table 5.1—with some subtle differences in attention. For example, news media held onto the Isla Vista story and Rodger's name much longer than #YesAllWomen. In the Twitter stream the Isla Vista shooter was part of the provocation for the hashtag, but as the stream moved on, his name was left behind. In news, Rodger's name remained a very frequent part of the discourse, perhaps because news is more dependent on "hooks" than Twitter.

Many of the news writers made personal connections to the #YesAllWomen stream—for example, one journalist began her story by talking about how she was harassed by her subject during an interview—or writers would share worries for their daughters and sons. Albert Dubreuil's tweet, for example, was often reprinted:

> Started reading the #YesAllWomen tweets b/c I've got a daughter, but now I see I should be reading them b/c I've got two sons.

There was, of course, some resistance to #YesAllWomen in antifeminist media —for example, in Fox News the anchors dismissed the stream as "whiners" and "man haters." In a more philosophical vein, #YesAllWomen was critiqued in the *Federalist* for making too many stereotypical generalizations. (This was also a highly linked piece among #YesAllWomen tweeters.) Though #YesAllWomen had never actually indicted all men—it was about recognizing how the system of male supremacy and the violent behavior of some men affected *all* women—the nuance of this distinction was often lost in coverage, and many of its critics saw #YesAllWomen as misandrist, so writers invoked good men that they knew as counterexamples.

Table 5.2 summarizes some of the common differences between the (majority) pro and (minority) anti #YesAllWomen media stories.

Table 5.2
Discursive Differences between Supportive and Critical Press Articles

Supportive News Articles	Critical Articles
Made personal connections	Identified own experience as different
Located in mainstream and liberal media	Located in conservative sites
Agreed with micro-macro links, misogyny as spectrum (catcalling to rape)	Refused micro-macro links, yelling, groping unrelated to rape/murder
Recirculated favorite #YesAll-Women tweets	Repeated #notallmen memes
Linked to/describe Rodger's manifesto, other misogynous murders, sees pattern	Sourced mental health professionals, focused on immediate victims
Key issues: misogyny, violence, fear #yesallwomen	Key issues: individual pathology, mental health, #notallmen

While supportive articles aligned with #YesAllWomen's feminist framework—seeing catcalling, stalking and date rape as on a spectrum, for example—critical commenters refused the larger structural frame of patriarchy and insisted that in gender crimes, as in others, there were simply good and bad guys. These writers were much more likely to see Elliot Rodger as mentally ill than a misogynist, and they stressed that he killed men as well as women.

III. Interactions between #YesAllWomen and Other Sites

As Table 5.3 illustrates, most of the tweets in the #YesAllWomen stream (54%) were "simple" tweets—that is, messages with no additional hashtags (other than #YesAllWomen) and no other attachments (pictures or

Table 5.3
How Tweeters Used #YesAllWomen

Types of Tweet	Percent of Whole
Simple tweet (#YesAllWomen and message)	54
One mention	8.6
One URL	6.9
Two hashtags	5.7
One mention + One URL	3.7
One media	2.1
One mention + One media	2.0
Two hashtag + One URL	2.0
Two mentions	1.8
Three hashtags	1.3
All other combinations (222 < 1% each)	11.1
Total	100

Table 5.4
Top Page Links in #YesAllWomen Tweets

1. *Slate* (738) Phil Plait, #YesAllWomen, May 27	6. Change.org (396) Change.com petition, sexual assault James Madison U.
2. *Time* magazine (594) Nolan Feeney, The Most Powerful #YesAllWomen Tweets, May 25	7. *The Daily Beast* (362) Unresolved link to page[*]
3. *Slate* (569) Amanda Hess, Why It's So Hard for Men to See Misogyny, May 27	8. brbr.co.1kuokcp (340) Unresolved link
4. *SF Globe* (519) 17 #YesAllWomen Tweets Everyone Must See, May 27	9. tumblr.com (320) whenwomenrefuse, May 27
5. *Upworthy* (451) Adam Mordecai, 70 of the 71 Mass Murderers in the US in the Last 30 Years Had One Thing in Common, May 27	10. *The Daily Beast* (314) Arthur Chu, Your Princess Is in Another Castle: Misogyny, Entitlement and Nerds, May 27

*Not all links could be resolved to a final page because of broken links.

images) or mentions (links to other individuals by name). The next biggest categories—tweets with one mention (a personal shout out indicated by an @ sign that will bring your message directly to that individual's stream) at 8.6 percent, one URL link (6.9%), or two hashtags (one other than #YesAllWomen) at 5.7 percent—make up all of the combinations over 5 percent. According to some web analytics,[22] around 30 percent of tweets on average usually include a link, so this is lower than we might expect. Twitter researchers have also tended to define tweets with more links or more hashtags as more important—noting that these people may serve as online "nodes" or brokers in the network.[23] While there were instances of individual tweets with multiple links and hashtags in #YesAllWomen—as many as 19 hashtags—most tweets in this corpus did not make connections, suggesting a more expressive than connective purpose.

The links that were made by #YesAllWomen tweeters were mostly to online articles, as Table 5.4 illustrates, with the exception of *Time* magazine, *Slate* was the most linked to site and *Salon*, *Upworthy*, and *The Daily Beast*, are all recent, online media. The stories linked to were analytical pieces about misogyny or masculinist culture. For example, #1 was a story by Phil Plait about the limits of a #notallmen approach; #2 was a story by Nolan Feeney on "The Most Powerful #YesAllWomen Tweets," in which he recirculated some key tweets; and #10, Arthur Chu's May 27, 2014, *Daily Beast* piece, *Your Princess Is in Another Castle: Misogyny, Entitlement, and Nerds* is one in which Chu deconstructs the masculinist culture of gaming culture, and gamergate was a typical example.

Table 5.5
Mainstream Media Page Link Ranks

Publication (#Links)	Rank First Links to Domain
Time magazine (594)	#2
The New Yorker (232)	#15
New Statesman (167)	#29
CNN (117)	#40
The Atlantic (116)	#41
New York Times (90)	#53
The Guardian (79)	#66
The Washington Post (70)	#72
BBC (57)	#88
People magazine (51)	#97

The lack of links to mainstream media by #YesAllWomen tweeters is interesting here. It is not that mainstream media was not linked to at all by #YesAllWomen participants—see Table 5.5 to the rankings of mainstream media—it is that online-only news sites and media pages were much *more* likely to be linked to. This indicates, perhaps, a shift in feminist attention (and perhaps social movements more generally) away from centralized media as a resource and toward "new" digital media.

CONCLUSIONS AND DISCUSSION

The Twitter event #YesAllWomen was a large-scale discursive event in which hundreds of thousands of citizens spoke out against violence and harassment against women. By linking many individual messages together, #YesAllWomen functioned not only as a massive online protest against existing gender/power relations, but it also proactively brought feminist terms and frames of analysis into public debate in a way that rarely happens. For example, as I describe in the chapter, the #YesAllWomen stream often used feminist terms (such as *patriarchy, intersectionality*) and drew on structural feminist analytical frames such as "the personal is political" that tie small, everyday practices to larger structural forces.

Because the #YesAllWomen event was also widely and positively covered by traditional media that recirculated key ideas and tweets from the stream, it reached audiences and policy makers well beyond its Twitter participants and impacted conversations in mainstream media and politics. #YesAllWomen participants also connected widely with online media sources, in particular with progressive online-only media sites such as *Slate*, *Upworthy*, and *The Daily Beast* showing that the campaign and its concerns was also a critical topic of debate online.

Overall, we conclude that #YesAllWomen provided a critical *counter-narrative* to dominant gender discourses that present male harassment as either not serious (e.g., objectification and street calling as joking or flattery) or as somehow unusual or untypical. The vast number of personal stories and examples of daily disempowerment in the #YesAllWomen stream counter these arguments. By showing how the threat and reality of male sexual violence limit women's freedom, the hashtag also counters postfeminist and antifeminist arguments that we already have gender equality.

#YesAllWomen was not an isolated incident. It emerged in the context of other recent feminist mobilizations around sexual violence—such as Title IX challenges on campus, SlutWalks, and high school feminist protests against "slut-shaming" dress codes—and as such was part of a general recentering of issues of violence and harassment in feminist movements around, what has been called "rape culture."[24] #YesAllWomen, as an aggregation of stories about the daily ways in which the threat and actuality of male violence circumscribe women's lives, was a compelling intervention into this larger political conversation.

Digital media platforms like Twitter, then, not only allow *more* communication for citizens and activists, but by linking together people who share concerns, analyses, and ideas—in short, who share politics—through hashtags, Twitter also encourages the development of new collectivities and new (counter) narratives. In her classic analysis of the public sphere and of counter public spheres, Nancy Fraser argued for the necessity in democracy of *subaltern spheres*, spaces for the development of political identity where oppressed groups could articulate their grievances and demands. But she also noted that there must be established routes between these spheres and the legitimated spheres of allocation, policy decisions, and resources (e.g., government, market, and institutions).[25] Hashtag campaigns like #YesAllWomen, and more generally, online spheres like Feminist Twitter can be understood within this framework not only as virtual counter spheres—important in their own right—but also serving as conduits to bring new collectivities into the mainstream public sphere.

NOTES

1. Stephen Coleman and Deen Feelon, *Handbook of Digital Politics* (Cheltenham, UK: Edward Elgar Publishing, 2015).

2. Bernadette Barker-Plummer, "Producing Public Voice: Resource Mobilization and Media Access in the National Organization for Women," *Journalism and Mass Communication Quarterly*, 79 (2002): 188–205; Lenor Camauer, "Women's Movements, Public Spheres and the Media: A Research Strategy for Studying Women's Movements' Publicist Practices," in *Gender, Politics and Communication*, eds. Annabelle Sreberny and Liesbet Van Zoonen (Cresskill, NJ: Hampton Press, 2000), 161–183; Charlotte Ryan, Michael Anastario, and Alfredo DaCunha, "Changing Coverage of Domestic Violence Murders: A Longitudinal Experiment in Participatory Communication," *Journal of Interpersonal Violence* 2 (2006): 209–228.

3. Jodie Dean, *Blog Theory: Feedback and Capture in the Circuit of Drives* (Cambridge, UK: Polity Press, 2010).

4. Anastasia Kavada, "Engagement, Bonding, and Identity across Mutiple Platforms; Avaaz on Facebook, YouTube, and MySpace," *Medie-Kultur* 52 (2012): 28–48.

5. Farhad Manjoo, "How Black People Use Twitter: The Latest Research on Race and Microblogging," *Slate,* August 10, 2010, accessed December 7, 2015, http:// http://www.slate.com/articles/technology/technology/2010/08/how _black_people_use_twitter.html; Andrea Grimes, "Hashtag Activism and the Lie of Solidarity," *RH Reality Check,* May 28, 2014, http://rhrealitycheck.org/article/ 2014/05/28/hashtag-activism-lie-solidarity/.

6. The Twitter sample contained 500,294 tweets and 1.48 million retweets; the news sample had 122 press stories from a LexisNexis search and 21 broadcast news stories (ABC, NBC, CBS, Fox). See Methods section for more details.

7. Malcolm Gladwell, "Small Change: Why the Revolution Will Not Be Tweeted," *The New Yorker,* October 4, 2010, http://www.newyorker.com/ magazine/2010/10/04/small-change-malcolm-gladwell.

8. A communicative understanding of politics and social change does not assume direct cause and effect between campaigns and actions but rather tracks shifts in public opinion and cultural attitudes over time and the underlying dynamics of media and political communication that are related to these shifts. See for example, Bernadette Barker-Plummer, "The Dialogic of Media and Social Movements," *Peace Review* 8 (1996): 27–33; Charles Stewart, Craig Allen Smith, and Robert Denton, *Persuasion and Social Movements* (Long Grove, IL: Waveland Press, 2012); Bill Gamson, "Movement Impact on Cultural Change," in *Culture, Power, and History,* eds. Stephen Pfohl et al. (Boston, MA: Brill Publishers, 2005).

9. Yarimar Bonil and Jonathan Rosa, "#Ferguson: Digital Protest, Hashtag Ethnography, and the Racial Politics of Social Media in the United States," *American Ethnologist* 42 (2015): 4–17.

10. Bonila and Rosa, "#Ferguson," 9.

11. Mark Tremayne, "Anatomy of a Protest in the Digital Era: A Network Analysis of Twitter and Occupy Wall Street," *Social Movement Studies* 13 (2014): 110–126.

12. Yannis Theocaris, Will Lowe, Jan van Deth, and Geema Garcia-Albacte, "Using Twitter to Mobilize Protest Action: Online Mobilization Patterns and Action Repertoires in the Occupy Wall Street, Indignados, and Aganaktismenoi Movements," *Information, Communication and Society* 18 (2015): 202–220; Aaron Veenstra, Narayanan Iyer, Mohammad Hossain, and Jiwoo Park, "Time, Place, Technology: Twitter as an Information Source in the Wisconsin Labor Protests," *Computers in Human Behavior* 31 (2013): 65–72.

13. GNIP Twitter data come in JSON format. We executed a Java program to analyze the data, extracting and counting structures of interest—for example, word frequencies for topics, comparing strings to collate retweets, extracting, resolving, and counting page links, and so on.

14. Topics were determined by selecting the most common nouns from the word list (ignoring prepositions, pronouns, conjunctions, etc.) and when these were identified, then identifying and collating the word's grammatical variations (e.g., feminist (s)/feminism(s) into the same category). Because so many of the top terms were gender related (e.g., *men/male*(s)/*man/guy*(s)/*boys*), we pulled these words together into two semantic categories (male/female) to allow more topics to be seen.

15. Names, where available, were extracted and run against a gendered database from the Social Security Administration from the mid-1990s. In Twitter, "handles" can be used instead of names and not all names were recognized, so these ratios are based on names that could be attributed.

16. Twitter defines retweets as only those with the same original ID. Any minor differences (extra space from cut and paste) would not count the tweets together even if they are substantially similar to the human eye. Twitter's lists of top retweets thus have several entries that are essentially the same—as when someone re-pastes an original tweet with a space and then that is retweeted, both the first and second groups of retweets are listed separately in Twitter's retweet lists. We wanted to collect tweets together by content (same meaning), so we searched all retweets for exact content (looking for the same string without spaces, punctuation, non-alpha characters) to find all retweets with the same word content but minor differences in punctuation (e.g., spaces, commas, dashes added by retweeters). In this analysis we dropped out of the top retweets list the "up vote" tweets—for example, retweets that said things like "This is amazing" or "This is the most important thing I have ever read." While these are important indicators of how valuable participants found the hashtag—these kind of messages accounted for three of the top 10 retweets before exclusion (2, 3, 6 ranks)—in this analysis we were interested in the most retweeted content/ideas, so we left these out.

17. Wodak Ruth and Michael Meyer, *Methods of Critical Discourse Analysis* (London: Sage, 2002).

18. Bonila and Rosa, "#Ferguson," 5.

19. Kaye, M., "On #YesAllWomen, One Year Later," *The Toast*, May 26, 2015, http://the-toast.net/2015/05/26/yesallwomen-one-year-later/.

20. There were other public forums—such as reddit and subreddit discussions—where #YesAllWomen was treated much more harshly, of course, but not in mainstream press or TV.

21. Alexandra Petri, "Why YesAllWomen Is Worth Reading," *Washington Post*, May 29, 2014, p. A19.

22. This is taken from hubspot.com—http://blog.hubspot.com/marketing/twitter-usage-stats—but it is a figure that has also been reported in other places.

23. Mark Tremayne, "Anatomy of a Protest in the Digital Era," 114.

24. See for example, Kate Harding, *Asking for It: Slut-Shaming, Victim-Blaming, and How We Can Change America's Rape Culture* (New York: Decapo Books, 2015). Rape culture theorists such as Harding point to the ways in which our culture constructs women as objects of desire or "prizes" to be won; that constructs men as having an expectation of access to women's bodies and companionship; that scrutinizes rape victims stories but worries about the future of their attackers; and that frames street harassment as flattery and excuses everyday instances of harassment with sentiments like "boys will be boys." The resonance between these descriptions or rape culture and the tweets in #YesAllWomen is remarkable.

25. Nancy Fraser, "Rethinking the Public Sphere: A Contribution to the Critique of Actually Existing Democracy," *Social Text*, 25/26 (1990): 56–80.

BIBLIOGRAPHY

Barker-Plummer, Bernadette. "The Dialogic of Media and Social Movements." *Peace Review* 8 (1996): 27–33.

Barker-Plummer, Bernadette. "Producing Public Voice: Resource Mobilization and Media Access in the National Organization for Women." *Journalism and Mass Communication Quarterly* 79 (2002): 188–205.

Barker-Plummer, Bernadette. "News and Feminism: A Historic Dialog." *Journalism and Communication Monographs* 12, no. 3 (2010): 145–120.

Bonil, Yarimar and Jonathan Rosa. "#Ferguson: Digital Protest, Hashtag Ethnography, and the Racial Politics of Social Media in the United States." *American Ethnologist* 42 (2015): 4–17.

Dean, Jodie. *Blog Theory: Feedback and Capture in the Circuit of Drives.* Cambridge, UK: Polity Press, 2010.

Gamson, William. "Movement Impact on Cultural Change." In *Culture, Power, and History,* edited by Stephen Pfohl et al. (Boston, MA: Brill Publishers, 2005).

Gladwell, Malcolm. "Small Change: Why the Revolution Will Not Be Tweeted." *The New Yorker,* October 4, 2010. http://www.newyorker.com/magazine/2010/10/04/small-change-malcolm-gladwell.

Grimes, Andrea. "Hashtag Activism and the Lie of Solidarity." *RH Reality Check,* May 28, 2014. http://rhrealitycheck.org/article/2014/05/28/hashtag-activism-lie-solidarity/.

Kaye, M. "On #YesAllWomen, One Year Later." *The Toast,* May 26, 2015. http://the-toast.net/2015/05/26/yesallwomen-one-year-later/.

Lenor, Camauer."Women's Movements, Public Spheres and the Media: A Research Strategy for Studying Women's Movements' Publicist Practices." In *Gender, Politics and Communication,* edited by Annabelle Sreberny and Liesbet Van Zoonen, 161–183. Cresskill, NJ: Hampton Press, 2002.

Rodino-Colocino, Michelle. "#YesAllWomen: Intersectional Mobilization against Sexual Assault Is Radical (Again)." *Feminist Media Studies* 14 (2014): 1113–1115.

Solnit, Rebecca, " #YesAllWomen Changes the Story of the Isla Vista Massacre." *The Nation Online,* June 6, 2014. http://www.tomdispatch.com/post/175850/tomgram%3A_rebecca_solnit,_%23yesallwomen_changes_the_story.

Theocaris, Yannis, Will Lowe, Jan van Deth, and Geema Garcia-Albacte. "Using Twitter to Mobilize Protest Action: Online Mobilization Patterns and Action Repertoires in the Occupy Wall Street, Indignados, and Aganaktismenoi Movements." *Information, Communication and Society* 18 (2015): 202–220.

Thrift, Samantha C. "#YesAllWomen as Feminist Meme Event." *Feminist Media Studies* 14 (2014): 1090–1092.

Tremayne, Mark. "Anatomy of a Protest in the Digital Era: A Network Analysis of Twitter and Occupy Wall Street." *Social Movement Studies* 13 (2014): 110–126.

Veenstra, Aaron, Narayanan Iyer, Mohammad Hossain, and Jiwoo Park. "Time, Place, Technology: Twitter as an Information Source in the Wisconsin Labor Protests." *Computers in Human Behavior* 31 (2014): 65–72.

Wodak, Ruth and Michael Meyer. *Methods of Critical Discourse Analysis.* London: Sage, 2002.

Chapter 6

The Politics of Authenticity in Facebook's Name Policy

Amber Davisson

In November 1993, *The New Yorker* published a cartoon that depicted two canines sitting in front of a computer with the caption "On the Internet, nobody knows you're a dog." The now iconic cartoon was an early symbol of both the exciting potential and growing fear of anonymity online. Online anonymity offered the potential to be anyone or anything. Just two years later, Sherry Turkle published *Life on the Screen*, a germinal work on digital technology, which touted the Internet as an escape from the cultural myth of a unified identity.[1] She argued that in leaving bodies behind, users gained the ability to not just be anyone but to be a plethora of anyones. Twenty years later, these visions of digital anonymity seem like quant relics of a distant past. Major corporations have built communication platforms, and designed an overarching infrastructure for the web, that increasingly forces users to integrate their offline and online identities. As we drag our physical bodies into digital spaces, with them come the violence and discrimination common to life offline. The push to see the digital as an extension of the physical, and to have one's digital identity correspond with a real world physical identity, has had serious consequences for the way that some Internet users are able to participate in the digital world. Facebook's authentic identity policy demonstrates the political implications of forcing individuals to unite the physical and the digital.

Originally called the "real" name policy, Facebook renamed their policy using the word *authentic* in hopes of broadening the types of names users could use on the site.[2] The word *authentic* in Facebook's policy, which is described in detail in the next section, carries with it a lot of baggage. Before getting into the discussion of the particulars of the policy, let us first dive into that term for a moment. Alice Marwick and danah boyd, in an essay on the way Twitter users construct communication, point out that authenticity on social media sites has a very particular meaning, which may be separate from the typical academic and theoretical conversation surrounding the concept.[3] On sites like Twitter and Facebook, one is likely to encounter a population of individuals who are using social media to develop a brand to capitalize on the technology. These users are seen as behaving in a way that is overly conscious of audience in an attempt to manipulate their *followers* or *friends*. To contrast, other users try to demonstrate authenticity by avoiding that sense of audience consciousness: authentic users will just be themselves regardless of who is watching. The simplicity of the instruction to just be yourself, your authentic self, your real self ignores the complexity of self and authenticity as context-dependent constructs.[4] Theo Van Leeuwen argues that "authenticity cannot be seen as an objective feature of talk."[5] Instead, it is a subjective feature that can be judged only by those experiencing it. Marwick and boyd argue that on Twitter, the users end up performing a version of authenticity that will be best received by the people they believe are in their audience. In using the word *authentic* as the building block for the development of a policy, Facebook has attempted to solidify the notion of authenticity. The process of taking something context and audience specific and transforming it into something objective and legalistic has had a number of problematic consequences.

The remainder of this essay explores those consequences in three sections. The first section outlines and analyzes Facebook's authentic name policy and public statements from the company outlining the reasoning behind its creation. This section argues that while Facebook's policy is meant to create a symbiotic relationship between offline and online life, it is actually altering the way users think about identity in both spaces. The second section, on narrowing the conversation, is a critical analysis of the mechanisms used to policy user name choices, authentic user name choices, and enforce the use of a particular name. This section argues that at each step along the way, the mechanisms behind this policy have encouraged members of minority groups to leave the site while simultaneously facilitating those who would harass minorities on the site. Finally, the last section deals with privacy and identity by focusing on the affordances of the Facebook site. This section argues that the focus on visibility, which is built into the culture of the site, creates an unsafe environment for some Facebook users. In each of these sections, one thing becomes apparent—Facebook's authentic name policy has consequences for all site users. Certain communities—particularly Native Americans, domestic violence survivors, and members of the gay, lesbian, bisexual, transexual, questioning, and intersex (GLBTQI) community—have experienced some of the worst consequences of the policy. However, as will become apparent throughout this chapter, no Facebook user is exempt from the impact of the policy.

FACEBOOK'S AUTHENTIC NAME POLICY

Since its founding in 2004, Facebook has had a policy that requires members to use their "authentic identities" when creating a profile.[6] By "authentic" identity, Facebook has specified that they mean that users must use the name they use "in real life; that way, you always know who you're connecting with."[7] The site asks users to refrain from using symbols in their names, characters from multiple languages, titles of any kind, words or phrases in place of middle names, and offensive words of any kind.[8] The name needs to be one that the user can verify with a government-issued ID or with other official documentation such as a library card or bank statement. While the question of what makes a name authentic might be difficult to determine, Facebook (2015) makes one thing clear: "Pretending to be anything or anyone isn't allowed."[9] The company has consistently argued that this "pretending" is dangerous to the overall ecology of Facebook.

In the early days of Facebook, user identity was verified by requiring people to sign up using a college e-mail address. In 2006, when the site switched over to allow anyone over the age of 13 to create a profile, the company changed their policy and now asks users to report any friends who are using aliases. Mark Zuckerberg, founder of Facebook, defended the policy in an interview with journalist David Kirkpatrick, saying that "having two identities for yourself is an example of a lack of integrity."[10] Nadia Drake, a science reporter at *Wired Magazine*, points out that one of the main reasons given by Facebook for requiring authentic names is because they believe anonymity can be dangerous.[11] The company narrative surrounding the policy is that a user will operate under a fake name so they can be a bully, or troll the site, and avoid consequences. Most site users were likely unaware of the real name rule before an incident in September 2014 when several drag performers had their accounts disabled.[12] The incident spurred widespread protesting on Facebook and Twitter.[13] Despite protests from site users that the policy was being used to unfairly target members of the queer community who used aliases online as a means to separate out different parts of their lives, Facebook stood by the rule, arguing that it was necessary to avoid fraud, bullying, or other malicious behavior.[14] On June 1, 2015, Justin Osofsky, vice president of Global Operations, and Monika Bickert, head of Global Product Policy, posted on the official Facebook blog a response to many of the critiques of the authentic name policy. They argued that "when people use their authentic names on Facebook they are more accountable for what they say. People can be assured that they're really connecting with their loved ones, and no one can hide behind an anonymous name to bully, taunt or say insensitive or inappropriate things. This creates a safer community for everyone."[15] The post listed some things the company is doing to help out those individuals harmed by the authentic name policy. In the wake of controversy surrounding the policy, Facebook has stated they will provide a seven-day grace period while someone proves their name, though reports indicate it is unclear how to get access to this grace period.[16] Prior to the controversy, Facebook let users submit only a government ID to prove their identity, and now they allow other forms of identification. For those protesting the Facebook policy, these changes did not go far enough.

The right to name oneself, or choose what to be called, has a long and contentious history. In conversations about race, the right to choose what to be called—such as the choice between Negro, African American, or black—signals a claiming of power.[17] In the United States, there has long been a struggle over the power issues involved in naming and renaming the homes and sacred lands of native peoples.[18] The choice to call oneself a feminist or to label something as sexist has serious political implications.[19] When media personalities choose to refer to someone who is transgender by their legal name instead of their chosen name, it sends a clear message that they are not recognizing the person's expressed gender identity. Naming practices are strongly connected to questions of power. When the issue of authenticity is brought into the discussion, the power issues only become clearer. If choosing what to be called or what to call something is about claiming power, then a system that recognizes or denies authenticity has the implication of denying that power. Karen Nemeth argues that names are about attempting to identify an idea, and as such they can change based on context. Facebook does not allow for that sense of context.[20] The Facebook authentic name policy enforces a strict sense of identity that says this is who you are and attempts to be something else are a lie.

To get at the power issues involved in Facebook's authentic name policy, it is important to consider the relationship between "digital life" and "real life." danah boyd points out that authentic name policies often stem from the notion that in real life we use our real names, so using our real names online will allow the digital to mimic real life. However, that is not an entirely accurate description of how we interact in real life:

"When someone walks into a cafe, they do reveal certain aspects of themselves while obfuscating other aspects of their identity."[21] Our public presentation of self reveals some aspects of identity and hides others. Similarly, "the practice of sharing one's name is embedded in rituals of relationship building. People do not share their names with every person they encounter. Rather, names are offered as an introductory gesture in specific situations to signal politeness and openness."[22] Karen Nemeth, who was previously an employee of Facebook, argues that the company is not just after your name for the purpose of advertising. The authentic name policy helps to reinforce the notion of authenticity on the site—you are talking to your real friends who you know in real life. "Facebook wants you to be your authentic self because they believe that authenticity is what makes the site appealing. No fake usernames or second profiles or profiles for things that aren't people means more eyeballs on the site."[23] All this operates under the assumption that in authentic interactions we reveal all this information about ourselves. Zuckerberg himself has articulated this exact assumption when responding to questions about the authentic name policy: "Real names help make the service easier to use. People use Facebook to look up friends and people they meet all the time. This is easy because you can just type their name into search and find them. This becomes much harder if people don't use their real names." The assumption here is that when people meet they exchange full legal names. Using this lens to view what makes interactions authentic is actually changing the way we interact in real life. As Nemeth explains, "As a technology, Facebook isn't neutral. It's actually changing the way we interact with names. Before Facebook how many of your friends' surnames did you actually know?"[24] Furthermore, "By forcing us to change our names on the site, Facebook changes the names we are known by in real life—whether we like it or not."[25] In Facebook's attempt to use naming practices as a signal of authenticity, they are actually altering how we understand notions of authenticity, privacy, and identity.

Even Mark Zuckerberg has acknowledged that the relationship between identity and name is not cut and dry. In a town hall style Q&A on the Facebook site, the founder told people:

> Your real name is whatever you go by and what your friends call you. If your friends all call you by a nickname and you want to use that name on Facebook, you should be able to do that. In this way, we should be able to support everyone using their own real names, including everyone in the transgender community. We are working on better and more ways for people to show us what their real name is so we can both keep this policy which protects so many people in our community while also serving the transgender community.

Zuckerberg's statement implies that the site protects a certain level of agency for individuals reporting their name. In October 2014, Facebook loosened its policy. At the time of the change, Chris Cox, chief product officer at Facebook, wrote that "the spirit of our policy is that everyone on Facebook uses the authentic name they use in real life. For Sister Roma, that's Sister Roma. For Lil Miss Hot Mess, that's Lil Miss Hot Mess."[26] While this may be the spirit of the policy, the way the policy has been written and enacted does not support that spirit.

NARROWING THE CONVERSATION

Since its inception in 2004, Facebook has become the place where many get their political news, engage in political discussions, and generally develop their understanding of the current political climate. A 2015 study from the Pew Research Center found that 60 percent of millennials and 39 percent of baby boomers get their political news from Facebook.[27] Where previously one might have relied on newspaper editors or news television producers to curate stories and decide what political news would receive the most attention, now many individuals are following the links to stories their friends consider to be the top news or stories that Facebook pushes through their trending topics feature. Probably the most immediate response to issues with the authentic name policy is that individuals who have a problem with the rule can just stop using the site. There are a number of issues with this advice. For someone who is the target of stalking or domestic violence, this is the choice between safety and the ability to participate in public political conversations. Beyond that, a number of the individuals targeted by the policy are members of minority groups, in particular GLBTQI communities, or members of racial and ethnic minority groups. To encourage these individuals to leave the site or capitulate to the policy would likely result in a number of minority voices removed from the political conversation. Some would argue that the mass removal of certain voices from the site would have little impact, because Facebook has several algorithms that determine what shows up in a user's news feed or trending topics.[28] This fails to take into account that while the site may be manipulating what content users see, it can only do that with the content that is available. Excluding particular groups from the conversation will necessarily alter the variety and types of material that circulates through the site. This section the mechanisms and procedures that are used to enforce Facebook's policy—from the reporting process to the name authentication process. Facebook is a critical site for current political conversation, and the system that has been built around the authentic name policy has made it a tool for excluding minority voices from the conversation.

While the authentic name policy may have been originally designed to deter bullying or malicious behavior, the reporting mechanism for the policy seems to actually enable these behaviors. In 2015, Facebook reported more than a billion users logging in each month. Assigning employees to find violations of the policy, or creating an algorithm to do so, has thus far proved inefficient given the sheer number of users on the site.[29] Instead, the company relies on the Facebook community to report users with suspicious names. Facebook's reliance on user reporting has created a situation where the authentic name policy is used to harass minority groups on the site. Some Facebook users have created groups specifically for the purpose of using the authentic name policy to harass other users—such as non-gender conforming individuals and political activists.[30] Shane Creepingbear said that he has had his name reported twice; both times it was after he had made a controversial political statement on his Facebook page.[31] In one instance, a single Facebook user reported several hundred accounts as fake, and no one at the company questioned the pattern.[32] Even users who are using their legal name on the site may find themselves locked out of their account while they go through the process of proving their identity. Forcing someone to deal with the identity authentication process is a quick way to, at least temporarily, kick people off the site if you do not like what they have to say. Nadia Drake points out that "perhaps the most frustrating part of this is that the person who flags your account is afforded more privacy than you are. Even when it's a matter of personal safety, Facebook will not reveal the accuser."[33] Instead of protecting users from anonymous harassment, by making the reporting process anonymous, they have created a method for anonymous harassment. The result is that "Facebook has handed an enormous hammer to those who would like to silence us, and time after time I see that hammer coming down on trans women who have just stepped out of line by suggesting that perhaps we're being mistreated. In fact, it happened to me shortly after commenting on a Facebooker's post that Facebook needs to step up on this issue."[34] Instead of decreasing anonymous bullying or harassment, the policy has facilitated it.

While the reporting process for the authentic name policy has created a hostile environment for some users, the verification process has proven just as problematic. One of the issues with Facebook's method for verifying authentic names is that some names that are legal do not conform to popular norms regarding naming. One group that has faced considerable issues with the name policy are Native American Facebook users. Native American users have been forced to spell their names in English instead of their native language.[35] Some Native American users with longer than traditional names have been made to either delete or join together parts of their names. In one case, "Oglala Lakota Lance Brown Eyes was booted from Facebook, and when he turned in his proof of identification they changed his name to Lance Brown. After contacting the Better Business Bureau and threatening Facebook with a class action lawsuit, they [Facebook] sent him an apology and let him use his given name again."[36] The issue here is that "like so many other norms that have the potential to primarily disenfranchise everyone except straight white guys, this 'authentic name' policy favors a certain type of user: Someone without a fluid identity, who can use their name online without fear—and as we've repeatedly seen, someone whose name doesn't sound 'weird' to a Facebook employee's ears."[37] Names that sound weird or seem to fall outside of dominant cultural norms are ruled as fake, or in some cases changed to fit with social expectations. As Matt Cagle points out, "By controlling the identity of the speaker with this policy, Facebook has the effect of both reducing speech and eliminating speakers from the platform altogether. This is a particularly concerning move to the ACLU because forums like Facebook serve as the modern-day equivalent of the public square for a lot of communities."[38] While the reporting process has been used as a tool of harassment, the verification process has been of forcing larger cultural norms on minority users.

For some Facebook users, a pseudonym is necessary to avoid digital threats crossing over into physical violence. When the Facebook verification process is completed, the company changes the user's name to the on official documentation that was submitted. When Facebook automatically changes the name, it can have serious consequences for those who use pseudonyms to protect their safety. Laurie Penny, a journalist who writes for the *New Statesman* and *The Guardian*, used a pseudonym on Facebook to avoid trolls who had leaked her private information, such as phone number and address, and used that information to threaten her. After Penny was forced to use her legal name on the site, she tweeted "Thanks to @facebook for forcing me to use my real name, I am now at more risk of rape and death threats. But enjoy flogging that data, guys."[39] For Penny, a pseudonym on Facebook made it possible to connect with family and friends while avoiding harassment from members of the public who might disagree with the views expressed in her articles. Other Facebook users report using pseudonyms to hide their identity from someone who may have stalked or abused them. Facebook users who fear for their safety may leave the site altogether to avoid the risk, meaning they are left out of discussions on the site. Alternatively, they may self-censor to avoid posts that could give away personal details or make them a target for threats of physical violence. The knowledge that Facebook will automatically change the name on your profile to the one on the documentation submitted encourages some users to avoid the process and simply leave the site.

Translating a subjective concept like authenticity into an objective policy is a complicated process. Facebook's procedures for identifying policy violators, verifying authentic names, and changing names have proven problematic for a number of users. At each step along the way, harassment, community norms, and the threat of potential violence encourage minority users to leave the site. As a result, the authentic name policy has a direct impact on the quality of political conversation on Facebook.

PRIVACY AND IDENTITY MANAGEMENT

When Facebook talks about authenticity, the primary point of reference they use in their policy is "real life." As in: "We require people to provide the name they use in real life."[40] At the center of the conversation about how digital life and real life correspond are issues of privacy and the question of how individuals use privacy to develop identity. Daniel Solove argues that, in Western cultures, conversations about privacy often hinge on the "nothing-to-hide" argument.[41] People say they do not worry about their privacy because they have "nothing-to-hide." Conversely, people who are worried about their privacy must have something to hide, and they should give up their privacy in the interest of security. Facebook asks users to give up any privacy associated with remaining anonymous because "this helps keep our community safe."[42] Potential privacy invasions, at places like airports, are justified under the logic that if you are not doing anything wrong you should not mind. The people who protest are believed to have insidious motives for their complaints. For Solove, the simplicity of the "nothing-to-hide" argument belies the larger issue that because the concept of privacy lacks a clear definition, individuals do not know how to identify it or protect it. In the battle between a concept that "is a plurality of things that do not share one element in common but that nevertheless bear a resemblance to each other" and a more concrete term like *security*, one's privacy becomes a difficult thing to defend.[43] Less discussed are the ways we use privacy in our everyday lives to build our identity within different contexts. Helen Nissenbaum has argued that privacy is less about the absolute release of information and more about the ability to control how much information is revealed within a given social context.[44] For instance, a person keeps certain parts of his or her life private while he or she is at work so that he or she can establish a professional identity. Individuals often adopt slightly different identities for different contexts in their life (e.g., one for work, one for spending time with family, one for hanging out with friends). For those identities to be distinct, parts of the self must be withheld and other parts of the self revealed. Nissenbaum explains that part of the choice about what to reveal and what to withhold has to do with social norms particular to a given social context. For example, it is generally inappropriate to talk about your sex life at work.[45] While it may be that the things we keep to ourselves are often not insidious, but merely inappropriate, in a "nothing-to-hide" society what is hidden is threatening. Controversy surrounding privacy often boils down to a conflict between the need to keep the community safe from those who would hide critical information and a need for individuals to protect their established identity by choosing what to reveal in a given context.

Life online can complicate attempts to create multiple contextualized selves. Siva Vaidhyanathan points out that "the online environments in which we work and play have broken down the barriers that separate the different social contexts in which we move ... most online environments are intentionally engineered to serve our professional, educational, and personal desires simultaneously."[46] Vaidhyanathan goes on to argue that this problem is compounded by services online that collect and organize information. A Google search does not distinguish between our "at work selves" and our "at the bar with friends selves." If a person investigates you on Google or Facebook, they are likely to find information from multiple facets of your life. In a face-to-face interaction, people may strategically reveal information to develop their identity, but once information is released online, it becomes difficult, even impossible, to be strategic about who sees it.[47] Some have tried to combat the problem by developing multiple personas under different names. Being known by different names helps to control visibility online. danah boyd, in her work on youth attitudes toward digital privacy, says that those who cannot strategically control their identity often experience something called contextual collapse. The collapse happens when multiple parts of one's life converge in the same place.[48] On a site like Facebook, a person may be confronted by work colleagues, family members, and friends all in the same space. It becomes difficult to target content, such as status updates or photos, in order to develop different aspects of identity. boyd found that some users avoid the negative consequences of contextual collapse by hiding all aspects of self, both in their offline and online behavior, that might be offensive. Faced with the inability to create multiple contextualized selves, they functionally lose any sense of a distinct self.

When it comes to developing a sense of self, the affordances of the Facebook site are geared toward developing the self in a very particular way. Angela Cirucci has argued that Facebook's "real you" policy is geared toward encouraging users to be as visible on the site as possible. The standard of realness becomes the willingness to constantly perform what is going on in "real" life through photos and updates.[49] While these affordances are willingly adopted by many users, the need to perform a certain level of realness may be intimidating for users whose sense of identity is more fluid. Joyce Y. M. Nip, in her research on the relationship between online and offline queer communities, has argued that the technical features of a platform have a significant impact on the development of communication habits.[50] In particular, she found that the ability of members of the queer community to develop social ties in online spaces was significantly influenced by the level of safety users felt when navigating the platform. One of the major safety issues has to do with how "out" a person is in their offline or day-to-day life. John Campbell, in his writing on gay male sexuality online, has argued that feeling safe from outing is necessary for a lot of users to feel safe exploring their identity online.[51] Furthermore, Mary Bryson, in her research on QLBT women online, found that even women who defined themselves as "out" were very protective of their online identities.[52] If a person is attempting to feel safe from outing, or going through the process of exploring multiple sex and gender identities, the authentic name policy can be problematic at best and dangerous at worst. As of July 2015, there are 75 countries with laws against sexual activity by lesbian, gay, bisexual, transgender, or intersex people. In eight of those countries, punishment is the death penalty.[53] At a protest outside of Facebook headquarters in June 2015, Sister Merry Peter talked about the dangers of the authentic name policy for LGBTQI individuals around the world, noting that "we have Sisters in Uruguay who are stalked by death squads because they are taking on the oppression of the Roman Catholic Church. Outing their real names on Facebook puts them in serious danger of mortal harm."[54] The threat posed by outing is not imagined or mere paranoia. Beyond the threat of legal consequences, there is the fear that exposure could result in the loss of employment, the end of friendships, or the alienation of family members. In the United States, there are multiple instances of individuals being fired after employers discovered they were gay or after they posted their views on same-sex marriage.[55]

For someone who is queer-identifying, the Internet might seem like a natural space to use one's privacy to explore new identities. Digital spaces hold out the potential to leave one's body behind and create an almost post-human identity. Kathryn Conrad has posited that for the queer community, digital post-humanism provided hope that individuals could create multiple bodies of information relating to different identities and form relationships where they could be someone who more closely resembles their sense of selves.[56] George Chauncey wrote that "there is no queer space; there are only spaces used by queers or put to queer use. Space has no natural characteristic, no inherent meaning, no intrinsic status as public or private."[57] Digital spaces are not private, and there is no guarantee that someone exploring multiple queer selves will find the privacy they need to develop those identities. Still, over the years, a number of digital platforms have been adopted by the queer community as spaces to develop community, share resources, and experiment with identity performance. Often, while these platforms have not offered themselves up as inherently queer spaces, the potential for anonymity or the use of aliases has made them simultaneously public and private in a way that lends itself to identity play. Much of the potential of these spaces has to do with established norms. Nissenbaum explains that the norms of a context determine our sense of privacy in that space: "These norms, which I call context-relative informational norms, define and sustain essential activities and key relationships and interests, protect people and groups against harm, and balance the distribution of power."[58] The norms that have evolved surrounding Facebook's naming practices and privacy raise questions about whether this is a safe space to be queer.

The authentic name policy was meant to create a safe space and to "help prevent people from creating fake or malicious accounts that may hurt your ability to enjoy sharing with your friends."[59] The affordances of the site are geared toward discouraging anonymity and making users as visible as possible. Still, there is a sizable population of individuals who troll the Facebook site, those who disrupt conversations and violate community norms, and do so while using names that violate the authentic name policy. Many suspicious names on the site are overlooked for humorous reasons. At any given time, one will find plenty of accounts for "Seymour Butts."[60] Users do not report these names because they are generally seen as funny. Whitney Phillips in her research on Internet trolling has found that communities of trolls are able to maintain strong ties despite the fact that their accounts are repeatedly deactivated for violations of the authentic name policy. Trolls will use multiple combinations and versions of a similar name to create several accounts; "having stable names to call each other meant that trolls suddenly had persistent social identities."[61] For trolls, the ability to maintain community links is more important than the body of information they have amassed on a single profile. So, when an account is deactivated for violating policy, nothing is really lost. They simply make another profile and reforge the links. Whereas, for a user who buys into the culture of visibility and amasses a significant amount of data on the site, losing a profile can be devastating. Those who would use the site for harassment and bullying are not as invested in their profiles. So, the punishment weighs heavier on those it needs to protect than on the people it was meant to deter.

For members of some minority groups, the choice is between safety and participation in an important site of political discussion. Privacy allows a certain level of safety that makes it possible to explore identity and engage with others at the same time. Almost everyone exercises a certain level of privacy or anonymity in their daily lives as a way of avoiding conflict, establishing a professional persona, or even just making new friends. Demands that people give up privacy, or be more authentic, are often couched in terms of safety. In this case, the demand for authenticity in the name of safety is allowing for the targeted harassment of some of the most vulnerable members of the Facebook community.

SUMMARY AND CONCLUDING THOUGHTS

In May 2015, Sister Roma led a group protesting Facebook's involvement in San Francisco PRIDE celebration.[62] Sister Roma has been a leader in an online movement called #mynameis, which has been particularly vocal in challenging the authentic name policy. While Facebook was ultimately allowed to participate in the festivities, one of the things they agreed to do in exchange was to meet with Sister Roma and other members of the LGBTQI community to discuss potential changes to the authentic name policy. After the meeting, Sister Roma reported some critical changes in the company's policy regarding authentic names.[63] In the meeting, which took place in November 2015, Facebook acknowledged that the option for name reporting on the site was being abused to target members of the LGBTQI community, and they are updating the reporting form to require people to state the motivation for reporting the name and why they think the name violates the policy. In addition, the name verification forms will now include a place for the user to identify as a domestic abuse survivor, Native American, or member of the LGBTQI community. In response to the overall controversy, Facebook has hired someone in charge of actually dealing with and responding to fake name reporting and identity confirmation. As Sister Roma noted, these changes show a drastic shift in Facebook's overall policy regarding authentic identity:

> Since we first met with Facebook they seem to have broadened their grasp on the concept of identity with relation to the LGBTQI and other affected communities. They acknowledge that identity is fluid and cannot always be proven with a piece of paper. As a result, when the changes roll out in December, someone who has been reported for using a "fake" name will have an opportunity to explain who they are. This will include options for LGBT, American Indian, Domestic Violence Survivor, etc. There will also be a text field for users to further share their stories of identity.[64]

These changes are all scheduled to go into place in December 2015. As of the writing of this essay, the possibilities for change are promising, but it is hard to tell if these reforms will solve all the problems. Facebook has taken up a difficult mission—turning a subjective concept into an objective policy—and the ultimate success of the mission is still hard to determine.

Often privacy is thought of as a right only invoked by those who have something to hide. What might not be considered here is that some of the most vulnerable members of our society hide things to protect themselves. That protection may be a matter of avoiding physical harm, and it may be a matter of finding the necessary safety to express one's beliefs. Regardless, privacy can be a necessary freedom. In the case of the Facebook policy, the conflict arises when the site is attempting to create a safe space, and their policy potentially harms the safety of many of their users. Often something is considered authentic online when it corresponds with practices offline. However, this raises questions about how we understand authenticity in day-to-day life, and what measures we use to prove it is happening.

NOTES

1. Sherry Turkle, *Life on the Screen* (New York: Simon & Schuster, 1995).
2. Abby Phillip, "Online 'Authenticity' and How Facebook's 'Real Name' Policy Hurts Native Americans," *Washington Post*, February 10, 2015, https://www .washingtonpost.com/news/morning-mix/wp/2015/02/10/online-authenticity -and-how-facebooks-real-name-policy-hurts-native-americans/.
3. Alice E. Marwick and danah boyd, "I Tweet Honestly, I Tweet Passionately: Twitter Users, Context Collapse, and the Imagined Audience," *New Media & Society* 13, no. 1 (2011): 120.
4. Vincent Joice Cheng, *Inauthentic: The Anxiety over Culture and Identity* (Rutgers, NJ: Rutgers University Press, 2004).
5. Theo Van Leeuwen, "What Is Authenticity?" *Discourse Studies* 3, no. 4 (2001): 396.
6. Facebook Help Center, "What Names Are Allowed on Facebook?" November 10, 2015, https://www.facebook.com/help/112146705538576.
7. Ibid.
8. Facebook Help Center, "What Types of ID Does Facebook Accept?" November 10, 2015, https://www.facebook.com/help/159096464162185.
9. Facebook Help Center, "What Names Are Allowed on Facebook?"
10. David Kirkpatrick, *The Facebook Effect: The Inside Story of the Company That Is Connecting the World* (New York: Simon and Schuster, 2010), 199.
11. Nadia Drake, "HELP, I'm Trapped in Facebook's Absurd Pseudonym Purgatory," *Wired Magazine,* June 19, 2015, http://www.wired.com/2015/06/ facebook-real-name-policy-problems/.
12. Valeriya Safronova, "Drag Performers Fight Facebook's 'Real Name' Policy," *New York Times*, September 24, 2014, http://www.nytimes.com/2014/09/25/ fashion/drag-performers-fight-facebooks-real-name-policy.html?_r=1.
13. Reed Albergotti, "Facebook Changes Real Name Policy after Uproar from Drag Queens," *Wall Street Journal,* October 2, 2014, http://www.wsj.com/articles/ facebook-changes-real-name-policy-after-uproar-from-drag-queens-1412223040.
14. Safronova, "Drag Performers Fight Facebook's 'Real Name' Policy"; Tony Merevick, "Despite Meeting with LGBT Activists, Facebook Won't Budge on Name Change Issue," *Buzzfeed*, September 17, 2014, http://www.buzzfeed.com/tonymere vick/despite-meeting-with-lgbt-activists-facebook-wont-budge-on-n#jzqy2r.
15. Justin Osofsky and Monika Bickert, *Facebook Blog*, June 1, 2015, https:// www.facebook.com/fbsafety/posts/861043117266861.

16. Drake, "HELP, I'm Trapped in Facebook's Absurd Pseudonym Purgatory."

17. Ben L. Martin, "From Negro to Black to African American: The Power of Names and Naming," *Political Science Quarterly* (1991): 83–107.

18. Winona LaDuke, *Recovering the Sacred: The Power of Naming and Claiming* (Cambridge, MA: South End Press, 2005).

19. Sara Mills, "Caught between Sexism, Anti-Sexism and Political Correctness: Feminist Women's Negotiations with Naming Practices," *Discourse & Society* 14, no. 1 (2003): 87–110.

20. Karen Nemeth, "My Name Is Only Real Enough to Work at Facebook, Not to Use on the Site," *The Medium*, June 27, 2015, https://medium.com/@zip/my-name-is-only-real-enough-to-work-at-facebook-not-to-use-on-the-site-c37daf3f4b03.

21. danah boyd, "The Politics of Real Names," *Communications of the ACM* 55, no. 8 (2012): 30.

22. Ibid.

23. Nemeth, "My Name Is Only Real Enough to Work at Facebook, Not to Use on the Site."

24. Ibid.

25. Ibid.

26. Jessica Guynn, "Facebook Apologizes to Drag Queens over Real Name Policy," *USA Today*, October 1, 2014, http://www.usatoday.com/story/tech/2014/10/01/facebook-drag-queens/16552927/.

27. Amy Mitchell, Jeffrey Gottfried, and Katerina Eva Matsa, "Millennials and Political News Social Media—the Local TV for the Next Generation?" *Pew Research Center*, June 1, 2015, http://www.journalism.org/2015/06/01/millennials-political-news/.

28. Amanda Hess, "Facebook's 'Trending' Is the Worst Place on the Internet," *Slate.com.*, October 22, 2015, http://www.slate.com/articles/technology/future_tense/2015/10/facebook_s_trending_algorithm_makes_me_ashamed.html; Vindu Goel, "Facebook Tinkers with Users' Emotions in News Feed Experiment, Stirring Outcry," *New York Times*, June 29, 2014, http://www.nytimes.com/2014/06/30/technology/facebook-tinkers-with-users-emotions-in-news-feed-experiment-stirring-outcry.html?_r=0.

29. Patrick McKenzie, "Falsehoods Programmers Believe about Names," *Kalzumeus*, June 17, 2010, http://www.kalzumeus.com/2010/06/17/falsehoods-programmers-believe-about-names/.

30. Nadia Kayyali, "Facebook's Name Policy Strikes Again, This Time at Native Americans," *Electronic Frontiers Foundation*, February 13, 2015, https://www.eff.org/deeplinks/2015/02/facebooks-name-policy-strikes-again-time-native-americans.

31. Phillip, "Online 'Authenticity' and How Facebook's 'Real Name' Policy Hurts Native Americans."

32. Jessica Guynn, "Facebook Apologizes to Drag Queens over Real Name Policy."

33. Drake, "HELP, I'm Trapped in Facebook's Absurd Pseudonym Purgatory."

34. Nemeth, "My Name Is Only Real Enough to Work at Facebook, Not to Use on the Site."

35. Dana Lone Hill, "Facebook Don't Believe in Indian Names," *Last Real Indians* (blog), July 2, 2015, http://lastrealindians.com/facebook-dont-believe-in-indian-names-by-dana-lone-hill/.

36. Ibid.

37. Drake, "HELP, I'm Trapped in Facebook's Absurd Pseudonym Purgatory."

38. Ibid.

39. Bethan McKernan, "A Journalist Who Used a Pseudonym to Avoid Rape and Death Threats Has Been Kicked off Facebook," *i100* (blog), June 24, 2015, http:// i100.independent.co.uk/article/a-journalist-who-used-a-pseudonym-to-avoid -rape-and-death-threats-has-been-kicked-off-facebook—bJZmbd2b1Me.

40. Facebook Help Center, "What Names Are Allowed on Facebook?"

41. Daniel Solove, *Nothing to Hide: The False Tradeoff between Privacy and Security* (Hartford, CT: Yale University Press, 2011), 21.

42. Facebook Help Center, "What Names Are Allowed on Facebook?"

43. Solove, *Nothing to Hide*, 22.

44. Helen Nissenbaum, *Privacy in Context: Technology, Policy, and the Integrity of Social Life* (Stanford, CA: Stanford University Press, 2009), 3.

45. Nissenbaum, *Privacy in Context*, 3.

46. Siva Vaidhyanathan, *The Googlization of Everything: (and Why We Should Worry)* (Berkley, CA: University of California Press, 2012), 95.

47. Vaidhyanathan, *The Googlization of Everything*, 95.

48. danah boyd, *It's Complicated* (New Haven, CT: Yale University Press, 2014), 49.

49. Angela M. Cirucci, "Facebook's Affordances, Visible Culture, and Anti-Anonymity," *Proceedings of the 2015 International Conference on Social Media & Society*, 11, ACM, 2015.

50. Joyce Yee-man Nip, "The Relationship between Online and Offline Communities: The Case of the Queer Sisters, *Media, Culture & Society* 26, no. 3 (2004): 409–428.

51. John Campbell, *Getting It on Online: Cyberspace, Gay Male Sexuality, and Embodied Identity* (New York: Routledge, 2004).

52. Mary Bryson, "When Jill Jacks In: Queer Women and the Net," *Feminist Media Studies* 4, no. 3 (2004): 239–254.

53. "79 Countries Where Homosexuality is Illegal," *Erasing 76 Crimes* (blog), July 9, 2015, http://76crimes.com/76-countries-where-homosexuality-is-illegal/.

54. Joe Kukura, "Protest at Facebook HQ Flags 'Real Names' Policy for Review," *SFist.com* (blog), June 1, 2015, http://sfist.com/2015/06/01/protest _at_facebook_headquarters_fl.php.

55. Duaa Eldeib, "2nd Catholic Church Employee Says He Was Fired over Same-Sex Marriage," *Chicago Tribune*, November 12, 2015, http://www.chicagotribune .com/news/local/breaking/ct-gay-catholic-church-employee-complaint-met -20151112-story.html; "Woman Fired over Her Same-Sex Marriage Speaks Out," *6ABC*, July 10, 2015, http://6abc.com/education/woman-fired-over-her-same -sex-marriage-speaks-out/839191/.

56. Kathryn Conrad, "Surveillance, Gender, and the Virtual Body in the Information Age," *Surveillance & Society* 6, no. 4 (2009): 382.

57. George Chauncey, "Privacy Could Only Be Had in Public: Gay Uses of the Streets," in *The People Place, and Space Reader,* eds. Jen Jack Gieseking, William Mangold, Cindi Katz, Setha Low, and Susan Saegert, 202–206 (New York: Routledge, 2014), 202.

58. Nissenbaum, *Privacy in Context*, 3.

59. Facebook Help Center, "Why Was My Name Rejected during Signup?" November 11, 2015, https://www.facebook.com/help/212848065405122.

60. Barbara Ortutay, "Real Users Caught in Facebook Fake-Name Purge," *San Francisco Gate,* May 25, 2009, http://www.sfgate.com/business/article/Real-users-caught-in-Facebook-fake-name-purge-3231397.php.

61. Whitney Phillips, *This Is Why We Can't Have Nice Things* (Cambridge, MA: MIT Press, 2015), 77–78.

62. JW Waxner-Herman, "Sister Roma and Others Want to Ban Facebook from Pride over Ongoing 'Real Name' Policy," *The Sword,* May 4, 2015, http://thesword.com/sister-roma-and-others-want-to-ban-facebook-from-pride-over-ongoing-real-name-policy.html.

63. Sister Roma, "Sister Roma: 'Facebook Is Finally Listening Re: #MyNameIs'," *The Sword*, November 3, 2015, http://thesword.com/sister-roma-facebook-is-finally-listening-re-mynameis.html.

64. Ibid.

Chapter 7

Allocating Identities within a Smartphone App Game: A Case Study of *Dark Summoner*

Keith Massie and Angela M. Cirucci

During the first half of 2015, numerous news stories emerged to focus the nation's attention on identity. Caitlyn Jenner, Rachel Dolezal, and the ideologically motivated mass murder at the historically African-American Emanuel African Methodist Episcopal Church in Charleston, South Carolina, opened a space for citizens to begin reflecting on and examining the intersection of identity and politics. This chapter analyzes and engages a space that, for some time, has had implications for the self and that constructs and reifies identity, yet is often overlooked: videogames.

For the purposes of this chapter, identity will be defined as some narrative process, wherein humans employ concepts from metanarratives that represent sociocultural expectations. That is, people construct their selves by allocating local, national, and global signifiers.[1] Although an individual's identity is shaped by numerous social institutions such as school, family, religion, and community, media—such as videogames—play a large role in the ways in which players see the world, themselves, and others.[2]

If the term *political* is, at its root, focused on the allocation and control of resources, then the ability of a gamer to control his or her own (virtual) identity and body is necessarily a political act.[3] In the same vein, the ability for game designers and programmers to afford users certain identity acts in-game is also a political act. Because videogames require that each and every identity aspect be quantified so as to code the related act, videogames become an important site of study—the allocation and control of identity is highlighted and often manipulated in these spaces.

As this book focuses on the intersection of social media and politics, this chapter will begin with a discussion of both social media and politics to establish how a videogame may exist as a site for both. After addressing these basic notions, the chapter focuses on the size, scope, content, and research of videogames. Although researchers are beginning to take notice of console and PC games, smartphone apps remain largely under researched. Smartphone addiction itself (i.e., not necessarily games) has been found to have a negative impact on university students;[4] however, to date, little research has been released that studies such representations within videogames designed exclusively for smartphones. The goal of this chapter, then, is to employ a case study of one such smartphone videogame app—*Dark Summoner*.

SOCIAL MEDIA AND POLITICS

A singular definition of social media is difficult to develop. For the purposes of this chapter, we will define social media in the simplest way by combining the overarching aspects of the term *social* with that of *media*. What does *social* mean? It is any act, attribute, or object whose function is to build and/or maintain relationships between parties. Such a definition is basic yet functional for our purposes. What does *media* mean? A medium is any technology that allows for the transference of meanings. So, *social media* are those technologies that enable the building and maintenance of relationships.

Politics as a concept has been around much longer than the phrase *social media*. At its root, politics deals with and examines the allocation of resources. There are four distinct aspects of videogames that intersect the political realm. Each aspect will be addressed beginning with the most obvious for videogame research to the more subtle.

Videogames and Civic Engagement

Videogame playing impacts the depth and rate of teens' civic and political engagement. One study found that "playing games with others in person was related to civic and political outcomes, but playing with others online was not."[5] In short, players who had physical, social interactions engaged in more civic activity (e.g., getting information about politics or raising money for a charity) than those who played games socially with others online (i.e., not physically present). If this fact holds and is causal in nature, mobile (or smartphone) game apps like *Dark Summoner*, which are rarely played with another physically present, may lower the players' likelihood to engage in civic matters.

Some elements of playing video games may assist in developing civic-mindedness. "Teens who have civic gaming experiences report much higher levels of civic and political engagement than teens who have not had these kinds of experiences."[6] Civic gaming experiences include, but are not limited to: (1) helping or guiding other players, (2) playing games wherein the player learns about a problem in society, (3) playing a game where the player has to think about moral or ethical issues, (4) playing a game where the player helps make decisions about how a community, city, or nation should be run, and/or (5) organizing game groups or guilds (sometimes called clans).

Videogames and Rating Systems

The intersection of politics and videogames can be seen in the allocation via regulation by game ratings for audience members. Videogames can be rated: EC (Early Childhood), E (Everyone), E10+ (Everyone 10+), T (Teen), M (Mature), or AO (Adult Only). These ratings function to assign who should have access to what content. However, such ratings may not be very effective. Sixty-one percent of males and 77 percent of females 12–17 years old have a favorite videogame that is rated M or AO.[7]

Although smartphone app games share a similar rating system, there is a significant difference between videogames sold in stores for PC or gaming consoles and those that are app games. Games sold in stores allow for a gatekeeper (i.e., the seller) to request proof of age when selling the item; however, smartphone app games are downloaded (often for free) with no human agent to regulate their dissemination.

One online store for downloading smartphone apps for Android, Google Play, suggests to developers that any app with "sexual & suggestive content" should be given a "high maturity" rating and "apps that focus on sexual or suggestive references or include sexualized images or pornography [are] not permitted on Google Play."[8] However, the latter part of this chapter will highlight the sexual elements within an app, *Dark Summoner*, allowed in the store. *Dark Summoner* is given a "T" rating, which is the same rating given to the app, *Best Dirty Jokes*—the apps icon has a pair of women's legs in heels with a red circle and "18+" in the corner. Here, the inconsistency is clear in the allocation of ratings to smartphone (game) apps.

Videogame Player's Selection of Available Avatars

Politics and videogames intersect when the player selects the identity of his or her avatar. Some games have limited choices for avatars, and other games have multifarious variations regarding the avatars available. Players often select avatars that are unlike their physical body, perhaps in an effort to perform an aspirational or hoped-for self.[9] A white male, for example, may select to play as a black male avatar or vice versa. Although such acts occur, little research examines such race-playing (partially due to the limited number of games with nonwhite avatars). In contrast, gender bending (or playing as an avatar of the opposite sex) is not only common but also highly researched. Researchers found that "57% of gamers had engaged in gender swapping [i.e., gender bending], and it is suggested that the online female persona has a number of positive social attributes in a male-oriented environment."[10] However, "more females than males had gender swapped their character . . . in order to prevent unsolicited male approaches."[11] In each of the aforementioned examples, individuals are crafting their identities by allocating how they will be perceived in the digital space.

Game Designers' Choices for Avatars

It is not only individuals who allocate how they will be engaged in a social, online space. The final place in which politics intersect videogames is through the choices of game designers who select how avatars will be depicted. "We must remember that games don't just entertain; intentional or not, they always express a set of values and present us with concepts of normalcy."[12] Choices made by the designer shape how various groups—such as women and racial minorities—are shown or whether such identities are depicted at all. As with any human-made structure, the designers and programmers necessarily embed their own culture, values, and beliefs into every aspect of the game.[13] It is this intersection of the political with videogames that will be the focus of this chapter.

VIDEOGAMES

When examining videogames, there are numerous areas to investigate. To provide context and perspective, we have selected to address (1) the overall size of the industry, (2) videogame playing and addiction, (3) social gaming, (4) videogame content and research, and (5) smartphone gaming apps. Each section functions to demonstrate the significance of the cultural artifacts that are videogames and why it is important that scholars and researchers examine them.

The Overall Size of the Videogame Industry

Unlike arcade games in the 1980s that drew a predominantly adolescent audience, videogames have been integrated into households via gaming consoles, PCs, and, more recently, smartphone apps. Approximately

65–72 percent of U.S. households play videogames.[14] In terms of total profit, videogames have surpassed both Hollywood productions and the music industry to be the largest entertainment industry. This scale of integration deems videogames ripe for study. In addition to the large number of households playing videogames, playing can become an addicting obsession.[15]

Videogame Playing and Addiction

Videogames are also important social artifacts because they can take up much of a gamer's life. As of November 2006, for instance, one *EverQuest* player, Ryuichl Drgonslayer, had played a combined 548 days, 14 hours, and 58 minutes of the game.[16] In other words, it is not unheard of for gamers to become so engrossed in the social and digital game world that they spend more than a year of their lives there. Some researchers argue that videogames isolate us from communities even more so than automobiles or televisions. Sherry Turkle compares engaging with digital content to drug addiction. "X amount of heroin use is never a good thing; this same amount of Internet activity [including videogames] can be a helpful or hurtful thing, depending on the *content* of the messages and the role of the activity in life of the person doing it" (emphasis added).[17] Thus, the addictive nature of videogames can have real-world consequences. Research, for instance, has found that college males with higher videogame addiction had lower college engagement and grade point averages (GPAs).[18]

Social Gaming

Contemporary videogames are very likely to have some social component. Many console and PC games allow players to play digitally with one another as either adversaries (attempting to defeat or outperform the other in a given task, like a race) or as allies (working in conjunction to beat either the tasks of the game or other players online). Playing a videogame with a friend is quite common. Research suggests that "just one-quarter (24%) of teens *only* play games alone."[19]

Indeed, unlike traditional arcade games and early console games, more recent videogames have also added an important component—sociality. While the latter part of MMORPG—Role Playing Game—could speak to any game that asks a player to take on a new persona, the former— Massively Multiplayer Online—reveals an important social aspect. Gamers are asked to collaborate, and at times battle, other, human players. In fact, many games require that users work in groups at some point in the game. *World of Warcraft* gamers, for example, must team up with other players to complete certain quests and destroy larger bosses. If players choose, they can also join "guilds." Guilds provide an even more social aspect, allowing players to join groups that consistently chat, quest together, battle bosses, and trade goods. At the most basic level, gamers (like those playing *World of Warcraft*) can engage with other players, asking questions, surveying gear, and trading goods.

Such social interactions in game worlds are far from superficial. Almost half of the teens that play online games collaborate with people they know offline, and a little over a quarter of teen gamers play with other gamers who they know only digitally.[20] MMORPGs are extremely social spaces that allow gamers to begin to build "strong friendships and emotional relationships."[21] Especially at such a developmentally important age, teen gamers may learn key social and collaboration skills in game worlds.

Videogame Content and Research

Content within console games, like Playstation and Xbox, as well as PC games, has been explored regarding addiction[22] as well as stereotypical, and harmful, representations.[23] MMORPGs have gained considerable attention from researchers. For example, the economist Edward Castronova determined the real exchange rate of digital goods and currency within *World of Warcraft*—the most popular MMORPG with approximately 7.1 million subscribers.[24] In short, he found the economic value of *World of Warcraft* "gold" to the U.S. dollar. This finding led to what is known as goldfarming (i.e., playing the game to generate real-world income). In addition, some researchers have studied representations within games. Researchers, for example, examined the ways in which race and gender are depicted within another popular MMORPG, *EverQuest*.[25]

Whether implicit or explicit, mediated content aids in shaping young adults' minds about the characteristics of various subject positions. Although race in videogames has been depicted through both stereotypical representations as well as through ways that disadvantage dark-skinned avatars, gender constructions are often more apparent as they appear more commonly within game spaces.[26] Such a notion is not to dismiss the significance of race as a social signifier, but rather to highlight that game designs are often more explicit in their gender depictions. In games that have a fantasy theme, many characters take on nonhuman forms that still work to depict gender. For example, in the popular game *World of Warcraft*, a gamer can choose to be a nonhuman avatar such as a panda, an orc, or a goblin. However, "female" or "male" must still be chosen, and the avatar is then allotted stereotypical visual social signifiers.

Both Taylor and Massie highlight sexualized representations in the game *EverQuest*.[27] For example, Massie points out that "Illusionist Lobaen [a Non-Playable Character or NPC who sells Enchanter spells in the library]...appears more like a stripper ready to sell lap dances [as] she appears to be wearing what resembles a black 'teddy' covered by a white, transparent robe."[28] More recently, Sarkeesian has investigated the dehumanizing and objectifying nature of sexualized female characters in videogames; she contends that "because traditionally, damsel characters become the central object or goal in a competition between men . . . the game of patriarchy, women are not the opposing team, they're actually the ball."[29] In many games, male avatars are not competing against female avatars, rather males are competing with other males to obtain the "prize" (a female avatar). For example, in the classic game *Super Mario Brothers*, the male avatar—Mario—is attempting to battle Bowser (another male avatar) to save Princess Peach. Here, the female character serves only as an object (i.e., ball) to drive conflict and competition between males.

Smartphone App Gaming

The adoption of smartphones in general implies a more social lifestyle. A large goal of owning a smartphone is to be more in touch with social worlds. Users can employ a variety of apps to stay connected with friends, coworkers, family, and so on. Thus, it is not a stretch to realize that many smartphone videogame apps are situated in the social world. Linking with users' friend lists, e-mail contacts, and phonebooks, smartphone apps make it even easier for gamers to add a social aspect to their gaming experiences. In fact, mobile (or smartphone) games have been increasing in popularity; 59 percent of online users from the United States and United Kingdom played such games in the past month during April 2012.[30] Lenhart et al. note that "48% [of US teens] use a cell phone . . . to play games."[31] Games like *Candy Crush*, *Words with Friends*, *Samurai Siege*, and *Farmville* are popular smartphone game apps that highlight the social dimension—gamers can connect to one another as opponents or as groups competing as allies.

DARK SUMMONER: A SMARTPHONE APP GAME

Dark Summoner is a popular, free game app for smartphones.[32] As described through its informational page on Google Play:

> *Dark Summoner* is set in a multidimensional world known as "Triaterra," where a war between rival factions has plunged everything into chaos. . . . In the role of summoner, you must call forth Monsters and creatures from distant dimensions to join your army and fight for you in Missions and Events. Battle other players in the Arena and make friends in Clans, where you cooperate with your Clan comrades to fight your way to the No. 1 spot and the glory that comes with supremacy! [33]

The game is available on both iPhone and Android operating systems. To date, the app has been downloaded more than 7,000,000 times. At this scale, the app's population is similar to that of Paraguay's (104th most populated country) or, in the United States, the state of Washington's, population (13th most populated state). The *Dark Summoner* app is available for download in three languages: English, Japanese, and Korean. The size and scope of this smartphone videogame deems it a significant social artifact for investigation.

To explore *Dark Summoner* and its gender portrayals, this chapter will investigate three elements of the game: (1) people as pets/slaves, (2) objectification and sexualization of the female form, and (3) virtual rape.

Pets and Slaves

Within videogames, players are expected to take on some role and identify with a digitally constructed avatar. Depending on the game, players have a certain level of customization in designing their avatar's appearance and skills. "Avatars are the embodiment, in text and/or graphic images, of a user's online presence in social spaces."[34] Gamers frequently are allotted the opportunity to sculpt their avatar as they see fit—both physically and skills-wise. Gamers, then, often create avatars that act as their counterparts in the game world. In other words, it is inevitable that some features of the avatar will reflect physical and emotional characteristics of its creator.[35] Similarly, just as offline identifications find their way into the online world, online characteristics can also make their way offline. Thus, the relationship between a gamer and her avatar is not unidirectional. Instead, it is highly likely that ideas she learns and events she experiences in-game will have implications for her offline self.

These effects can manifest themselves through different avenues. In some cases, the avatar is played through a first person perspective, and the player sees only "outwardly" (e.g., *Call of Duty*). In other games, the game places the player in the role of the character, which the player controls through a third person perspective (e.g., *Super Mario Brothers*). Regardless of perspective, this type of avatar is known as a Player (or Playable) Character or PC. In contrast, NPCs, or Non-Playable Characters, are toons that have predetermined actions set by algorithms within the game. NPCs are designed to both help and battle PCs. A clear example is highlighted in the popular *Pacman* game—Pacman is a PC and the "ghosts" are NPCs.

Beyond these two characters, recent games have developed a third toon type—Pets or Slaves. Many gamers tend to just use the term *pets*, but a distinction between the two can be useful in highlighting an important difference between non-hominid (Pets) and hominid (Slaves) avatars. Such characters are not completely controlled by the player nor are they entirely controlled by algorithms. Examples of Pets/Slaves are common in the popular *World of Warcraft* game. Players who select to be a Hunter can "tame" animals (i.e., Pets) which then follow the player's avatar and can be commanded to attack. Gamers who select to be a Warlock in game can cast a spell that summons a demon (i.e., Slave) that follows the player's avatar around and will attack adversaries on command. In short, the Pet/Slave is subordinate to the PC but it not itself the PC. This is a significant distinction because *Dark Summoner* focuses almost entirely on the player acquiring and using Pets/Slaves.

Gendered Representations

In *Dark Summoner*, the player takes a (pseudo-) first person perspective as a conjuror or summoner of creatures that will fight for her. One goal of the player is to collect the most Pets/Slaves as to have a greater selection for her Top Five that will be used in combat. Each potential Pet/Slave is depicted via a still image. The images of male Pets/Slaves and those of female Pets/Slaves are represented along clear stereotypically gendered lines.

Male Pets/Slaves are consistently brawny with large, muscular frames. The male avatars are commonly posed as if in battle: aggressive, assertive, and engaged. In addition, male Pets/Slaves regularly don armor or other gear that covers much of their form. Although there are some exceptions, each never seems sexualized or objectified because they are styled to look like their only purpose is to battle.

In contrast to their male counterparts, female Pets/Slaves are distinctly sexualized and objectified. Unlike the well-armored or clothed male, female Pets/Slaves wear nearly no clothing and often appear in lingerie-like attire. Female Pets/Slaves are also displayed in passive poses that are counterintuitive—they are supposed to exist for battle yet they are designed to look timid. Some images even depict female Pets/Slaves in nearly naked dyads, suggesting lesbian interactions.[36] Moreover, nearly all female Pets/Slaves have light colored skin, perhaps suggesting that only white females are aesthetically appealing or useful.

In an attempt to defend the scantily clad female Pets/Slaves, some gamers argue that it is a sign that females actually have *greater* skills than their male counterparts—males are less avid warriors and need more armor to protect themselves, while females, being extraordinarily skilled, need no armor and almost no clothing.

The symbolism of women becoming more powerful as they lose their clothing has been depicted for decades. Take, for example, the classic television program *Wonder Woman* (1975–1979). Wonder Woman is disguised as Navy secretary Diana Prince, dressed in conservative, naval attire. But, in order to "change" to Wonder Woman, she must spin in such a way as to remove much of her clothing. This cultural artifact suggests that female characters gain power as they remove clothing. The process of females losing clothing, or at the very least changing into more provocative clothing, to gain power and become their alter egos can also be seen in media artifacts, including *Powerpuff Girls*, *Winx Club*, *She-Ra*, and *Catwoman*, among others.

Similar events occur within *Dark Summoner*. A few "special" Pets/Slaves can evolve. If a player captures these Pets/Slaves, the PC can acquire virtual materials (e.g., potions and gems) that allow the Pets/Slaves to change into super powerful characters. Every Pet/Slave that can perform this ability is female. In addition, in each of the three stages of "evolution," the female Pet/Slave loses clothing. As the female Pet/Slave evolves, she also gains attributes that are more valuable in combat.

Pets/Slaves lose clothing while also gaining power and skills, thus becoming more valuable to the gamer. In other words, the female form is most valuable to the gamer when she is baring more skin and less traditional combat gear. Females, then, are deemed *dangerous* simply due to their bodies—most of the female Pets/Slaves carry no weapons or are only armed with musical instruments.[37] Since no female Pet/Slave appears to be elderly or even middle-aged in appearance, a female's only source of power is portrayed to exist in her youthful appearance and sexuality.

Virtual Rape

The idea that females become more powerful when they strip off clothing in-game is directly challenged by two events that have transpired in *Dark Summoner*. Generally, events in the game are task-driven, reward-generating, and time-sensitive challenges organized by the game's designers. Events may be as short as one hour and as long as one week. Advertisements for these events continue the theme of representing female characters as sexual objects. Interestingly, the event titled *Forest of Phantoms*, which lacks the sexualized imagery, may be most noteworthy. Within this event, gamers could take part in a subevent—*Phantom Princess Appears*. The subevent is described in the game as follows:

Phantom Princess Appears
Limit Time event
2/12 12:59 AM ET
Special Feature!
Break Off The Armor!

To complete this subevent, the player must attack the Phantom Princess. Her original depiction is well-armored; but, after the first strike, a couple of the Princess's pieces of armor are knocked off, exposing her shoulders, cleavage, and the edges of her black bra. At the same time, her health decreases. When the Princess is hit again, a perfectly formed triangle is removed that reveals her midriff, and the upper portion of her black bra is destroyed so that it appears she is now wearing a corset that reveals more than half of her breasts. Again, her health diminishes. A third strike defeats her, and the player is rewarded with an enigmatic chest (a box housing virtual goods like potions or currency).

The *Phantom Princess Appears* is not the only event with such depictions. *Dark Festivities* contains similar content. Within this event, the gamer much defeat a female NPC named Crystal Tonakai and has two hours to complete the task. The process of defeating her is similar to that of the Phantom Princess. The gamer must strike her violently, each time removing a piece of her clothing and diminishing her health. Unlike the previous event, Crystal Tonakai bats her eye lashes after every strike, adding an extra sexual layer.

Using film as her primary example, Mulvey (2010) explores the ways in which women, much more than men, seem to be objectified and sexualized through film.[38] There is pleasure in both looking at the human form and being noticed. But, she argues, because (especially at the time) it is mostly men behind the camera, women are the bodies that are to be erotically gazed upon. The woman in the narrative actually means nothing in and of herself; she is merely what she inspires in the "hero" (the man). In line with some "male gaze," then, the predominately male gamer-base experiences a metaphoric "conquering" of a female (i.e., disrobing her to have sex with her). With the accompanying violence, the player is also participating in acts that are closely tied to rape. Not only is the goal to "defeat" the female by removing her armor, the gamer is also decreasing her health, making her more vulnerable.

The clandestine nature of these events is not to be left out. In a search for these two in-game events, a researcher would come up empty-handed. Although the game's Facebook page lists seemingly every event that has occurred, there are two exceptions—(1) any subevent [this includes *Phantom Princess Appears*] and (2) the *Dark Festivities* event. Moreover, these two events do not appear in any promotion material of the game.[39] They are only up for investigation in this chapter because Keith (the first author) happened to be playing *Dark Summoner* when the events were introduced.

Virtual rape, cyber-rape, or the depiction of rape-like scenarios is not completely new. One of the first documented cases of such a digital event occurred on LambdaMOO (an early online game). Within the games, a player—Mr. Bungle—used a voodoo doll subprogram to do his will against other players who lost control over their avatars.[40] Interestingly, few researchers have considered this phenomenon. One researcher whose work notes such phenomena is Anita Sarkeesian (who vlogs via "feministfrequency" on YouTube). Sarkeesian states that "violence against women [in videogames] is, essentially, used as a set piece to establish or punctuate the seedy atmosphere of crime and chaos-ridden, fictional universes."[41]

In some videogames, violence against women is depicted via a slap in the face from one avatar to another; however, in other games, violence against women is shown via images of rape and sexual assault. Sarkeesian argues that "rape and sexual assault are also frequently used as a sort of narrative currency to try and raise the emotional stakes and heighten the dramatic tension for gamers."[42] Such graphic representations by game designers may minimize perceptions of the impact such actions have in both online and offline worlds. "These women [i.e., female avatars in videogames] and their bodies are sacrificed in the name of infusing mature themes into gaming stories, but there is nothing mature about flippantly evoking shades of female trauma. It ends up sensationalizing an issue which is painfully familiar to large percentage of women on this planet, while also normalizing and trivializing their experiences."[43]

Concluding Thoughts: Social Smartphone Videogames and Political Events

The ability for gamers to control their avatars' identities is a political event—they are given the agency to control and allocate aspects of their avatars. In the same vein, when others, including game designers, afford certain acts and control avatars' acts, these too are political events. The less choice a gamer has in the avatar-creation process, the less agency she has regarding the persona she must digitally embody.

Through our research, we found that *Dark Summoner* actively chooses to allocate identification resources in a way that directly objectifies and sexualizes female Pets/Slaves. Male Pets/Slaves are depicted as assertive, active, engaged, and strong. They are shown wearing more armor and wielding weapons. Female Pets/Slaves, on the other hand, are depicted as less battle-ready. They are passive and sexualized, wearing little to no armor and owning no weapons. Thus, at first read, female Pets/Slaves are only to be captured and employed because of their dangerous bodies and femininity. Male Pets/Slaves are instead captured because they don armor and weapons, thus making them powerful because they have been afforded the ability to *own* something. We argue that this symbolic representation connotes the idea that the gamers themselves collect better gear when a male Pet/Slave is captured, but simply a better female slave when a female Pet/Slave is captured. In other words, collecting males is to collect gear, but collecting females is to collect bodies. It is clear, then, that female bodies become objects in this process.

We also found that both the depiction of female Pets/Slaves and the interaction with female bosses (within game events) are rooted in rape culture. Rival females in *Dark Summoner* are also scantily clad but are defeated through a series of violently sexual acts that disrobe them while also decreasing their health. As noted earlier, one conclusion may be that

women are the more powerful Pets/Slaves because their bodies are dangerous. Besides our analysis that shows this example actually works to objectify
the female body, the battles with female rivals are in direct opposition to this
"female empowerment" argument. When gamers must defeat a female
NPC, they are instructed to make her *less* powerful by removing her clothing
and stripping her down to the real prize—her objectified body. Thus, in both
examples, the female body is the prize or "the ball" to be won, whether she
is made more or less powerful through armor and weapons.

As discussed early on in this chapter, smartphone games like *Dark
Summoner* are often downloaded and played by teens. Gamers early on
in their lives are being introduced to a problematic worldview that promotes the objectification of women's bodies and that normalizes rape culture. These messages are harder to police than traditional PC and console
games because the rating system is more of a suggested age than a law
that shopkeepers can enforce.

Mulvey notes that images of women in film are always passive while
the man, including his gaze and subsequently the audience's gaze, is
active.[44] These representations demand the following of some traditional,
patriarchal order. As we have shown in this chapter, these problematic
images are still present in modern day media. Smartphone app games,
like *Dark Summoner*, compel gamers to believe in specific stereotypical representations of some binary female to male comparison. Because these
smartphone app games are interactive and social and are tied very closely
with gamer identifications, it is important that we better understand the
identity politics that are subtly embedded within game structures and
potentially influencing the associations and perspective of young gamers.

Dark Summoner chooses to allocate specific resources to the male Pets/
Slaves while denying these same resources to the female Pets/Slaves.
The politic, or embedded values, therein arguably reify the notion that
women are to be objectified, allotted less resources (e.g., lower wages),
and stripped naked of the few resources they do have. The gamers controlling these Pets/Slaves are forced to take on some dominating, stereotypically masculine role that affords them certain values in the
identification process. These identification resources are then applied
throughout gamers' narratives, affecting the cultural expectations and
assumptions in both their online and offline realities.

NOTES

1. Michael Bamberg, "Stories: Big or Small: Why Do We Care?" *Narrative
Inquiry* 16, no. 1 (2006): 139–147; Mark Freeman, "Life 'On Holiday?': In Defense
of Big Stories," *Narrative Inquiry* 16, no. 1 (2006): 131–138; James Holstein and Jaber
Gubrium, *The Self We Live By: Narrative Identity in a Postmodern World* (New York:
Oxford University Press, 2000).

2. T. L. Taylor, *Play between Worlds: Exploring Online Game Culture* (London: MIT Press, 2006).

3. James Anderson and Elaine Englehardt, *The Organizational Self and Ethical Conduct* (Orlando, FL: Harcourt College Publishers, 2001).

4. Jeongmin Lee, Boram Cho, Youngju Kim, and Jiyea Noh, "Smartphone Addiction in University Students and Its Implication for Learning," in *Emerging Issues in Smart Learning*, eds. Guang Chen, Vive Kumar, Ronghuai Huang, Siu-Cheung Kong, and Kinshuk (Heidelberg, Germany: Springer-Verlag, 2015), 297–306.

5. Amanda Lenhart, Joseph Kahne, Ellen Middaugh, Alexandra Macgill, Chris Evans, and Jessica Vitak, "Teens, Video Games, and Civics: Teens' Gaming Experiences Are Diverse and Include Significant Social Interaction and Civic Engagement," *Pew Internet & American Life Project* (Washington, DC, September 16, 2008): vi.

6. Ibid., 44.

7. Ibid., 25.

8. "Content Ratings for Apps and Games," *Google Play*, last modified 2015, https://support.google.com/googleplay/android-developer/answer/188189?hl=en.

9. Nick Yee, Jeremy N. Bailenson, and Nicolas Ducheneaut, "The Proteus Effect: Implications of Transformed Digital Self-Representation on Online and Offline Behavior," *Communication Research* 36, no. 2 (2009): 285–312.

10. Zaheer Hussain and Mark Griffiths, "Gender Swapping and Socializing in Cyberspace: An Exploratory Study," *CyberPsychology & Behavior* 11, no. 1 (2008): 47.

11. Ibid, 52.

12. Anita Sarkeesian, "Women as Background Decoration: Part 2-Tropes vs Women in Video Games," *Youtube.com*, August 25, 2014, https://www.youtube.com/watch?v=5i_RPr9DwMA.

13. Langdon Winner, "Do Artifacts Have Politics?" *Daedalus* 109, no. 1 (1980): 121–136.

14. "Education Database Online," *Videogame Statistics*, last modified 2015, http://www.onlineeducation.net/videogame; Ryan Winslett, "72 Percent of American Households Play Games,"*Gaming News,* July 7, 2011, http://www.joystickdivision.com/2011/07/72_percent_of_american_househo.php.

15. Daniel King, Paul Delfabbro, and Mark Griffiths, "Trajectories of Problem Video Gaming among Adult Regular Gamers: An 18-Month Longitudinal Study," *Cyberpsychology, Behavior, and Social Networking* 16, no. 1 (2013): 72–76.

16. Keith Massie, "Representations of Race and Gender within the Gamespace of the MMO EverQuest," in *Online Gaming in Context: The Social and Cultural Significance of Online Games,* eds. Garry Crawford, Victoria Gosling, and Ben Light (New York: Routledge, 2011), 249–265.

17. Andrew Wood and Matthew Smith, *Online Communication: Linking Technology, Identity, and Culture,* 2nd ed. (New York: Routledge, 2005), 108.

18. Zachary Schmitt and Michael Livingston, "Video Game Addiction and College Performance among Males: Results from a 1 Year Longitudinal Study," *Cyberpsychology, Behavior, and Social Networking* 18, no. 1 (2015): 25–29.

19. Lenhart, Kahne, Middaugh, Macgill, Evans, and Vitak, "Teens, Video Games, and Civics," iii.

20. Ibid.

21. Helena Cole and Mark Griffiths, "Social Interactions in Massively Multiplayer Online Role-Playing Games," *CyberPsychology & Behavior* 10, no. 4 (2007): 575.

22. Mark Griffiths, "Addiction and Overuse of Online Games," in *The International Encyclopedia of Digital Communication and Society,* 1st ed. (New York: John Wiley & Sons, Inc., 2014).

23. Cassie Rodenberg, "Grand Theft Auto V Makes It Cool to Pick Up – Even Kill – Prostitutes," *The Guardian,* December 27, 2013, http://www.theguardian .com/commentisfree/2013/dec/27/grand-theft-auto-v-prostitutes-killed; Sarkeesian, "Women as Background Decoration."

24. Gergo Vas, "Why World of Warcraft Lost So Many Subscribers," *Kotaku: Gawker Media,* May 7, 2015, http://kotaku.com/why-world-of-warcraft-lost-so-many-subscribers-1702814469; Edward Castronova, "Gold from Thin Air: The Economies of Virtual Worlds," *Pop!Tech, ITConversations,* October 31, 2005, http://web.archive.org/web/20130729205609id_/http://itc.conversationsnetwork.org/shows/detail772.html.

25. Massie, "Representations of Race and Gender within the Gamespace of the MMO EverQuest," 249–265; Taylor, *Play between Worlds.*

26. Ibid.

27. Ibid.

28. Massie, "Representations of Race and Gender within the Gamespace of the MMO EverQuest," 261.

29. Sarkeesian, "Women as Background Decoration."

30. Hui-Fei Lin, "The Effect of Product Placement on Persuasion for Mobile Phone Games," *Journal of Advertising* 33, no. 1 (2014): 37–60.

31. Lenhart, Kahne, Middaugh, Macgill, Evans, and Vitak, "Teens, Video Games, and Civics," i.

32. Like the business model of other smartphone apps, the game is initially free; however, one can pay real world currency to purchase items (i.e., virtual goods) to advance in the game more quickly.

33. "Dark Summoner," *Google Play,* last modified 2015, https://play.google.com/store/apps/details?id=com.darksummoner.

34. Lisa Nakamura, *Cybertypes: Race, Ethnicity, and Identity on the Internet* (New York: Routledge, 2002), 31.

35. Stephen Kline, Nick Dyer-Witheford, and Greig de Peuter, *Digital Play: The Interaction of Technology, Culture, and Marketing* (Quebec, Canada: McGill-Queen's Press-MQUP, 2003).

36. Lesbian tryst images may initially suggest acceptance of various sexual orientation; yet, there is no male equivalent, and the (heterosexual) male gaze is magnified by such lesbian depictions.

37. Those with musical instruments are playing the flute or piccolo. Within the game, musical instruments serve no purpose. As an image, the instruments suggest both the "woman as muse trope" as well as, given the type of instrument, serve as a phallic symbol.

38. Laura Mulvey, "Visual Pleasure and Narrative Cinema," in *The Feminism and Visual Culture Reader,* 2nd ed., ed. Amelia Jones (New York: Psychology Press, 2010), 44–53.

39. There is one tweet by @ADarkSummoner1 on December 18, 2013, that states: "Dark Festivities Underway." The official *Dark Summoner* Twitter account, however, appears to be @DarkSummoner_.

40. Julian Dibbell. "A Rape in Cyberspace: How an Evil Clown, a Haitian Trickster Spirit, Two Wizards, and a Cast of Dozens Turned a Database into a Society," *The Village Voice*, December 23, 1993, http://www.juliandibbell.com/texts/bungle_vv.html.

41. Sarkeesian, "Women as Background Decoration."

42. Ibid.

43. Ibid.

44. Mulvey, "Visual Pleasure and Narrative Cinema," 44–53.

BIBLIOGRAPHY

Anderson, James, and Elaine Englehardt. *The Organizational Self and Ethical Conduct.* Orlando, FL: Harcourt College Publishers, 2001.

Bamberg, Michael. "Stories: Big or Small: Why Do We Care?" *Narrative Inquiry* 16, no. 1 (2006): 139–147.

Castronova, Edward. "Gold from Thin Air: The Economies of Virtual Worlds." *Pop!Tech. ITConversations*, October 31, 2005. http://web.archive.org/web/20130729205609id_/http://itc.conversationsnetwork.org/shows/detail772.html.

Chiong, Cynthia, and Carly Shuler. *Learning: Is There an App for That? Investigations of Young Children's Usage and Learning with Mobile Devices and Apps.* New York: The Jan Ganz Cooney Center at Sesame Workshop, 2010.

Cole, Helena, and Mark Griffiths. "Social Interactions in Massively Multiplayer Online Role-Playing Games." *CyberPsychology & Behavior* 10, no. 4 (2007): 575–583.

"Content Ratings for Apps and Games." *Google Play.* Last modified 2016. https://support.google.com/googleplay/android-developer/answer/188189?hl=en.

"Dark Summoner." Google Play. Last modified 2016. https://play.google.com/store/apps/details?id=com.darksummoner.

Dibbell, Julian. "A Rape in Cyberspace: How an Evil Clown, a Haitian Trickster Spirit, Two Wizards, and a Cast of Dozens Turned a Database into a Society." *The Village Voice*, December 23, 1993. http://www.juliandibbell.com/texts/bungle_vv.html.

"Education Database Online." *Videogame Statistics.* Last modified, 2015. http://www.onlineeducation.net/videogame.

Freeman, Mark. "Life 'On Holiday?': In Defense of Big Stories." *Narrative Inquiry* 16, no. 1 (2006): 131–138.

Griffiths, Mark. "Addiction and Overuse of Online Games." In *The International Encyclopedia of Digital Communication and Society,* 1st ed. New York: John Wiley & Sons, Inc., 2014.

Holstein, James, and Jaber Gubrium. *The Self We Live By: Narrative Identity in a Postmodern World.* New York: Oxford University Press, 2000.

Hussain, Zaheer, and Mark Griffiths. "Gender Swapping and Socializing in Cyberspace: An Exploratory Study." *CyberPsychology & Behavior* 11, no. 1 (2008): 47–53.

King, Daniel, Paul Delfabbro, and Mark Griffiths. "Trajectories of Problem Video
    Gaming among Adult Regular Gamers: An 18-Month Longitudinal Study."
    Cyberpsychology, Behavior, and Social Networking 16, no. 1 (2013): 72–76.
Kline, Stephen, Nick Dyer-Witheford, and Greig de Peuter. *Digital Play: The Interac-
    tion of Technology, Culture, and Marketing*. Quebec, Canada: McGill-Queen's
    Press-MQUP, 2003.
Lee, Jeongmin, Boram Cho, Youngju Kim, and Jiyea Noh. "Smartphone Addiction
    in University Students and Its Implication for Learning." In *Emerging
    Issues in Smart Learning*, edited by Guang Chen, Vive Kumar, Ronghuai
    Huang, Siu-Cheung Kong, and Kinshuk, 297–306. Heidelberg, Germany:
    Springer-Verlag, 2015.
Lenhart, Amanda, Joseph Kahne, Ellen Middaugh, Alexandra Macgill, Chris
    Evans, and Jessica Vitak. "Teens, Video Games, and Civics: Teens' Gaming
    Experiences Are Diverse and Include Significant Social Interaction and
    Civic Engagement." *Pew Internet & American Life Project.* Washington, DC,
    September 16, 2008.
Lin, Hui-Fei. "The Effect of Product Placement on Persuasion for Mobile Phone
    Games." *Journal of Advertising* 33, no. 1 (2014): 37–60.
Massie, Keith. "Representations of Race and Gender within the Gamespace of the
    MMO *EverQuest*." In *Online Gaming in Context: The Social and Cultural
    Significance of Online Games*, edited by Garry Crawford, Victoria Gosling,
    and Ben Light, 249–265. New York: Routledge, 2011.
Mulvey, Laura. "Visual Pleasure and Narrative Cinema." In *The Feminism and
    Visual Culture Reader*, 2nd ed., edited by Amelia Jones, 44–53. New York:
    Psychology Press, 2010.
Nakamura, Lisa. *Cybertypes: Race, Ethnicity, and Identity on the Internet*. New York:
    Routledge, 2002.
Rodenberg, Cassie. "Grand Theft Auto V Makes It Cool to Pick Up – Even Kill –
    Prostitutes." *The Guardian*, December 27, 2013. http://www.theguardian
    .com/commentisfree/2013/dec/27/grand-theft-auto-v-prostitutes-killed.
Sarkeesian, Anita. "Women as Background Decoration: Part 2-Tropes vs Women in
    Video Games." *Youtube.com*, August 25, 2014. https://www.youtube.com/
    watch?v=5i_RPr9DwMA.
Schmitt, Zachary, and Michael Livingston. "Video Game Addiction and College
    Performance among Males: Results from a 1 Year Longitudinal Study."
    Cyberpsychology, Behavior, and Social Networking 18, no. 1 (2015): 25–29.
Taylor, T. L. *Play between Worlds: Exploring Online Game Culture*. London: MIT
    Press, 2006.
Vas, Gergo. "Why World of Warcraft Lost So Many Subscribers." *Kotaku; Gawker
    Media*, May 7, 2015. http://kotaku.com/why-world-of-warcraft-lost-so
    -many-subscribers-1702814469.
Winner, Langdon. "Do Artifacts Have Politics?" *Daedalus* 109, no. 1 (1980): 121–136.
Winslett, Ryan. "72 Percent of American Households Play Games." *Gaming News*,
    July 7, 2011. http://www.joystickdivision.com/2011/07/72_percent_of
    _american_househo.php.
Wood, Andrew, and Matthew Smith. *Online Communication: Linking Technology,
    Identity, and Culture*, 2nd ed. New York: Routledge, 2005.
Yee, Nick, Jeremy N. Bailenson, and Nicolas Ducheneaut. "The Proteus Effect:
    Implications of Transformed Digital Self-Representation on Online and
    Offline Behavior." *Communication Research* 36, no. 2 (2009): 285–312.

Chapter 8

Memes and the 2012 Presidential Election

Bobbie Foster

INTRODUCTION

One feature of American politics has always been true; a politician's image means everything to his or her political career.[1] Anderson and Sheeler[2] argue that candidate image is shaped by "image fragments generated by the individual politician, his or her campaign communication, news framing, and popular culture," however, increasingly "a politician's image can also be shaped by non-elite discourses" generated by social media websites like Facebook, Twitter, and Tumblr. Social media has introduced new ways for voters and nonvoters to influence media coverage during election cycles, and this form of participation can often take the shape of Internet memes.[3]

There are two different competing definitions of memes, a traditional look at memes as elements of culture,[4] and a popular culture definition of memes as user-generated media or Internet memes.[5] In his book *The Selfish Gene*, Dawkins[6] suggested that memes were a vehicle for cultural transmission that would replicate and evolve over time, just as dominant genes adapt and spread during evolution to benefit the host. The examples Dawkins cites for memes are fashion, religion, and other cultural artifacts like art. However, in recent years, the term *meme* has taken on a new definition in popular culture that restricts it to the use of online media and often specifically image macros.[7] This makes the study of memes difficult because the idea developed by Dawkins is very broad, and the use of the term in popular culture is very fluid.

The popular culture definition of a meme uses online content such as GIFs, image macros, text posts on social media websites such as Twitter, Tumblr, Reddit, or Facebook, videos from YouTube or Vine, and e-mail chains to help define mimetic behavior. Shifman[8] found that the memes she examined contained six common features: a focus on ordinary people, flawed masculinity, humor, simplicity, repetitiveness, and whimsical content. Other meme studies have also found humor[9] to be a key element of meme making as well as simplicity and manipulation of content from other sources such as popular movies, news websites, or photographs pulled from Google searches or social media.[10] This chapter, however, is not focused on the larger cultural definitions of the term *meme*, but the use of the word to define viral activities online, and more specifically the contents of image macros posted to 2012 presidential election Facebook pages. Therefore, the work in this chapter is aimed at contributing to the popular culture definition of a meme and the understanding of how traditional media framing[11] contributes to the construction of memes for politically driven posts on Facebook.

IMAGE FRAMING AND MEMES

Image macro memes are used to add commentary to an existing photograph.[12] Sometimes the image used is a stock photo, like in the case of the *First World Problems*[13] meme used to convey complaints about nonissues experienced by middle- to upper-class privileged individuals, and sometimes the images are news photographs like in the case of the *Texts from Hillary*[14] image macro meme. The manipulation of news or stock photographs of candidates is an increasingly important part of online participation and image generation during election cycles.[15] Because past studies have found that Internet memes contain elements of manipulated content,[16] it is reasonable to believe that meme-makers are developing or manipulating news images of candidates for their own political purposes and distributing that content to be replicated or shared online.

Decker-Maurere[17] argued that common design characteristics in memes like font, linguistic style, and intertextuality allowed users viewing the memes to build and advertise a political identity the same way they would with campaign stickers and yard signs. If memes allow users to build an online identity or advertise a point of view to followers, it is possible that meme-makers are acting as gatekeepers[18] and developing frames in which they want others to view the information passed along in the meme they create. In the past, gatekeepers would be newspaper editors or television producers who generate stories based on gathered facts and quotes from witnesses or sources, but now each social media user can act as a gatekeeper to their followers. For example, Facebook group administrators can choose what to post to the group, and then the individual group members can choose to share that information outside of the group with their followers by taking actions such as liking, commenting, or sharing the meme to their wall.

In traditional media, defined as newspapers, radio, and television, gatekeepers can frame stories by highlighting some parts of an issue or person and ignoring others.[19] For example, when the news media focuses on mental health after a mass shooting instead of gun control it is framing the story, because the media is emphasizing the contribution the shooter's mental health made to his or her actions rather than other contributing aspects like gun control laws. The news media, however, are not the only driving force behind candidate media frames; politicians and campaign managers also use frames to persuade voters.[20] For example, a campaign ad might focus on a candidate's family but ignore the candidate's voting record on domestic policy issues like paid family leave; this is framing because the ad places emphasis on positive aspects of a candidate's personal life while ignoring what the candidate's voting record might say about his or her broader view of domestic policy. Political media framing does not end with debates, ads, and speeches; now candidates can release information on social media. In an analysis of photos posted by campaigns to the official Facebook pages of Mitt Romney and Barack Obama, Goodnow found that Romney posted 300 images to his Facebook Timeline and most often used patriotic symbols like flags to associate the candidate with leadership qualities. President Obama's campaign posted fewer than half of that number, and most of his images depicted him in the White House looking away from the camera down at papers on his desk, talking with world leaders, or with his back turned to the camera while standing in the oval office. The Obama campaign did not feel the need to emphasize his leadership qualities in the same way as the Romney campaign because Obama was already president.

Most studies focus on verbal or textual analysis to find media frames and leave out the influence of visual communication such as news photographs and videos.[21] Images are a powerful tool for communication and can have a great impact on voters' perception of a candidate's ability to lead.[22] Grabe and Bucy[23] argue that most studies of media framing of candidate personality traits focus on positive and negative imagery and not the more "nuanced character frame-building dimensions" used by campaigns through the media to help define the characteristics of a candidate. By examining television coverage of several campaigns in the 1990s and 2000s, Grabe and Bucy[24] developed three different frames used most in the media. Those frames were the ideal candidate, the populist campaigner, and the sure loser. The ideal candidate not only shows compassion by hugging supporters and kissing babies but also presents him or herself in a stately manner by wearing suits and being seen with other established political leaders.[25] The populist campaigner frame is used to convey ordinariness by wearing informal clothes, visiting factories and farms, and associating with large crowds or celebrities with mass appeal. [26] The sure loser frame is exactly how it sounds, the candidate makes inappropriate facial displays, such as frowning or scowling at inopportune times, and he or she is seen with small or disapproving crowds.[27] These are the same frames Goodnow[28] found in her study of images released by Mitt Romney and President Barack Obama on Facebook during the 2012 presidential campaign. She found that Mitt Romney often used the populist campaigner frame and that President Obama often used the ideal candidate frame.

It is unclear if these frames appear in memes posted to social media, or if new frames have begun populating chat rooms and newsfeeds. Some politicians have taken advantage of an existing meme and use it to control a frame themselves, most notably Hillary Clinton. Anderson and Sheeler[29] analyzed Hillary Clinton's reuse of the *Text from Hillary* meme to create her own meme when she joined Twitter with the hashtag; "#tweetsfrom-Hillary." They[30] argue that "Clinton's Twitter debut illustrates a new type of strategic image management [. . .] in which politicians attempt to capitalize on existing memes that originate from outside the sphere of information elites." Clinton in particular has a number of existing memes[31] to choose from because of her pop culture icon status as a fixture of American politics and nearly eight-year involvement with the Obama administration. She is also included in the Beyoncé Voter's meme,[32] and her pantsuits are a meme of their own within popular culture.

A number of past studies using the popular culture definition of a meme have found that online memes contain an element of manipulation of a popular video or photograph to change the original meaning of the image or comment on a particular aspect of culture.[33] If politics are visual and campaigns struggle to control a candidate's image, then the struggle would continue online, as more voters are able to actively participate in election coverage by creating their own frames. For example, a photograph of Hillary Clinton frowning during the Bengazi tribunals might be paired with the word *bitter* or *exhausted* in traditional media, but the same photograph online could become an image macro accompanied by positive messages of power and influence featuring words like *fierce* or *boss* written above or below the same photograph from the news. For example, the Beyoncé Voter[34] memes of Hillary Clinton sometimes contain unflattering images of Clinton with empowering words or messages superimposed on the photograph. In this chapter, I examine the content of memes posted to user-created Facebook pages for both Mitt Romney and President Barack Obama during the last week of the 2012 presidential election to find if the frames of the ideal candidate, the populist campaigner, and the sure loser can be found in the memes or if users are indeed acting as gatekeepers and developing their own frames for consumption online.

RESULTS

The 16 Facebook pages selected yielded a small sample of 69 memes. The Facebook pages were then divided by the candidate name, and if the title and description of the page was for or against the candidate. Pro-Obama pages posted 27 memes, anti-Romney pages posted 24 memes, and there was an even split of 9 memes each for pro-Romney and anti-Obama pages posted during the last week of the 2012 presidential election. The analysis of candidate frames proved to be very difficult because of the manipulation of pictures in image macro memes posted to Facebook. For example, how do you analyze the candidates when they are featured in a meme together? How is a frame determined by examining a meme featuring only the candidate's face without other context clues for the original news photograph?

Researchers should develop a better system for the content analysis of memes because the anarchy introduced by Adobe Photoshop and other photo-manipulation software made the analysis of the images very difficult. The candidates were often pieced together from other photographs to create chaos of candidate images for one meme. Finally, I settled on examining each candidate individually in the memes, so there is some crossover of memes that feature both candidates, but use images from news or campaign photographs that present the candidate in the frames of ideal candidate, populist campaigner, and sure loser.

The results show the ideal candidate frame was present in 36 (52.2%), the populist campaigner frame was used in 46 (66.7%), and the sure loser frame was present in 52 (75.4%) of the 69 memes sampled. As expected the majority of pro-Obama pages posted ideal candidate image memes (18 or 26.1%), with anti-Romney pages having 9 (13%) memes of Obama as the ideal candidate. However, the majority of anti-Romney pages depicted Romney as the populist campaigner (23 or 33.3%) rather than a sure loser (17 or 24.6%). This percentage of the populist campaigner frame was higher than on any other pro or anti-candidate Facebook pages. The sure loser frame was used most frequently (7 or 10.1%) on other pro or anti-candidate Facebook pages. However, the number of sure loser frames (17 or 24.6%) to populist campaigner frames (23 or 33.3%) was very low when compared on the anti-Romney pages. Because the majority of Romney photographs posted during the campaign focused on the populist campaigner frame, that is the image of Romney most available for users to manipulate into a meme and repost.[35]

There was no significant relationship between the ideal candidate frame and pro or anti-candidate pages, but the relationship between the populist campaigner frame and pro or anti-candidate pages was significant with the populist campaigner frame appearing more frequently than expected on anti-Romney Facebook pages. The relationship between the sure loser frame and pro and anti-candidate pages was also not significant, according to the data in this study. All three of the frames created by Grabe and Bucy[36] were found in the study, but unlike Goodnow[37] the results found that memes using those frames were posted in unexpected places. For example, the anti-Romney pages posted frames featuring the populist campaigner rather than the sure loser frame.

When I examined the use of photographic manipulation, qualified as the addition or subtraction of characters to a photograph or the manipulation of a candidate's body or face, 53.6% of the memes in the sample could be categorized as having too many manipulated elements to fit into one category of manipulation, meaning the image had been significantly changed to included added and subtracted elements and manipulation of the candidate's face and body. Nine (13%) featured a manipulation to only the background of an image, 4 (5.8%) featured only an additional character that was not in the original photograph, and 3 (4.3%) featured the manipulation to the candidate's face or body alone. Only 16 (23.3%) of the total 69 memes featured no photographic manipulation of any kind apart from the addition of the text to the photograph to create the image macro. The data found no significant relationship to Romney's image and photo manipulation, but there was a significant relationship between President Obama's image and photographic manipulation. This would indicate that although Obama appeared as the ideal candidate in most of the memes, his image was also the most manipulated by the addition or subtraction of characters and his body or face. Most of Obama's images were on pro-Obama pages, so it would appear that despite supporting a candidate users would manipulate a news image to make a meme.

Next, to understand the manipulation of candidate images into memes, I created a category for incongruity, which was then broken into three subcategories, a text incongruity was a meme that featured an incongruous statement superimposed on a photograph. A photo incongruity was a meme that featured a visual incongruity added to the photograph, and finally memes without incongruities were labeled. Most of the memes, 32 (46.6%), did not feature an incongruity. Text incongruities were most common with 19 (27.5%) of the 69 memes gathered featuring a funny or awkward saying above the image used. Photographic incongruities were not far behind with 18 (26.1%) of the 69 memes in the sample featuring an incongruous photo manipulation. The data show no significant relationship between Romney's image or Obama's image and the amount of incongruities in the memes. However, the majority of Romney's memes featuring the populist campaigner frame also contained either a text or photo incongruity. This would seem to indicate that users are playing with the populist campaigner frame by creating an incongruity within the meme featuring the populist campaigner image of Romney.

MEME-FRAMES, MEME-GENRES, AND PRESIDENTIAL ELECTIONS

Upon closer examination, it appears that users are playing with frames by emphasizing different aspects of the original image generated by traditional media frames. Users work within the ideal candidate, populist campaigner, or sure loser to make a comment about the candidates, but are adding new emphasis on these frames to create their own meme-frames. For example, the meme posted by the Facebook page *Mitt Romney Sucks* features Romney standing near a barn surrounded by tractors, like the populist campaigner frame used most by anti-Romney Facebook pages during the 2012 presidential election,[38] but it includes a new emphasis on the unordinary aspects of Mitt Romney in a rural setting by calling Romney a liar. If Mitt Romney was shown only as the populist campaigner in news media and his campaign,[39] then the memes reflect that those were the images most circulated on Facebook in 2012, but with a new element of awareness added as an incongruity to the original image—the un-populist campaigner frame. This frame appears to coincide with the rhetoric used in another popular Romney meme from 2012, Relatable Romney.[40]

Each meme indicates that Romney is too rich and out-of-touch with the common man to be elected, but in the Relatable Romney meme Romney is framed as a sure loser because of the face he is making standing alone in the image reaching out to the camera. In contrast, the un-populist campaigner frame pulls rhetoric from Relatable Romney, but adds a new dimension because the meme-frame is emphasizing something from the original populist campaigner frame, like the presence of farms or factories and informal dress, with new information added to the image to frame to create the meme.

To continue the study of memes in the context of the popular culture definition, I propose a two-part understanding of how memes can be divided between frames and genres. For example, the candidate that appeared most often in the memes who was not running for office at the time was Chris Christie. The memes posted in the last week of October 2012 featured a lot of photographs of President Obama and Chris Christie, and some of them featured Christie alone. The meme posted by the Facebook page *Mitt Romney Is a Silicon-Based Life Form or Robot*, for example, has a lot to offer for analysis of candidate image in memes.

In the meme, Christie's head is placed on the meme *Bad Luck Brain's*[41] body. The incongruity of the size of Christie's head on the small child's body is not only strange and humorous but also very unflattering for any candidate with hopes of running for office. However, the meme itself suggests empathy for Christie's political predicament of working with the president to secure aid for his state or stand hard with party lines to refuse to work with the Democrats. So does the meme help or hurt Christie's image? How would his image be categorized according to the traditional media frames of populist campaigner, sure loser, or ideal candidate?

To start, we could argue that Christie as *Bad Luck Brian* is wearing informal clothing like the populist campaigner would, but the inappropriate and strange nature of his head on the body could confuse voters like the sure loser frame, yet the words suggest the meme-creator is supporting Christie's decisions so the intended effect is to have positive influence on Christie's image. The image would seem almost impossible to analyze if we do not try to break apart what aspects of Christie the creator is emphasizing, and what aspects of the meme are simply a vehicle for that frame. We must first tear apart the image by dividing it into a meme-frame and meme-genre.

Meme-genera are existing memes that can be used to convey a range of political or cultural ideals because the meme itself is so popular. In the aforementioned example, *Bad Luck Brian* is existing meme-genera within the confines of the Internet. There are many *Bad Luck Brian* memes that promote a lot of different ideologies or specific obscure cultural references. For example, *Bad Luck Brian* can be used to express feelings about movies, video games, or political candidates, but the meme-genera itself does not have a specific connection to a larger framework to view an issue or candidate. Most of the meme-frames of Christie in this sample place him as the "above politics guy," in other words he fights for what is right for New Jersey and is above the petty nature of political party strife. He was added to the meme-genre *Bad Luck Brian*, who attempts to do something right but it always turns out wrong, and using the meme-genera of *Bad Luck Brian*, the user is able to build a meme-frame of Christie as the "above politics guy" punished by the system for operating outside of it.

The meme posted by *One Million Strong Defeated Mitt Romney in 2012* features Christie and Obama together, surrounded by victims of Hurricane Sandy. Obama is embracing a woman and Christie is looking into the distance with the words: "What we used to be before the tea party, before the Koch brothers, before Rush Limbaugh, before the birthers—Americans." This meme was the most liked, shared, and commented meme in the sample with 34,746 likes, 18,880 shares, and over 2,500 comments. This same image of Christie working with Obama is still used in jokes on late night television about Christie's bid for the 2016 Republican nomination. Clearly, an event as large as Hurricane Sandy would have a lasting effect on the candidates in 2012, but it appears to have reached beyond Obama's second term to still touch Christie's image in the media today as he runs for office in 2016.

More studies of image macros or memes posted to user-created Facebook pages for the 2016 election would be needed to understand the importance of these images and the meme-frame of the "above politics guy" to Christie's 2016 run, but in this snapshot of online activity in the last week of the 2012 election cycle shows that Christie had a lot of support, particularly among anti-Romney pages, for his actions of working with President Obama. It is possible that both Democrats and Republicans created anti-Romney pages during the 2012 election, and Republicans could be posting the most memes supporting Christie because although they do not support Romney, they may still hold hope for the future of the party.

An existing meme-genre was not used to create the Obama-Christie meme. Instead, the user has chosen to keep the image very simple by adding text to state their opinion and leave out any other forms of manipulation. However, it can be argued that the meme-frame of the "above politics guys" is still present in the meme because Christie and Obama together symbolize a reaching across the aisle, however, this meme also provides evidence to argue the populist campaigner frame is at work because both candidates are in plain clothing surrounded by ordinary people in a large crowd. Obama is showing compassion by hugging a woman, which also leans the frame toward the ideal candidate. In this instance, the meme-frame is a favor to both politicians. It can be argued that both Christie and Obama are borrowing goodwill from the image to perpetuate the ideal candidate frame of a leader that will work with other political elites to accomplish goals. Although there is no humor present in the meme, it is still manipulated, replicated content online, and so again the popular culture definition of a meme is vague in its description of online content passed between users. Is the image a meme because it is manipulated or is it a meme because it spread through the Facebook communities viewing the image macro? The answer is a little bit of both. Although past studies have found that humor[42] is an important element to understanding Internet memes, clearly powerful images such as the one used to create that meme can have replicating power.

The majority of the memes posted to the political Facebook pages in 2012 took campaign materials and news photographs to create the memes, indicating that users are actively participating in image creation during campaigns. The 2016 field of candidates will feature meme superstars like Hillary Clinton and Donald Trump, who have been a part of the media consciousness long enough to develop and, at times, manipulate their image both in traditional media and online.[43] At this point, it is unclear if the meme-genre of *Text from Hillary* will help or hurt in the creation of new frames for the candidate as she runs for office in 2016.

Users are participating in political discussion online more frequently,[44] and according to the data in this study, the traditional media frames of the ideal candidate, populist campaigner, and sure loser[45] are used as a base to build their commentary. But the political memes appear to be more nuanced in their messages than the use of three political frames found in traditional media. Users are blending good and bad images to build something new and different—for example, the use of Christie's head on *Bad Luck Brian*'s body. Many memes featuring Hillary Clinton also feature unflattering images of Clinton with positive emphasis placed on her leadership characteristics.[46] It is unclear if users are aware of the media frames, but it appears they are in some cases purposely playing with the original photographs, like in the case of Romney's image as the un-populist campaigner.

The term *meme* is very flexible used both in a traditional sense[47] to describe cultural evolution and in popular culture[48] to describe image macros, .GIFs, and other user-generated content online. In either definition, memes are used to describe infectious behavior among humans. To broaden the understanding of the popular culture definition of a meme, a two-part naming system should be used to separate the genre or existing meme and the content or frame within it. Just as in the analysis of the Chris Christie *Bad Luck Brian* meme, where *Bad Luck Brian* is an existing meme-genre, but the frame or content of the meme focuses on Christie's punishment by the Republican Party for working with President Obama during the final weeks of the 2012 election after Hurricane Sandy. Although further study is needed, social media users appear to be acting as their own gatekeepers by passing on information they view as important to their followers, but not without manipulating the information to frame the issue or candidate how they see fit. The memes in this sample may have been used to gather a popular vote of approval by group users liking, sharing, or commenting on the meme, but the contents of the memes suggest that users are aware of the traditional media frame, just like in the case of the un-populist campaigner frame that emerged on anti-Romney Facebook pages in this sample. With each passing election, social media becomes more important[49] to a winning campaign strategy, so more scholarship should develop a deeper understanding of how memes are used to send information, what effect they have on voters, and finally how can candidates successfully use memes to their advantage the way that Hillary Clinton appears to have tried with her "#tweetsfromHillary" meme.

NOTES

1. Shanto Iyengar and Jennifer McGrady, *Media Politics: A Citizen's Guide* (New York: W.W. Norton, 2007).

2. K. V. Anderson and K. H. Sheeler, "Texts (and Tweets) from Hillary: Meta-meming and Postfeminist Political Culture," *Presidential Studies Quarterly* 44, no. 2 (2014): 224–243.

3. Limor Shifman, *Memes in Digital Culture* (Cambridge, MA: The MIT Press, 2014); Limor Shifman, "An Anatomy of a YouTube Meme," *New Media & Society* 14, no. 2 (2011): 187–203; M. Knobel and C. Lankshear, "Online Memes, Affinities and Cultural Production," in *A New Literacies Sampler* (New York: Peter Lang Publishing, Inc., 2007), 199–227.; P. Dias Da Silva and J. L. Garcia, "YouTubers as Satirists: Humor and Remix in Online Video," *Jedem* 4, no. 1 (2012): 89–114; H. E. Decker-Maurere, "I Can Haz Rhetoric: How Image Macros Address Social Issues in an Age of Participatory Culture," unpublished manuscript, 2012.

4. Richard Dawkins, *The Selfish Gene*, new ed. (Oxford: Oxford University Press, 1989); S. Blackmore, *The Meme Machine* (New York: Oxford University Press, 1999).

5. Anderson and Sheeler, "Texts (and Tweets) from Hillary," 224–243; Shifman, *Memes in Digital Culture*; Shifman, "An Anatomy of a YouTube Meme," 187–203.

Knobel and Lankshear, "Online Memes, Affinities and Cultural Production," 199–227; Dias Da Silva and Garcia, "YouTubers as Satirists," 89–114; Decker-Maurere, "I Can Haz Rhetoric."

6. Dawkins, *The Selfish Gene*.

7. Kim Wilkins, "Valhallolz: Medievalist Humor on the Internet," *Postmedieval* 5, no. 2 (2014): 199–214; Lilian, Weng, Filippo Menczer, and Yong-Yeol Ahn, "Virality Prediction and Community Structure in Social Networks," *Scientific Reports* 3 (2013): 1–7; L. Weng, A. Flammini, A. Vespignani, and F. Menczer. "Competition among Memes in a World with Limited Attention," *Scientific Reports* 3 (2003): 1–8; Dias Da Silva and Garcia, "YouTubers as Satirists," 89–114; Decker-Maurere, "I Can Haz Rhetoric"; Anderson and Sheeler, "Texts (and Tweets) from Hillary," 224–243; Shifman, *Memes in Digital Culture*; Shifman, "An Anatomy of a YouTube Meme," 187–203; Knobel and Lankshear, "Online Memes, Affinities and Cultural Production," 199–227.

8. Shifman, "An Anatomy of a YouTube Meme."

9. Knobel and Lankshear, "Online Memes, Affinities and Cultural Production," 199–227; Dias Da Silva and Garcia, "YouTubers as Satirists," 89–114.

10. Decker-Maurere, "I Can Haz Rhetoric"; Wilkins, "Valhallolz," 199–214; Anderson and Sheeler, "Texts (and Tweets) from Hillary," 224–243.

11. Rebecca Verser and Robert H. Wicks, "Managing Voter Impressions: The Use of Images on Presidential Candidate Web Sites during the 2000 Campaign," *Journal of Communication* 56, no. 1 (2006): 178–197; Maria Elizabeth Grabe and Erik P. Bucy, *Image Bite Politics News and the Visual Framing of Elections* (Oxford: Oxford University Press, 2009); J. R. Azari and J. S. Vaughn, "Barack Obama and Rhetoric of Electoral Logic," *Social Science Quarterly* 95, no. 2 (2014): 523; Iyengar and McGrady, *Media Politics: A Citizen's Guide*.

12. Anderson and Sheeler, "Texts (and Tweets) from Hillary," 224–243; Decker-Maurere, "I Can Haz Rhetoric."

13. "Know Your Meme Online Database: First World Problems," *Know Your Meme*, 2001, accessed November 5, 2015, http://knowyourmeme.com/memes/first-world-problems.

14. B. Amanda, "Know Your Meme Online Database: Texts from Hillary," *Know Your Meme*, 2012, accessed November 5, 2015, http://knowyourmeme.com/memes/texts-from-hillary.

15. Julia Woolley, Anthony Limperos, and Mary Beth Oliver, "The 2008 Presidential Election, 2.0: A Content Analysis of User-Generated Political Facebook Groups," *Mass Communication and Society* 13, no. 5 (2010): 631–652; Dias Da Silva and Garcia, "YouTubers as Satirists," 89–114; Shifman, *Memes in Digital Culture*.

16. Anderson and Sheeler, "Texts (and Tweets) from Hillary," 224–243; Dias Da Silva and Garcia, "YouTubers as Satirists," 89–114; Knobel and Lankshear, "Online Memes, Affinities and Cultural Production," 199–227; Shifman, "An Anatomy of a YouTube Meme," 187–203; Shifman, *Memes in Digital Culture*.

17. Decker-Maurere, "I Can Haz Rhetoric."

18. Verser and Wicks, "Managing Voter Impressions," 178–197; Grabe and Bucy, *Image Bite Politics News and the Visual Framing of Elections*; Azari and Vaughn, "Barack Obama and Rhetoric of Electoral Logic," 523; Iyengar and McGrady, *Media Politics: A Citizen's Guide*.

19. Iyengar and McGrady, *Media Politics: A Citizen's Guide*.

20. Grabe and Bucy, *Image Bite Politics News and the Visual Framing of Elections*; T. Goodnow, "Facing Off: A Comparative Analysis of Obama and Romney Facebook Timeline Photographs," *American Behavioral Scientist*: 57, no. 11, 1584–1595.

21. Grabe and Bucy, *Image Bite Politics News and the Visual Framing of Elections*.

22. Goodnow, "Facing Off," 1584–1595; Grabe and Bucy, *Image Bite Politics News and the Visual Framing of Elections*; Iyengar and McGrady, *Media Politics: A Citizen's Guide*.

23. Grabe and Bucy, *Image Bite Politics News and the Visual Framing of Elections*.

24. Ibid.

25. Ibid.

26. Ibid.

27. Ibid.; P. A. Stewart, "The Influence of Self- and Other-deprecatory Humor on Presidential Candidate Evaluation during the 2008 US Election," *Social Science Information* 50, no. 2 (2011), 201–222.

28. Goodnow, "Facing Off," 1584–1595.

29. Anderson and Sheeler, "Texts (and Tweets) from Hillary," 224–243.

30. Ibid., 225.

31. "Know Your Meme Online Database: Hillary Clinton's New York Times Magazine Cover," *Know Your Meme*, 2014, accessed November 5, 2015, http://knowyourmeme.com/memes/hillary-clintons-new-york-times-magazine-cover.

32. Jenny Kutner, "The 'Beyoncé Voters' Tumblr Is a Piece of Internet You Should See," *Salon*, July 9, 2014, http://www.salon.com/2014/07/09/the_beyonce_voters_tumblr_is_a_piece_of_internet_you_should_see/.

33. Anderson and Sheeler, "Texts (and Tweets) from Hillary," 224–243; Dias Da Silva and Garcia, "YouTubers as Satirists," 89–114; Knobel and Lankshear, "Online Memes, Affinities and Cultural Production," 199–227; Shifman, "An Anatomy of a YouTube Meme," 187–203; Shifman, *Memes in Digital Culture*.

34. Kutner, "The 'Beyoncé Voters' Tumblr Is a Piece of Internet You Should See."

35. Goodnow, "Facing Off," 1584–1595.

36. Grabe and Bucy, *Image Bite Politics News and the Visual Framing of Elections*.

37. Goodnow, "Facing Off," 1584–1595.

38. Ibid.

39. Ibid.

40. "Know Your Meme Online Database: Relatable Romney," *Know Your Meme*, 2012, accessed November 5, 2015, http://knowyourmeme.com/memes/relatable-romney.

41. "Know Your Meme Online Database: Bad Luck Brian," *Know Your Meme*, 2012, accessed November 5, 2015, http://knowyourmeme.com/memes/bad-luck-brian.

42. Dias Da Silva and Garcia, "YouTubers as Satirists," 89–114; Knobel and Lankshear, "Online Memes, Affinities and Cultural Production," 199–227; Shifman, "An Anatomy of a YouTube Meme," 187–203; Shifman, *Memes in Digital Culture*.

43. Anderson and Sheeler, "Texts (and Tweets) from Hillary," 224–243.

44. Dias Da Silva and Garcia, "YouTubers as Satirists," 89–114; "One-in-Ten Dual Screened the Presidential Debate," *Pew Research Center*, October 11, 2012, http://www.people-press.org/2012/10/11/one-in-ten-dual-screened-the-presidential-debate/; Shifman, *Memes in Digital Culture*; Woolley, Limperos, and Oliver, "The 2008 Presidential Election, 2.0," 631–652.

45. Grabe and Bucy, *Image Bite Politics News and the Visual Framing of Elections*.

46. Kutner, "The 'Beyoncé Voters' Tumblr Is a Piece of Internet You Should See"; "Know Your Meme Online Database: Hillary Clinton's New York Times Magazine Cover."

47. Dawkins, *The Selfish Gene*; Blackmore, *The Meme Machine*.

48. Wilkins, "Valhallolz: Medievalist Humor on the Internet," 199–214; Weng, Menczer, and Yong-Yeol Ahn, "Virality Prediction and Community Structure in Social Networks"; Weng, Flammini, Vespignani, and Menczer, "Competition among Memes in a World with Limited Attention"; Dias Da Silva and Garcia, "YouTubers as Satirists," 89–114; Decker-Maurere, "I Can Haz Rhetoric"; Anderson and Sheeler, "Texts (and Tweets) from Hillary: Meta-meming and Postfeminist Political Culture," 224–243; Shifman, *Memes in Digital Culture*; Shifman, "An Anatomy of a YouTube Meme,"187–203; Knobel and Lankshear, "Online Memes, Affinities and Cultural Production," 199–227.

49. Anderson and Sheeler, "Texts (and Tweets) from Hillary," 224–243; Goodnow, "Facing Off," 1584–1595; "One-in-ten Dual Screened the Presidential Debate"; Woolley, Limperos, and Oliver, "The 2008 Presidential Election, 2.0," 631–652.

BIBLIOGRAPHY

Amanda, B. "Know Your Meme Online Database: Texts from Hillary." *Know Your Meme*, 2012. Accessed November 5, 2015. http://knowyourmeme.com/memes/texts-from-hillary.

Anderson, K. V., and K. H. Sheeler. "Texts (and Tweets) from Hillary: Meta-meming and Postfeminist Political Culture." *Presidential Studies Quarterly* 44, no. 2 (2014): 224–243.

Azari, J. R., and J. S. Vaughn. "Barack Obama and Rhetoric of Electoral Logic." *Social Science Quarterly* 95, no. 2 (2014): 523.

Ball, J. "Quantifying the Claim that Nixon Looked Bad: A Visual Analysis of the 1960 Debates." Unpublished master's thesis, 2010.

Blackmore, S. *The Meme Machine*. New York: Oxford University Press, 1999.

Bronstein, Jenny. "Like Me! Analyzing the 2012 Presidential Candidates' Facebook Pages." *Online Information Review* 37, no. 2 (2013): 173–192.

Dawkins, Richard. *The Selfish Gene,* new ed. Oxford: Oxford University Press, 1989.

Decker-Maurere, H. E. "I Can Haz Rhetoric: How Image Macros Address Social Issues in an Age of Participatory Culture." Unpublished manuscript, 2012.

Dias Da Silva, P., and J. L. Garcia. "YouTubers as Satirists: Humor and Remix in Online Video." *Jedem* 4, no. 1 (2012): 89–114.

Goodnow, T. "Facing Off: A Comparative Analysis of Obama and Romney Facebook Timeline Photographs." *American Behavioral Scientist* 57, no. 11 (2013): 1584–1595.

Grabe, Maria Elizabeth, and Erik P. Bucy. *Image Bite Politics News and the Visual Framing of Elections.* Oxford: Oxford University Press, 2009.

Iyengar, Shanto, and Jennifer McGrady. *Media Politics: A Citizen's Guide.* New York: W.W. Norton, 2007.

Journalism & Media, Staff. "The Master Character Narratives in Campaign 2012." *Pew Research Center: Journalism and Media,* August 12, 2012. http://www.journalism.org/2012/08/23/2012-campaign-character-narratives/.

Kaye, B. K., and B. S. Sapolsky. "Talking a 'Blue' Streak: Context and Offensive Language in Prime Time Network Television Programs." *Journalism & Mass Communication Quarterly* 81, no. 4 (2004): 911–927.

Knobel, M., and C. Lankshear. "Online Memes, Affinities and Cultural Production." *A New Literacies Sampler* (New York: Peter Lang Publishing, Inc., 2007), 199–227.

"Know Your Meme Online Database: Bad Luck Brian." *Know Your Meme,* 2012. Accessed November 5, 2015. http://knowyourmeme.com/memes/bad-luck-brian.

"Know Your Meme Online Database: First World Problems." *Know Your Meme,* 2001. Accessed November 5, 2015. http://knowyourmeme.com/memes/first-world-problems.

"Know Your Meme Online Database: Hillary Clinton's New York Times Magazine Cover." *Know Your Meme,* 2014. Accessed November 5, 2015. http://knowyourmeme.com/memes/hillary-clintons-new-york-times-magazine-cover.

"Know Your Meme Online Database: Relatable Romney." *Know Your Meme,* 2012. Accessed November 5, 2015. http://knowyourmeme.com/memes/relatable-romney.

Kutner, Jenny. "The 'Beyoncé Voters' Tumblr Is a Piece of Internet You Should See." *Salon,* July 9, 2014. http://www.salon.com/2014/07/09/the_beyonce_voters_tumblr_is_a_piece_of_internet_you_should_see/.

Mitchell, A., and P. Hitlin. "Twitter Reaction to Events Often at Odds with Overall Public Opinion." *Pew Research Center,* March 4, 2013. http://www.pewresearch.org/2013/03/04/twitter-reaction-to-events-often-at-odds-with-overall-public-opinion/.

"One-in-Ten Dual Screened the Presidential Debate." *Pew Research Center,* October 11, 2012. http://www.people-press.org/2012/10/11/one-in-ten-dual-screened-the-presidential-debate/.

Rainie, L., A. Smith, and M. Duggan. "Coming and Going on Facebook." *Pew Research Center,* February 5, 2013. http://www.pewinternet.org/files/old-media/Files/Reports/2013/PIP_Coming_and_going_on_facebook.pdf.

Sapolsky, Barry S., Daniel M. Shafer, and Barbara K. Kaye. "Rating Offensive Words in Three Television Program Contexts." *Mass Communication and Society* 14, no. 1 (2010): 45–70.

Shifman, L. "An Anatomy of a YouTube Meme." *New Media & Society* 14, no. 2 (2011): 187–203.

Shifman, Limor. *Memes in Digital Culture.* Cambridge, MA: The MIT Press, 2014.

Shifman, Limor, and Mike Thelwall. "Assessing Global Diffusion with Web Memetics: The Spread and Evolution of a Popular Joke." *Journal of the American Society for Information Science and Technology* 60, no. 12 (2009): 2567–2576.

Shifman, Limor, Stephen Coleman, and Stephen Ward. "Only Joking? Online Humour in the 2005 UK General Election." *Information, Communication & Society* 10, no. 4 (2007): 465–487.

Stewart, P. A. "The Influence of Self- and Other-deprecatory Humor on Presidential Candidate Evaluation during the 2008 US Election." *Social Science Information* 50, no. 2 (2011): 201–222.

Verser, Rebecca, and Robert H. Wicks. "Managing Voter Impressions: The Use of Images on Presidential Candidate Web Sites during the 2000 Campaign." *Journal of Communication* 56, no. 1 (2006): 178–197.

Weng, L., A. Flammini, A. Vespignani, and F. Menczer. "Competition among Memes in a World with Limited Attention." *Scientific Reports* 3 (2003): 1–8.

Weng, Lilian, Filippo Menczer, and Yong-Yeol Ahn. "Virality Prediction and Community Structure in Social Networks." *Scientific Reports* 3 (2013).

Wilkins, Kim. "Valhallolz: Medievalist Humor on the Internet." *Postmedieval* 5, no. 2 (2014): 199–214.

Woolley, Julia, Anthony Limperos, and Mary Beth Oliver. "The 2008 Presidential Election, 2.0: A Content Analysis of User-Generated Political Facebook Groups." *Mass Communication and Society* 13, no. 5 (2010): 631–652.

Chapter 9

@TeaParty.org's Performance of Its *Virtual Identity* on Twitter

Gina Masullo Chen and Paromita Pain

For millennia, people have found ways to distort or manage how others see them. As early as ancient times, people used paint or decoration to adorn themselves and suggest greater wealth or power. In much the same way, social media offer people—or even groups—great potential to manage or perform themselves through the digitized process of creating a profile and communicating via snippets of information online. Social networks, such as Twitter, collapse the boundaries between the public and private identity[1]—offering a rich opportunity to understand the presentation of identity through this digital format. Communication scholar Zizi Papacharissi[2] theorizes that even thinking of public and private spheres as a binary is problematic online because private can only be defined in reference to what is public, so the line between the two becomes elusive or even nonexistent in the digital sphere of social media where almost everything can be made public.[3] As a result, social media offer greater fluidity than the offline world for impression management because the online identity is often not bounded by the limits of geography, time, or space.[4] Who we are online offers no physical form, so we can distort, re-create, and imagine a new identity for ourselves. When considered in the context of politics, social media offer fertile ground for understanding how political groups present and manufacture their own identities online. Just like an individual, a group can take advantage of the untethered aspects of social media to craft an identity that may not only mirror their offline identity but also warps it much like a fun-house mirror leaves a person's image awry.

For political organizations, like TeaParty.org, Twitter offers a chance to project a collective sense of who the group is and what it represents through a computer-mediated lens. We call this *virtual identity* because it is identity constructed through the virtual space of social media. We define virtual in its most literal sense—"existing or occurring on computers or on the Internet."[5] As a term, *virtual* has been applied to how people experience and interact with computers since the days of virtual community groups,[6] a precursor to social media. In this chapter, we use this term to explore how @TeaParty.org, one of dozens of Twitter accounts using some form of the name "tea party" in their handles, defines its group identity in the virtual—rather than physical—world through the computer-mediated space of Twitter. The term *virtual* also means to approximate something, "without actually being it."[7] We use this sense of virtual as well, to suggest that TeaParty.org's online identity may merely approximate its true identity. We define this computer-mediated identity as Papacharissi does, as "performance, projected to known and imagined audiences via Twitter."[8]

While identity is often associated with individuals, groups also have identities. Computer-mediated discourse, which lacks the cues of face-to-face communication, such as tone of voice or facial expressions, has been found to depersonalize interactions, so people become less aware of the line between individual and group.[9] People also may associate a Twitter account with a single entity, even when it refers to a group because they may interact with the account, much as they would with an individual. Twitter in particular fosters a conversation between people,[10] so those using it may be seen as having a single identity even when they represent a group. Prior scholars have explored group identity online in regard to a variety of topics, from white supremacist organizations, blogging communities, and the Tea Party members on Facebook.[11] Based on this logic, we sought to understand how TeaParty.org performed its *virtual identity* through its Twitter account.

To understand this *virtual identity*, we qualitatively analyze more than 3,000 tweets posted over three months at @TeaParty.org, which calls itself the official Twitter account of the U.S.-based conservative political group, TeaParty.org. It should be noted that we analyze only tweets from @TeaParty.org, although dozens of other accounts include the terms *tea party* in their names, including some that appear to represent state or city Tea Party organizations. Because the Tea Party is a "natural outgrowth of the growing size and conservatism of the activist base of the Republican

Party,"[12] rather than a formal party, there is no one definitive Twitter account that represents all people who may espouse Tea Party beliefs. In fact, there is no definitive core of Tea Party beliefs, as different factions focus on varying issues.[13] So this analysis is intended to provide insight into how one faction of the Tea Party movement performs its identity, not to be generalized to other Tea Party-related Twitter accounts or the movement as a whole.

We choose this particular account because it purports to have a national reach and it has a larger number of followers, 40,600, compared to some smaller accounts. Yet it is not the largest, so it retains some of the original grassroots appeal that launched the movement.[14] Therefore, we judged it as a suitable account to interpret how TeaParty.org's identity is communicated through Twitter. Also, it is important to understand that people who consider themselves Tea Partiers may not agree on all topics.[15] TeaParty.org, which is under study in this chapter and is also known as 1776 Tea Party, is the national faction most directly linked to the anti-immigration movement, while Tea Party Express has driven electoral politics more than other Tea Partiers and Tea Party Patriots focuses on property rights.[16] We also note that we do not analyze how the use of term *tea party* was used generally in tweets, because anyone—even those opposed to the group—could use that term, so analyzing the term itself does not explain how @TeaParty.org defines its identity through its use of Twitter.

Our aim is to explore how the organization performs its *virtual identity*. Much like the private identity, the *virtual identity* is malleable, a chameleon of sorts open to interpretation as others view or perceive it. We draw on sociologist Erving Goffman's[17] concept of the performance of identity to understand how @TeaParty.org presents and performs its identity through its tweets, hashtags, and language on Twitter. Because many of the nonverbal cues identified with offline speech are absent or altered online,[18] Twitter and other digital formats offer a rich atmosphere for "identity play."[19] This performance is "both an agent of and a product of the social and political surround in which it circulates."[20]

We begin by providing a brief history of the Tea Party more generally. Next we discuss theories of presentation and impression management that are relevant to this work. We then explain the tweets at the core of this study and explore themes we found, interpreting them using theory. Finally, we offer suggestions for what these findings mean for public discourse and society as a whole.

THE TEA PARTY: EVOLUTION OF A MOVEMENT

The Tea Party is not a party in the traditional sense but rather a loose collection of grassroots organizations that wield considerable political sway in national, regional, and statewide elections.[21] It was spawned in

2009 in the aftermath of the $700 billion spending stimulus bill that President Obama signed into law to curb the Great Recession.[22] Within weeks, hundreds of local Tea Party groups formed. Members of the Tea Party movement oppose the Obama administration's healthcare reform law, the financial bailout, proposed cap-and-trade legislation to address greenhouse gas emissions, excessive taxes, and the national debt, although different factions place an emphasis on some topics more than others.[23] The emergence of the Tea Party was an outgrowth of "increased conservatism of the Republican electoral base"[24] and a move toward greater polarization in the U.S. electorate.[25] Tea Partiers make a clear distinction between government aid—such as Social Security and Medicare—that they see as helping deserving people and welfare, which they see as a handout perpetuating irresponsibility.[26] Tea Partiers propose a narrow view of America that takes a strong stand against undocumented immigrants and affords little tolerance for differences in race or sexual orientation.[27] While race and racist rhetoric have long been a part of American politics and public policy,[28] race became hyper-salient when the nation's first African-American president, Barack Obama, was elected twice. Racist depictions of Obama are frequent at Tea Party events and its fliers. These depictions along with the movement's nearly all-white membership has led to charges of "racism that has dogged the movement,"[29] although the group's leaders try to diffuse this connection.

The movement grew out of what Tea Party proponent John M. O'Hara calls a widespread anxiety that America stood on the precipice of transforming into something unrecognizably foreign.[30] However, critics charge the Tea Party espouses a paranoid style of politics that hearkens to the Goldwater movement of the 1960s[31] and unites members through an exaggerated sense of conspiracy.[32] The name itself is both a nod to the Boston Tea Party of 1773 where Americans dressed as Mohawks and dumped 342 chests of tea into Boston Harbor to protest taxation without representation and an acronym for Taxed Enough Already.[33]

Tea Partiers tend to be made up of white, affluent, educated voters who mirror the conservative side of the Republican Party.[34] However, compared to the mainstream GOP, Tea Party supporters tend to be more affluent and religious, slightly less likely to have graduated from college, and more likely to be male and to own a gun.[35] What really sets Tea Partiers apart are their far right-wing political views, even compared to other conservatives.[36] In the primary battles of 2014, the Tea Party's candidates clashed markedly with traditional GOP nominees, creating a wedge between the Tea Party and the Republican Party.[37] In the early months of the 2016 presidential election, the Tea Party gained some of the national clout it had long sought, as some of the declared Republican candidates at the time owed their current political jobs to Tea Party support.[38]

However, later those candidates dropped out of the race, usurped by Donald Trump, the GOP nominee.

Analyzing how the group presents its *virtual identity* on Twitter is particularly salient because the Tea Party is the first political entity that is not a formal political party to leverage the power of digital media to the extent that it has.[39] In fact, "the Tea Party may be the first U.S.-based, insurgent political organization that has developed within a political milieu that incorporates [social-networking sites] into everyday campaign communication."[40] At the same time, little empirical study has examined the concept of presentation of political groups, such as the Tea Party, on social media, adding more urgency to this topic. Prior studies have examined the party's racist rhetoric and online political identity as it is presented through Facebook posts,[41] yet little has specifically addressed the mutable *virtual identity*, as interpreted through the computer-mediated discourse of Twitter.

TWITTER AS A POLITICAL PERFORMANCE SPACE

Goffman defined performance as "all the activity of a given participant on a given occasion which serves to influence in any way any of the other participants."[42] He asserted that people attach certain rights and duties to a particular status, and that people enact them as they perform their public identity. Philosopher and gender theorist Judith Butler viewed performance somewhat differently, proposing that performance is an unconscious, rather than deliberate, act.[43] In other words, people perform themselves somewhat unwittingly through their actions. In all definitions, performance produces identity through repeated behaviors.[44] People exist in this somewhat fluid social space where they recreate and reenact themselves again and again, creating different versions of themselves. In all this plasticity, identity is "the one constant in the midst of the ongoing reflexivity."[45] In essence, performance is a way to reveal—perhaps without directly telling others—private thoughts or "public dreaming."[46]

When applied to politics, performance transforms the abstraction of the political into something more concrete.[47] For example, a group like the Tea Party may espouse certain beliefs in public, through its website, news releases, or quotes. But its performance of its *virtual identity* may unveil a more nuanced description of who the group really is. The group's performance online may express aspects of its identity to others that the group wants conveyed—the idealized or true identity, under Goffman's understanding of performance.[48] The group's online performance may also exhibit hidden aspects—the unconscious identity, using Butler's concept of performativity.[49] The idealized and true identities are the same, produced at a conscious level, but they differ from the unconscious identity. Goffman believed that when people perform their identity they are aware they are doing so, while Butler suggests this performance happens outside of conscious thought. This chapter will examine both aspects of the @TeaParty.org's public performance of its *virtual identity* on Twitter.

IMPRESSION MANAGEMENT ONLINE

Presentation of identity has become an increasingly popular method for understanding online participation.[50] Like earlier forms of media, the digital sphere offers a means for people to reveal their private selves or expose what happens *backstage*, to use Goffman's dramaturgical analogy.[51] Researchers debate how Goffman's metaphor of *backstage* relates to online discourse. Some argue that privacy settings on social media create a *backstage* or private space,[52] but we agree with Internet scholar Bernie Hogan's[53] interpretation that backstage should not be conflated with a private sphere online because privacy online does not really exist. Rather, backstage refers to the "real work necessary to keep up appearances"[54] in the public space. In other words, in the digital world, private space becomes how individuals and groups conceive of and concoct their presentations in their own heads before they perform them in the public virtual space of the Internet.

Social media, such as Twitter, differ from earlier forms of media because they offer both mass and interpersonal communication.[55] When a person or a group speaks out on Twitter, they imagine they are speaking directly to a hypothetical audience that may number in the dozens or thousands.[56] This "imagined audience is the mental conceptualization of the people with whom we are communicating."[57] Social media create an illusion of intimacy[58] that blurs the lines between public and private,[59] so when people converse online they may feel as if they are speaking to a friend, even when they are not. In addition, the growing use of Twitter by politicians, political strategists, journalists, and voters make the medium a key forum for how political identities are publicly navigated.[60] Twitter's limitation as a vehicle for expressing identity may also be its strength. For example, tweets are short and contain much less content than a news article or blog. Much of a tweet is often a link to other information, so it is not really content in the traditional sense.[61] However, we argue that Twitter's brevity may make it more revealing because users have less space to distort their meaning when they craft their tweets. In addition, what people—or groups—choose to share on social media provides a powerful means by which to perform or even manipulate the presentation of identity. As Papacharissi explains: "Twitter affords a platform for the condensed yet potentially rich and variably public and private performances" of identity.[62] This "shareability"[63] provides a glimpse into the core identity of the sharer.

GROUP IDENTITY ONLINE

While identity is often associated with individuals, groups also manage their own identity, particularly on social media, where the lines between individual and group may blur.[64] Digital media disrupts the notion of identity of individual or group because everyone is disembodied online, so identity is assessed through words not bodies.[65] Research has found that impression management is a function of interpersonal relationships involved in a group.[66] People protect their own identity by associating with others who share similar beliefs.[67] In the same way, groups protect or manage their identity by putting forth beliefs that coincide with those of their members. The use of impression management has been explored in other groups,[68] including the Tea Party on Facebook,[69] paving the way for this current study.

@TEAPARTY.ORG'S TWEETS

For this chapter, we analyze 3,013 tweets, all tweets posted by @TeaParty.org during March, April, and May 2015. These months were chosen because they were the most recent during the study period, not for any particular news event going on during that time. We employ both textual and discourse analysis of the tweets, so we examine both the words and the attributes of the tweets—such as hashtags, @replies, retweets, and text[70]—as well as the larger discourse in which the tweets operate. Our interest is not just in the manifest content of the tweets but also the "underlying ideological and cultural assumptions"[71] of both the tweets themselves and the content that was tweeted. In this method, text is seen as the result of discursive strategies that operate in a particular context, so researchers can uncover the implied meaning and make broader inferences rather than merely note details.[72] In addition, we examine attributes unique to computer-mediated speech, such use of capital letters to indicate a raised tone.[73]

To conduct this analysis, we read through the tweets repeatedly, looking for commonalities or themes in our data, using a native anthropological approach.[74] In this approach, researchers immerse themselves in the computer-mediated text, much as anthropologists embed themselves in a culture. With this method, the researchers become both the observer and the measuring device for the data, interpreting the data through the lens of their own experiences.[75] This type of qualitative analysis is subjective in nature and useful for interpreting meaning in text,[76] focusing on the "underlying ideological and cultural assumptions in the text," and seeing text as a "complex set of discursive strategies that is situated in a special cultural context."[77] It is also useful for analyzing the absence of features in text and for uncovering "thematic patterns, repetition, and redundancy in observed trends."[78] However, unlike quantitative content analysis, this method is not objective or intended to produce generalizable results.[79] Nor is this design aimed at inferring meaning only through frequency of certain words or communication features. In contrast, meaning is inferred from the context of the words and communication features. The value, however, of these qualitative approaches is in making sense of text and the discourses that shape these messages[80] as well as the ideologies reproduced through the text,[81] not in offering statistical inference. This is important to understand when interpreting our results.

The key questions driving our research are: How does TeaParty.org perform its *virtual identity?* What does that *virtual identity* reveal about the group's idealized and unconscious identity?

THEMES IN THE TWITTER STREAM

Our analysis finds @TeaParty.org tweeted 972 times in March, 817 in April, and 1,224 in May. Because Twitter is a medium of conversation and connection with others,[82] we include in our analysis whether other people responded to the party's tweets through retweeting (repeating them) or replying directly to them (@replying). Our themes encompass both the content of the Twitter stream as well as how the party uses the medium of Twitter—or fails to use it—to shape its *virtual identity*. Three main themes emerge in the data. The first is that the party uses Twitter mainly as a broadcasting tool, not as an engagement mechanism. It uses Twitter to promote its message but not to interact with its followers. Our second theme reveals the party uses Twitter to criticize messages and policies with which it disagrees. Our third theme suggests the party uses hyperbole and provocation to makes its points. We discuss each theme at length next. We explain the frequency of specific features of text in our analysis as a means to convey understanding to the reader. However, it is important to appreciate that discourse analysis looks beyond the mere frequency of features in text and analyzes the tone, context, and discourse that precedes media content.[83] Therefore, a percentage provides only part of the understanding of why a certain theme surfaces.

BROADCASTING ON TWITTER

When Twitter launched in 2006, its aim was for people to share what they were doing at that very moment, but the medium soon grew more engaging. Certainly some people still use Twitter to send out messages, without conversing with their followers, or to merely glean information.[84] However, ample research has found the medium is used most successfully for engaging with others through two-way communication. For example, research has found that when people use the tools of Twitter, such as the

@reply and the retweet, they are more likely to feel an "informal sense of camaraderie, called connection" with other Twitter users.[85] Similarly, the @reply, which is used to speak directly to another Twitter user, has been shown to signal the start of a Twitter conversation.[86] Our analysis shows the @TeaParty.org may have failed to make the switch to engagement. It is clear from our data that the group's Twitter account uses few of the tools available on Twitter to facilitate engagement. For example, consider the hashtag, which is a word or series of words prefixed with a hash symbol (#).[87] Hashtags started as a way to sort information on Twitter, but they have evolved into a method to add emotion, sarcasm, or humor to tweets.[88] They add richness to the scant computer-mediated speech of Twitter, which lacks the social cues—such as inflection or facial expression—of face-to-face speech.[89] A majority of tweets (80%) in our sample include #tcot, which stands for Top Conservative on Twitter,[90] but only seven tweets use #Wake-UpAmerica and two use #TeaParty. Hashtags have been found to be a powerful means to communicate political messages[91] and have played a central role in mobilizing political and social protests, starting with the Arab Spring in 2011.[92] #WakeUpAmerica suggests an effort to harness the galvanizing power of Twitter through the hashtag, but #tcot and #TeaParty appear to merely label the tweets. The very infrequent use of both #WakeUpAmerica is telling. This gap in the party's Twitter stream suggests the audience the @TeaParty.org imagines it is speaking to on Twitter comprises its supporters, not the general public. Of course, it is also plausible that TeaParty.org is not a savvy Twitter user. However, the reason makes little difference because the result is the same: @TeaParty.org fails to engage its audience using hashtags as well as it might.

In addition, the @TeaParty.org's Twitter stream shows an absence of retweets or @replies, further suggesting that it presents itself through Twitter as the broadcaster of its own message, not as a group that wants to converse or engage with others. In fact, every tweet in our sample was merely a link to a news story, blog, or the @TeaParty.org's own site. This again suggests the @TeaParty.org is communicating only in one direction—out—and not utilizing the two-way communication or social-ness intrinsic to Twitter. While other people @replied to the party's tweets 169 times, the party did not retweet or @reply even once during the three months we studied. Because our corpus of tweets is substantial, it seems reasonable that these three months were not an aberration when it comes to retweeting and @replies. These two aspects of Twitter are vital to online engagement because they are the grammar of Twitter conversations, and the more frequently people use these features, the more connected they feel to other users.[93] The fact that other Twitter accounts reached out by @replying, but @TeaParty.org did not respond, underscores the @TeaParty.org's presentation of a *virtual identity* that is detached and not engaged with its public. In the face-to-face world, this behavior is akin to a person speaking to another person and that person making no response. While undoubtedly ideological groups often use Twitter to reach their followers, rather than to recruit, what we find notable here is that @TeaParty.org fails to even engage with its own supporters by responding to their @replies. If Twitter is a conversation, as a great deal of research suggests,[94] @TeaParty.org is offering a monologue in a space intended for two-way discourse.

Finally, of the 3,013 tweets in our sample, only 11 contain words in all capital letters, a sign of a raised tone or yelling online.[95] Words in all capital letters are significant in computer-mediated speech because they violate norms of politeness that people expect others will follow both on-line and off.[96] The absence of words in all capital letters suggests the @TeaParty.org's presentation of its *virtual identity* is more formally polite than what is common online, where impoliteness often reigns.[97] Certainly, politeness is not a fault, but this finding indicates the @TeaParty.org manages its Twitter presentation using a less conversational or colloquial tone. This contrasts with the name-calling found in an analysis of the movement's Facebook posts,[98] suggesting @TeaParty.org may project a more formal *virtual identity* on Twitter than other Tea Partiers did on Facebook.

Taken together, the @TeaParty.org's use of Twitter presents a *virtual identity* that is cool, detached, and not engaged. It sees itself as sending messages out—in a broadcasting style—to an imagined audience that likely supports its views, rather than trying to engage its followers or even convert opponents. Furthermore, it fails to take advantage of the social-ness of Twitter, as it does not foster camaraderie with followers. In some ways, this suggests that @TeaParty.org's Twitter stream is more akin to a headline news service than a true "masspersonal"[99] space for interaction and discussion. This lack of engagement might be an unconscious act of performance.[100]

CRITICISM MESSAGES

All the @TeaParty.org's tweets were links to news stories or blog posts, not informal comments, but the stories and headlines the account tweets is revealing. It is unsurprising the many media sources the account picked to tweet—such as commentator Glenn Beck's *The Blaze* or Breitbart News Network—are conservative politically, as that fits the TeaParty.org's public identity. However, the content of the tweets it posts is telling. Through-out the tweets, a criticism theme surfaces strongly in the data that belies the formal politeness demonstrated through the absence of words in all capital letters to indicate yelling in computer-mediated speech. This dis-connect—critical tone with lack of yelling—suggests the Twitter account may be aiming to communicate passion rather than impoliteness through its verbiage. This theme is evident in 953 tweets, which constitutes nearly a third (32%) of the sample. @TeaParty.org takes particular critical aim at President Barack Obama (180 tweets); Democratic presidential hopeful Hillary Clinton (132 tweets); immigration (111 tweets); gay rights (74 tweets); Obama's healthcare plan, the Affordable Care Act (59 tweets); and global warming (39 tweets). This finding supports earlier research that has found similar themes in a Tea Party Facebook page,[101] suggesting consistency with @TeaParty.org's *virtual identity*. It should be noted that tweets also took aim at other targets, but these issues were less pronounced overall in the data. For example, a criticism theme surfaces in regard to gun rights in 37 tweets, race in 32 tweets, Muslims or Islam in 29 tweets, a claim of a war on Christianity in 27 tweets, abortion in 21 tweets, First Lady Michelle Obama in 16 tweets, and the media in 13 tweets. In addition, two-thirds of the tweets merely reported the news, without tone or context. Certainly, a political group criticizing its opponents is not unusual because to do so bolsters its own group identity.[102] Yet, the topics @TeaParty.org chooses to focus on in its tweets offer a glimpse of what policies and people it considers its main targets. We discuss each as subthemes.

Disdain for Obama

The largest target of @TeaParty.org's disdain was clearly President Barack Obama. This theme was evident in 19 percent of the total criticism tweets. This confirms early findings that Facebook posts associated with the movement portray Obama as an "overarching national bogeyman."[103] The tweets in our sample blame Obama for ruining the economy, compromising the country's security, devaluing the United States' role as an international arbiter of peace, and foolishly valuing the environment. Scorn is clear in the tweets. For example, the party tweeted: "Rush [Limbaugh]: Obama's Lies on the Economy Revealed" (April 3), "Obama Admin Asserts Dominion Over Creeks, Streams, Wetland, Ditches—Even Big Puddles" (May 27), and "Obama Legacy in Legal Jeopardy" (May 26). This finding suggests that while economic concerns motivated the founding of the Tea Party movement, @TeaParty.org's *virtual identity* is most vested in a single symbol—dislike for President Obama.[104]

Hillary Clinton

The timing of our data collection—amid the 2016 presidential election campaign season—undoubtedly influenced this finding, as Clinton is among the panel of hopefuls. Certainly, it seems logical that @TeaParty.org would take aim at a Democrat who became the nominee. However, it is notable that the criticism theme in regard to Clinton comprised 14 percent of total criticism tweets, while the sample had only two tweets that criticized Bernie Sanders, another Democratic presidential hopeful. Yet Clinton's stature in the Democratic Party, stemming both from her tenure as U.S. secretary of state, a U.S. senator, and first lady to former president Bill Clinton, likely explain this discrepancy. Criticism tweets regarding Hillary Clinton referred to her use of a private server for e-mails while she was secretary of state, her release to the government of e-mails related to that issue, and her handling of the 2012 attacks on U.S. government outposts in Benghazi, Libya,[105] as well as her bid for president. For example, @TeaParty.org tweeted: "RNC on Clinton: Even Nixon Didn't Destroy the Tapes" (March 28) and "Intel Experts: Hillary Clinton's Emails Server A Counterintelligence Disaster of Truly Epic Proportions" (April 8). These tweets are examples of many others that cast the e-mail scandal as very serious. By referencing the secret tapes that former president Richard M. Nixon made and turned over to the government during the Watergate investigation,[106] @TeaParty.org seems to be suggesting that Clinton's failure to turn over all e-mails makes her somehow worse than Nixon, a Republican who resigned in 1974 after the scandal. These tweets point to a *virtual identity* of the @Tea Party.org that focuses on criticizing its opponents in a striking way.

Immigration

The @TeaParty.org's tweets pointedly blame immigration as a major reason for U.S. unemployment and other societal ills. These tweets make up 12 percent of the tweets exhibiting a criticism theme, supporting other research that shows @TeaParty.org is a segment of the movement focused on immigration.[107] For example, the party tweeted on "Illegal Alien Here for One Month, Has Already Raped a 10-Year-Old Girl" (March 11), "Pew Researcher: Illegal Alien Males in Workforce 12 Percent Higher Than U.S.-Born Males" (March 29), and "Illegal Alien Child Molester Avoids Prison . . . Gets Deported . . . Re-Enters USA" (April 2). In addition, tweets show undocumented immigrants as deviating from the norm, which paints immigrants as a threat to the social fabric of the country.[108] Tweets like "Obama announces plan to bring in hundreds of thousands of new guest workers" (March 24), "Illegals Demand Safer Ways to Sneak into United States" (March 11), and "Deaths, Gang Activity Surge as Illegals Flood Border, 30,000 expected" (May 27) depict immigration as a symbolic as well as realistic threat to the economy as well as the country's culture. Symbolic threats challenge national culture or values, while realistic threats jeopardize economic, social, or political resources of whites.[109] These tweets point to a *virtual identity* of the @TeaParty.org that perpetuates the beliefs and even misconceptions of its base.

Same-Sex Marriage and Gay Rights

This topic was particularly salient during our study period, which comprised the months before the U.S. Supreme Court's June 2015 ruling that legalized same-sex marriage nationwide.[110] Tea Party supporters in general frequently claim nominal tolerance of gays and lesbians while categorically defining them as deviating from the norm.[111] Our data reveal this viewpoint strongly, with criticism tweets on this topic making up 8 percent of the total criticism theme. For example, the party tweeted: "Rand Paul: Gay Marriage a Moral Crisis" (March 28), "[Ann] Coulter: Hands Up, Don't Discriminate Against the Gays" (April 1), and "Next Frontier: Gays Use Law to Silence Christians at Work" (April 3). These tweets perpetuate a discourse that ignores systemic discrimination against sexual minorities[112] and denies political action to gay men and lesbians.[113] In so doing, these tweets reveal perhaps an unconscious *virtual identity* that flouts rights for gays, defying a more public script of tenuous tolerance.

Affordable Care Act

While Tea Partiers operated on the fringes of U.S. politics for much of 2009, they became a nationally recognizable movement following President Obama's signing of the Affordable Care Act—dubbed "Obamacare"—on March 30, 2010.[114] That focus is evident in the *virtual identity* @TeaParty.org performs through its tweets. In our sample, a recurring focus was claims the public is being forced into Obamacare and the program is flawed and broken beyond repair. This topic is featured in 6 percent of the criticism tweets. For example, the party tweeted: "Obamacare Begins a Death Spiral" (March 27), "GOP Finally Has Tool to Repeal Obamacare" (March 29), and "Report: 31 Million Uninsured Even With Obamacare" (May 20). It is notable that the party's wrath against this new federal social program is juxtaposed against its considerable acceptance of longstanding federal social programs that predate Obama's presidency, such as Social Security and Medicare.[115]

Global Warming

Another aspect of the @TeaParty.org's criticism theme is how it challenges the belief that climate change is caused by people. The tweets that exhibit this theme comprise 4 percent of the criticism tweets and use sarcasm to diminish those who believe humans are causing environmental harm. For example, the party's tweets, "New Climate Paper Gives Global Warming Alarmists 'One Helluva Beating' " (March 20), "Lefty Lawmaker Warns: Climate Change Makes Women Prostitutes" (March 27), and "Climate Blockbuster: New NASA Data Shows Polar Ice Has Not Receded Since 1979" (May 20), emphasize this denial. Again, this casts the party's *virtual identity* as reinforcing the beliefs of its members and challenging any who deviate.

Collectively, the criticism theme and subthemes found in the @Tea Party.org's Twitter stream depict a *virtual identity* that defines itself by what it dislikes. The party did not use Twitter to proclaim its beliefs, as much as to highlight what it sees as the erroneous conclusions of those with whom it disagrees. By focusing on the negative, rather than the positive in its tweets, @TeaParty.org distances itself from its critics, creating its own identity. By focusing on issues key to its base, it creates an "insular environment in an open community."[116] This also demonstrates political scientist Alan I. Abramowitz's assertion that "the Tea Party movement can best be understood in the context of the long-term growth of partisan-ideological polarization within the American electorate and especially the growing conservatism of the activist base of the Republican Party."[117] Prior research[118] on the Tea Party's more general performance of its identity through Facebook posts found that the party distanced itself from both the Democrats and mainstream Republicans. In our data, we saw much less of this. Eight tweets demonstrate the Tea Party detaching itself from the GOP. For example, the party tweeted: "Glenn Beck QUITS Republican Party: 'They Are Not Good' " (March 18), "[Donald] TRUMP: GOP Establishment 'Folds at Every Corner' on Every Major Issue" (April 16), and "Only Two Republicans Admit They Actually Read Secret Obama Trade Deal" (May 8). However, primarily, our data show that @ TeaParty.org's main target is Obama and the Democrats, not the GOP. One possible explanation for this discrepancy with the Facebook findings may be the timing of our analysis. In the lead up to the 2016 presidential election, Tea Partiers may not want to undermine a Republican bid.

HYPERBOLE AND PROVOCATION

Our final theme reveals a *virtual identity* shaped by exaggerated claims in 77 tweets that spark attention, even if they stretch the truth. We include this theme not because of its frequency but because of the severity of the tone of these tweets.

A glaring example of this was a pictorial meme tweeted on March 13 that shows President Obama crying with the words beside him reading, "Will Obama Leave Office Willingly in January 2017." The link[119] provided in the tweet connects to a poll on TeaParty.org's site that asks people whether they think Obama will willingly leave office at the end of the term. The next day, the party tweeted a similar pictorial meme showing a winking, mischievous Obama and the header, "Does Not Leave in 2017?" This tweet linked to another TeaParty.org poll[120] that asks what should be done if Obama refuses to leave office. Nowhere in either tweet or either webpage is there any substantiation for this fear. These types of tweets betray a perhaps unconscious paranoid *virtual identity* where people panic that they live in a world where they are "spied upon, plotted against, betrayed, and very likely destined for total ruin."[121] This stems from fear that they have nothing left to which they can anchor their American identity, so they flounder frantically to maintain the status quo.

Other tweets also suggest that the party chooses particularly provocative topics and words to rally its followers and distance itself from opponents. It is important to note that this rallying uses tweets to spark followers' emotions but does not rise to level of true online engagement because it lacks the two-way conversation.[122] In some cases, the tweets seem to do this by portraying the @TeaParty.org's beliefs as being criticized. Illustrating this point are the following tweets: "Prof: God of Religious Right Is Fictional 'A-hole'" (April 8), "Shock Study: Cops 25x Less Likely to Shoot Unarmed Blacks than Whites'" (April 8), and "[Mike] Huckabee: American Moving Toward 'Criminalization of Christianity'" (April 24). These tweets further the idea of the @TeaParty.org's *virtual identity* as a paranoid political group—perceiving a conspiracy to be targeted at the whole party and the national as a whole, not just the individual.[123]

@TEAPARTY.ORG'S *VIRTUAL IDENTITY*

Overall, these findings suggest that both idealized[124] and unconscious[125] forces shape the presentation of the @TeaParty.org's *virtual identity*, as shown through its Twitter use and stream. Most notable is @TeaParty.org's lack of engagement through Twitter. Twitter is primarily a social medium that has proven useful to mobilizing the masses for political action[126] and fostering connection between people.[127] However, the party's use of Twitter largely ignores these aspects of the platform. For example, the party uses the #hashtag, a tool of engagement, mainly to label its tweets with #tcot rather than imbue them with emotion.[128] @TeaParty.org does not engage with followers using @replies or retweets or even respond to the nearly 200 @replies from followers it receives. Some have argued the web helps create more of a conversational democracy where "citizens and political leaders interact in new and exciting ways."[129] According to our data, this has largely failed in the @TeaParty.org's Twitter stream. What does this mean for this faction of the larger Tea Party movement's *virtual identity*? It suggests @TeaParty.org performs this identity in a formal way, creating a certain Balkanization of views by posting tweets favorable to its followers but making little attempt to foster a community through a true exchange of dialogue or ideas.

The @TeaParty.org's online performance fits much of its self-proclaimed agenda to support key conservative beliefs, such as lower taxes and spending. Yet, its tweets focused more on oppositional issues—such as criticisms of undocumented immigrants, same-sex marriage, and, in particular,

President Obama—than these core topics. This betrays perhaps an unconscious identity that defines itself more by what it disagrees with than what it supports. While the Tea Party movement formed out of fiscal concerns[130] in an effort to save America, @TeaParty.org's tweets seem more aimed at pleasing its base of followers. Our results dovetail with prior research of a Tea Party Facebook page: "Instead of forming cogent arguments and discussing those arguments, most of the comments were designed to strengthen the group's identity at the expense of productive debate."[131] The tweets' frequent use of hyperbole and provocation further support this point, suggesting a paranoid political organization with "heated exaggeration, suspiciousness, and the conspiratorial fantasy."[132]

NOTES

1. Zizi A. Papacharissi, "Without You, I'm Nothing: Performance of the Self on Twitter," *International Journal of Communication* 6 (2012): 1989–2006.

2. Zizi A. Papacharissi, *A Private Sphere: Democracy in a Digital Age* (Malden, MA: Polity Press, 2010).

3. Gina Masullo Chen and Hinda Mandell, "Conclusion: Predicting a New Scandal Environment in the 21st Century," in *Scandal in a Digital Age*, eds. Hinda Mandell and Gina Masullo Chen (New York: Palgrave Macmillan, 2016).

4. Nancy K. Baym, "Interpersonal Life Online," in *The Handbook of New Media*, eds. Leah A. Lievrouw and Sonia Livingstone (Washington, DC: Sage Publications, 2010), 35–54; Natalya N. Bazarova, Jessie G. Taft, Young Hyung Choi, and Dan Cosley, "Managing Impressions and Relationships: Self-Presentation and Relational Concerns Revealed through the Analysis of Language Style," *New Media & Society* 32 (2010): 12–141.

5. Definition of "virtual," *Merriam-Webster*, accessed November 6, 2015, http://www.merriam-webster.com/dictionary/virtual.

6. Howard Rheingold, *The Virtual Community: Homesteading on the Electronic Frontier* (Cambridge, MA: The MIT Press, 2000).

7. Definition of "virtual," *Merriam-Webster*, accessed November 6, 2015, http://www.merriam-webster.com/dictionary/virtual.

8. Gina Masullo Chen, Paromita Pain, and Deepa Fadnis, "Over-Sharing in a Political Sex Scandal," in *Scandal in a Digital Age*, eds. Hinda Mandell and Gina Masullo Chen (New York: Palgrave Macmillan, 2016); Papacharissi, "Without You, I'm Nothing: Performance of the Self on Twitter," 1989; Bernie Hogan, "The Presentation of the Self in the Age of Social Media: Distinguishing Performance and Exhibitions Online," *Bulletin of Science, Technology & Society* 30, no. 6 (2010): 377–386.

9. Andrea B. Hollingworth and Noshir S. Contractor, "New Media and Small Group Organizing," in *The Handbook of New Media*, eds. Leah A. Lievrouw and Sonia Livingstone (Washington, DC: Sage Publications, 2010): 114–133.

10. Janet Fouts, *Social Media Success! Practical Advice and Real-World Examples of Social Media Engagement* (Cupertino, CA: HappyAbout.Info, 2009).

11. David T. Morin and Mark A. Flynn, "We Are the Tea Party! The Use of Facebook as an Online Political Forum for the Construction and Maintenance of

In-Group Identification during 'GOTV' Weekend," *Communication Quarterly* 62 (2014): 115–133; Karen M. Douglas, Craig McGarty, Ana-Maria Bliuc, and Girish Lala, "Understanding Cyberhate: Social Competition and Social Creativity in On-line White Supremacist Groups," *Social Science Computer Review* 23, no. 1 (2005): 68–76; Hee-Woong Kim, Jun Raymond Zheng, and Sumeet Gupta, "Examining Knowledge Contribution from the Perspective of an Online Identity in Blogging Communities," *Computers in Human Behavior* 27, no. 5 (2011): 1760–1770.

12. Alan I. Abramowitz, "Grand Old Tea Party: Partisan Polarization and the Rise of the Tea Party Movement," in *Steep: The Precipitous Rise of the Tea Party*, eds. Lawrence Rosenthal and Christine Trost (Los Angeles, CA: University of California Press, 2012), 209.

13. Devin Burghart, "View from the Top," in *Steep: The Precipitous Rise of the Tea Party*, eds. Lawrence Rosenthal and Christine Trost (Los Angeles, CA: University of California Press, 2012), 67–97.

14. Burghart, "View from the Top," 67–97; Theda Skocpol and Vanessa Williamson, *The Tea Party and the Remaking of Republican Conservatism* (New York: Oxford University Press, 2012).

15. Skocpol and Williamson, *The Tea Party and the Remaking of Republican Conservatism*.

16. Burghart, "View from the Top."

17. Erving Goffman, *The Presentation of the Self in Everyday Life* (New York: Anchor Books, 1959).

18. Baym, "Interpersonal Life Online," 35–38.

19. Baym, "Interpersonal Life Online," 41; Papacharissi, "Without You, I'm Nothing: Performance of the Self on Twitter," 1995.

20. Judith A. Hamera, and Dwight Conquergood, "Performance and Politics: Themes and Arguments," in *The Sage Handbook of Performance Studies*, eds. D. Soyini Madison and Judith A. Hamera (Thousand Oaks, CA: Sage, 2006), 422.

21. Matt A. Barreto, Betsy L. Cooper, Benjamin Gonzalez, Christopher S. Parker, and Christopher Towler, "The Tea Party in the Age of Obama: Mainstream Conservatism or Group Anxiety," *Political Power and Social Theory* 22 (2011): 105–137; Christopher F. Karpowitz, J. Quin Monson, Kelly D. Patterson, and Jeremy C. Pope, "Tea Time in America? The Tea Party Movement and Midterm Elections," *PS Political Science and Politics* 44 (2011): 303–309; Knickerbocker, "What Is the 'Tea Party' and How Is It Shaking up American Politics?" *Christian Science Monitor*, September 15, 2010, http://www.csmonitor.com/USA/Elections/2010/0915/What-is-the-tea-party-and-how-is-it-shaking-up-American-politics; Morin and Flynn, "We Are the Tea Party! The Use of Facebook as an Online Political Forum for the Construction and Maintenance of In-Group Identification during 'GOTV' Weekend"; Skocpol and Williamson, *The Tea Party and the Remaking of Republican Conservatism*.

22. Jared A. Goldstein, "The Tea Party Movement and the Perils of Popular Originalism," *Arizona Law Review* 53 (2011): 827.

23. Burghart, "View from the Top"; Jeffrey M. Jones, "Debt, Government Power among Tea Party Supporters' Top Concerns," *Gallup Poll*, July 5, 2010.

24. Alan I. Abramowitz, "Partisan Polarization and the Rise of the Tea Party Movement," American Political Science Association annual meeting, Berkeley, CA, September 1–4, 2011.

25. Alan I. Abramowitz and Steven Webster, "All Politics Is National: The Rise of Negative Partisanship and the Nationalization of U.S. House and Senate Elections in the 21st Century," Midwest Political Science Association annual meeting, Chicago, IL, April 16–19, 2015.

26. Skocpol and Williamson, *The Tea Party and the Remaking of Republican Conservatism.*

27. Goldstein, "The Tea Party Movement and the Perils of Popular Originalism," 827.

28. Tali Mendelberg, *The Race Card: Campaign Strategy, Implicit Messages, and the Norm of Equality* (Princeton, NJ: Princeton University Press, 2001); Jill Quadagno, *The Color of Welfare: How Racism Undermined the War on Poverty* (New York: Oxford University Press, 1994); Ira Katznelson, *Fear Itself: The New Deal and the Origins of Our Time* (New York: W.W. Norton & Co., 2013); Rogers M. Smith, *Civic Ideals: Conflicting Visions of Citizenship in U.S. History* (New Haven, CT: Yale University Press, 1997).

29. Christine Trost and Lawrence Rosenthal, "The Rise of the Tea Party," in *Steep: The Precipitous Rise of the Tea Party,* eds. Lawrence Rosenthal and Christine Trost (Los Angeles, CA: University of California Press, 2012), 1–22.

30. John M. O'Hara, *A New American Tea Party: The Counterrevolution against Bailouts, Handouts, Reckless Spending, and More Taxes* (Hoboken, NJ: John Wiley & Sons, 2010).

31. Richard Hofstadter, *The Paranoid Style in American Politics* (New York: Anchor Books, 1965), 26.

32. Barreto, Cooper, Gonzalez, Parker, and Towler, "The Tea Party in the Age of Obama: Mainstream Conservatism of Out-grout Anxiety?" 105–137.

33. Tea Party Movement, *Encyclopaedia Brittanica,* accessed July 20, 2015, http://www.britannica.com/topic/Tea-Party-movement.

34. Morin and Flynn, "We are the Tea Party!" 117.

35. Abramowitz, "Grand Old Tea Party: Partisan Polarization and the Rise of the Tea Party Movement."

36. Vanessa Williamson, Theda Skocpol, and John Coggin, "The Tea Party and the Remaking of Republican Conservatism," *Perspectives on Politics* 9 (2011): 25–43; Skocpol and Williamson, *The Tea Party and the Remaking of Republican Conservatism.*

37. Bruce Drake, "In the Polls, Tea Party Support Falls Among Republicans," *Pew Research Center,* May 21, 2014, http://www.pewresearch.org/fact-tank/2014/05/21/in-the-polls-tea-party-support-falls-among-republicans/.

38. Martha T. Moore, "Tea Party Sets Sights on White House," *USA Today,* May 11, 2015, http://www.usatoday.com/story/news/politics/elections/2015/05/11/tea-party-2016-presidential-election/70884260/.

39. Corbin Hiar, "How the Tea Party Utilized Digital Media to Gain Power," *MediaShift,* October 28, 2010, http://mediashift.org/2010/10/how-the-tea-party-utilized-digital-media-to-gain-power301/; Morin and Flynn, "We are the Tea Party!" 117.

40. Morin and Flynn, "We Are the Tea Party!" 117.

41. Darrel Enck-Wanzer, "Barack Obama, the Tea party, and the Threat of Race: On Racial Neoliberalism and Born Again Racism,"*Communication, Culture, & Critique* 4 (2011): 23–30; Morin and Flynn, "We Are the Tea Party!" 117.

42. Goffman, *Presentation of the Self in Everyday Life,* 15.

43. Judith Butler, *Bodies that Matter: On the Discursive Limits of Sex* (New York, NY: Routledge, 1993); Judith Butler, *The Psychic Life of Power* (Stanford, CA: Stanford University Press, 1997).

44. Hamera and Conquergood, "Performance and Politics: Themes and Arguments," 419–425; Papacharissi, "Without You, I'm Nothing: Performances of the Self on Twitter," 1990.

45. Papacharissi, *A Private Sphere: Democracy in a Digital Age*, 77.

46. Richard Schechner, *Performance Theory* (New York: Routledge, 2003), 265; Papacharissi, "Without You, I'm Nothing: Performances of the Self on Twitter," 1991.

47. Hamera and Conquergood, "Performance and Politics: Themes and Arguments," 419–425.

48. Bernie Hogan, "The Presentation of the Self in the Age of Social Media: Distinguishing Performances and Exhibitions Online"; Goffman, *Presentation of the Self in Everyday Life*, 30; Papacharissi, "Without You, I'm Nothing: Performance of the Self on Twitter," 1191.

49. Butler, *Bodies that Matter: On the Discursive Limits of Sex*; Butler, *The Psychic Life of Power*; Papacharissi, "Without You, I'm Nothing: Performance of the Self on Twitter," 1191.

50. Hogan, "The Presentation of the Self in the Age of Social Media: Distinguishing Performances and Exhibitions Online," 378.

51. Hogan, "The Presentation of the Self in the Age of Social Media: Distinguishing Performances and Exhibitions Online," 379; Goffman, *Presentation of the Self in Everyday Life*.

52. Kevin Lewis, Jason Kaufman, and Nicholas Christakis, "The Taste for Privacy: An Analysis of College Students' Privacy Settings in an Online Social Network," *Journal of Computer-Mediated Communication* 14 (2008): 79–100.

53. Hogan, "The Presentation of the Self in the Age of Social Media: Distinguishing Performance and Exhibitions Online."

54. Ibid., 378.

55. Gina Masullo Chen, "Tweet This: A Uses and Gratifications Perspective on How Active Twitter Use Gratifies a Need to Connect with Others," *Computers in Human Behavior* 27 (2011): 755–672.

56. Alice E. Marwick and danah boyd, "It Tweet Honestly, I Tweet Passionately: Twitter Users, Context Collapse, and the Imagined Audience," *New Media & Society* 13 (2011): 114–133.

57. Eden Litt, "Knock, Knock. Who's There? The Imagined Audience," *Journal of Broadcasting & Electronic Media* 56 (2012): 330–345.

58. Alice E. Marwick and danah boyd, "To See and Be Seen: Celebrity Practice on Twitter," *Convergence* 17 (2011): 139–158.

59. Chen, Pain, and Fadnis, "Over-Sharing in a Political Sex Scandal."

60. Julian Ausserhofer and Axel Maireder, "National Politics on Twitter: Structures and Topics of a Networked Public Sphere," *Information, Communication, & Society* 16 (2013): 291–314.

61. Andranik Tumasjan, Timm O. Sprenger, Philipp G. Sandner, and Isabell M. Welpe, "Predicting Elections with Twitter: What 140 Characters Reveal about Political Sentiment," *Proceedings of the Fourth International AAAI Conference on Weblogs and Social Media*, 178–185.

62. Papacharissi, "Without You, I'm Nothing: Performances of the Self on Twitter," 1989.

63. Ibid., 1992.

64. Hollingworth and Contractor, "New Media and Small Group Organizing."

65. Nancy K. Baym, *Personal Connections in the Digital Age* (Malden, MA: Polity, 2015).

66. Nhung T. Nyuyen, Anson Seers, and Nathan S. Hartman, "Putting a Good Face on Impression Management: Team Citizenship and Team Satisfaction," *Journal of Behavioral and Applied Management* 9, no. 2 (2008): 148–168.

67. Sarita Yardi and danah boyd, "Dynamic Debates: An Analysis of Group Polarization Over Time on Twitter," *Bulletin of Science, Technology & Society* 30, no. 5 (2010): 316–327.

68. Douglas, McGarty, Bliuc, and Lala, "Understanding Cyberhate: Social Competition and Social Creativity in Online White Supremacist Groups"; Kim, Zheng, and Gupta, "Examining Knowledge Contribution from the Perspective of an Online Identity in Blogging Communities."

69. Morin and Flynn, "We Are the Tea Party!"

70. Papacharissi, "Without You, I'm Nothing: Performances of the Self on Twitter," 1995.

71. Elfriede Fursich, "In Defense of Textual Analysis," *Journalism Studies* 10 (2009): 240.

72. Kent Lindkvist, "Approaches to Textual Analysis," in *Advances in Content Analysis*, ed. Karl Erik Rosengren (Beverly Hills, CA: Sage, 1981); Donald G. McTavish and Ellen B. Pirro, "Contextual Content Analysis,"*Quality & Quantity* 24 (1990): 245–265.

73. Erika Darics, "Politeness in Computer-Mediated Discourse of a Virtual Team," *Journal of Politeness Research* 6 (2010): 129–150.

74. Joan Cassell, "The Relationship of Observer to Observed in Peer Group Research," *Human Organization* 36 (1977): 412–416.

75. Cassell, "The Relationship of Observer to Observed in Peer Group Research"; Gina Masullo Chen, "Don't Call Me That: A Techno-Feminist Critique of the Term Mommy Blogger," *Mass Communication and Society* 16 (2013): 510–523.

76. Papacharissi, "Without You, I'm Nothing: Performance of the Self on Twitter."

77. Fursich, "In Defense of Textual Analysis," 240.

78. Papacharissi, "Without You, I'm Nothing: Performance of the Self on Twitter," 1997.

79. Bernard Berelson, *Content Analysis in Communication Research* (Glencoe, ILL: Free Press, 1952).

80. Chen, "Don't Call Me That: A Techno-Feminist Critique of the Term Mommy Blogger."

81. Papacharissi, "Without You, I'm Nothing: Performance of the Self on Twitter."

82. Chen, "Tweet This: A Uses and Gratifications Perspective on How Active Twitter Use Gratifies a Need to Connect with Others," 755–672.

83. Cassell, "The Relationship of Observer to Observed in Peer Group Research"; Chen, "Don't Call Me That: A Techno-Feminist Critique of the Term Mommy Blogger"; Fursich, "In Defense of Textual Analysis"; Lindkvist,

"Approaches to Textual Analysis"; Papacharissi, "Without You, I'm Nothing: Performances of the Self on Twitter."

84. Gina Masullo Chen, "Why Do Women Bloggers Use Social Media? Recreation and Information Motivations Outweigh Engagement Motivations," *New Media & Society* 17, no. 1 (2015): 24–40.

85. Chen, "Tweet This: A Uses and Gratifications Perspective on How Active Twitter Use Gratifies a Need to Connect with Others," 755.

86. danah boyd, Scott Golder, and Gilad Lotan, "Tweet, Tweet, Retweet: Conversational Aspects of Retweeting on Twitter," *Proceedings of the Forty-Second Hawai'i International Conference on System Sciences* (Kauai, HI: IEEE Press, 2009); Courtenay Honeycutt and Susan C. Herring, "Beyond Microblogging: Conversation and Collaboration via Twitter," *Proceedings of the Forty-Second Hawai'i International Conference on System Sciences* (Los Alamitos, CA: IEEE Press, 2009).

87. Marco Toledo Bastos, Rafael Luis Galdini Raimundo, and Rodrigo Travitzki, "Gatekeeping on Twitter: Message Diffusion in Political Hashtags," *Media, Culture & Society* 35 (2013): 260–270; Evandro Cunha, Gabriel Magno, Giovanni Comarela, Virgilio Almeida, Marcos Ande Goncalves, and Fabricio Benevenuto, "Analyzing the Dynamic Evolution of Hashtages on Twitter: A Language-based Approach," *Proceedings of the Workshop on Language in Social Media* (2011): 58–65.

88. Andre Brock, "From the Blackhand Side: Twitter as a Cultural Conversation," *Journal of Broadcasting and Electronic Media* 46 (2012): 529–549.

89. Baym, "Interpersonal Life Online," 38.

90. Yobie Benjamin, "The Secret Twitter War for America's Independents: #tcot vs. #p2," *SFGate.com*, accessed July 24, 2015, http://blog.sfgate.com/ybenjamin/2010/07/27/the-secret-twitter-war-for-americas-independents-tcot-vs-p2/.

91. Bastos, Raimundo, and Travitzki, "Gatekeeping on Twitter: Message Diffusion in Political Hashtags," 264.

92. Irfan Chaudhry, "#Hashtags for Change: Can Twitter Promote Social Progress in Saudi Arabia," *International Journal of Communication* 8 (2014): 943–961; Gina Masullo Chen, "Social Media," in *The Routledge Companion to Race and Media*, ed. Christopher P. Campbell (New York: Routledge, forthcoming in 2016); Sherri Williams, "Digital Defense: Black Feminists Resist Violence with Hashtag Activism," *Feminist Media Studies* 15 (2015): 341–358.

93. Chen, "Tweet This: A Uses and Gratifications Perspective on How Active Twitter Use Gratifies a Need to Connect with Others," 755–672.

94. boyd, Scott Golder, and Gilad Lotan, "Tweet, Tweet, Retweet: Conversational Aspects of Retweeting on Twitter"; Chen, "Tweet This: A Uses and Gratifications Perspective on How Active Twitter Use Gratifies a Need to Connect with Others"; Fouts, *Social Media Success! Practical Advice and Real-World Examples of Social Media Engagement*; Honeycutt and Herring, "Beyond Microblogging: Conversation and Collaboration via Twitter"; Marwick and boyd, "It Tweet Honestly, I Tweet Passionately: Twitter Users, Context Collapse, and the Imagined Audience."

95. Darics, "Politeness in Computer-Mediated Discourse of a Virtual Team," 138.

96. Ibid.

97. Kevin Coe, Kate Kenski, and Stephen A. Rains, "Online and Uncivil? Patterns and Determinants of Incivility in Newspaper Website Comments," *Journal of Communication* 64 (2014): 658–679.

98. Morin and Flynn, "We Are the Tea Party!" 122.

99. Joseph B. Walther, Caleb T. Carr, Scott Seung W. Choi, David C. DeAndrea, Jinsuk Kim, Stephanie Tom Tong, and Brandon Van Der Heide, "Interaction of Interpersonal Peer, and Media Influence Sources Online," in *Networked Self: Identity, Community, and Culture on Social Network Sites*, ed. Zizi A. Papacharissi (New York: Routledge, 2010), 34.

100. Butler, *Bodies that Matter: On the Discursive Limits of Sex*; Butler, *The Psychic Life of Power*.

101. Morin and Flynn, "We Are the Tea Party!" 122.

102. Ibid.

103. Ibid., 123.

104. Barreto, Cooper, Gonzalez, Parker, and Towler, "The Tea Party in the Age of Obama: Mainstream Conservatism or Group Anxiety," 105–137; Angie Maxwell and T. Wayne Parent, "The Obama Trigger: Presidential Approval and Tea Party Membership," *Social Science Quarterly* 93 (2012): 1384–1401.

105. Eric Lipton, Noam Scheiber, and Michael S. Schmidt, "Clinton Emails Became the New Focus of Benghazi Inquiry," *The New York Times*, October 11, 2015, http://www.nytimes.com/2015/10/12/us/politics/clinton-emails-became -the-new-focus-of-benghazi-inquiry.html?_r=0.

106. Carl Bernstein and Bob Woodward, *All the President's Men* (New York: Simon & Schuster, 1974).

107. Burghart, "View from the Top."

108. Michael A. Zarate, Berenice Garcia, Azenett A. Garza, and Robert T. Hitlan, "Cultural Threat and Perceived Realistic Group Conflict as Dual Predictors of Prejudice," *Journal of Experimental Social Psychology* 40 (2004): 99–105.

109. Lawrence D. Bobo, "Group Conflict, Prejudice, and the Paradox of Contemporary Racial Attitudes," in *Eliminating Racism*, eds. Phyllis A. Katz and Dalmas A. Taylor (New York: Springer, 1988), 85–109; Lawrence D. Bobo and Cybelle Fox, "Race, Racism, and Discrimination: Bridging Problems, Methods, and Theory in Social Psychological Research," *Social Psychology Quarterly* 66 (2003): 319–332.

110. Robert Barnes, "Supreme Courts Rules Gay Couples Nationwide Have Right to Marry," *The Washington Post*, accessed July 25, 2015, http://www.washington post.com/politics/gay-marriage-and-other-major-rulings-at-the-supreme-court/ 2015/06/25/ef75a120-1b6d-11e5-bd7f-4611a60dd8e5_story.html.

111. Barreto, Cooper, Gonzalez, Parker, and Towler, "The Tea Party in the Age of Obama: Mainstream Conservatism or Group Anxiety," 105–137.

112. S. G. Massey, "Polymorphous Prejudice: Liberating the Measurement of Heterosexuals' Attitudes toward Lesbians and Gay Men," *Journal of Homosexuality* 56 (2009): 147–172.

113. Kimberly B. Dugan, "Just Like You: The Dimensions of Identity Presentations in an Antigay Contested Context," in *Identity Work in Social Movements*, eds. Jo Reger, Daniel J. Myers, and Rachel L. Einwohner (Minneapolis, MN: University of Minnesota Press, 2008), 21–46.

114. Barreto, Cooper, Gonzalez, Parker, and Towler, "The Tea Party in the Age of Obama: Mainstream Conservatism or Group Anxiety," 105–137.

115. Williamson, Skocpol, and Coggin, "The Tea Party and the Remaking of Republican Conservatism"; Skocpol and Williamson, *The Tea Party and the Remaking of Republican Conservatism*.

116. Morin and Flynn, "We Are the Tea Party!" 127.

117. Abramowitz, "Grand Old Tea Party: Partisan Polarization and the Rise of the Tea Party Movement," 197; see also Abramowitz, "Partisan Polarization and the Rise of the Tea Party Movement"; Abramowitz and Webster, "All Politics Is National: The Rise of Negative Partisanship and the Nationalization of U.S. House and Senate Elections in the 21st Century."

118. Morin and Flynn, "We Are the Tea Party!" 127.

119. "Will Obama Leave Office Willingly in January 2017?" *TeaPartyInfo.Org*, accessed July 25, 2015, http://teapartyinfo.org/polling/10370_will_obama _leave_office_willingly_in_January_2017_.php.

120. "What Can Be Done if Obama Does Not Leave Office in 2017?" *TeaPartyInfo.Org*, accessed July 25, 2015, http://teapartyinfo.org/polling/ 10371_what_can_be_done_if_obama_does_not_leave_office_in_2017_.php.

121. Hofstadter, *The Paranoid Style in American Politics*, 45.

122. boyd, Golder, and Lotan, "Tweet, Tweet, Retweet: Conversational Aspects of Retweeting on Twitter"; Honeycutt and Herring, "Beyond Microblogging: Conversation and Collaboration via Twitter."

123. Hofstadter, *The Paranoid Style in American Politics*, 26.

124. Goffman, *The Presentation of the Self in Everyday Life*.

125. Butler, *Bodies that Matter: On the Discursive Limits of Sex*; Butler, *The Psychic Life of Power*.

126. Chaudhry, "#Hashtags for Change: Can Twitter Promote Social Progress in Saudi Arabia"; Chen, "Social Media"; and Williams, "Digital Defense: Black Feminists Resist Violence with Hashtag Activism."

127. Chen, "Tweet This: A Uses and Gratifications Perspective on How Active Twitter Use Gratifies a Need to Connect with Others," 755–672.

128. Brock, "From the Blackhand Side: Twitter as a Cultural Conversation," 529–549.

129. Anthony Corrado and Charles M. Firestone, eds., *Elections in Cyberspace: Toward a New Era in American Politics* (Washington, DC: Aspen Institute, 1996), 17.

130. Goldstein, "The Tea Party Movement and the Perils of Popular Originalism," 827.

131. Morin and Flynn, "We Are the Tea Party!" 127.

132. Hofstadter, *The Paranoid Style in American Politics*, 3.

Chapter 10

Screaming at Obama: The Tea Party and the Affordable Care Act

Glenn W. Richardson Jr.

The emergence of social media in the twenty-first century has opened up the world of political communication to scholars in ways never before possible. Where previously, measurement of public opinion was principally done through survey research, and typically based on surveys taken at a single moment in time, scholars are now able to observe popular attitudes as they are organically expressed (rather than in response to researcher's questions), as they flow from person to person, and as they evolve over time. Processes that had previously been obscured are revealed, and the entire political communication ecosystem has been transformed into an increasingly interactive and more diverse one, albeit also one heavily monitored and tracked by marketers and manipulators of various types.

This chapter seeks to take advantage of the incredible opportunity afforded by social media (in particular Twitter) in an attempt to try to reveal important aspects of one of the defining political movements of early twenty-first century U.S. politics, the Tea Party. Our effort will track the movement's evolution during the year leading up to the 2010 midterm congressional elections. There can be no mistaking the pivotal role the election of Barack Obama played in this process, and in particular the virulent opposition to the president's proposed health law that animated the insurrection. Probing further, we will explore the relative influence of political philosophy or ideology in Tea Party discourse as well as the language of religious and ethnic identity.

TEA PARTY RISING

The election in 2008 of Barack Hussein Obama as the 44th president of the United States, in the midst of a historic financial meltdown, concomitant economic dislocation, and social upheaval at home and abroad, constituted a political cauldron that germinated the most talked about mass movement in a generation. It began with a scream.

On February 19, 2009, barely a month after Obama's inauguration, CNBC analyst Rick Santelli, reporting from the floor of the Chicago Mercantile Exchange, unleashed "the rant." He denounced the American Recovery and Reinvestment Act of 2009 (aka "the stimulus") as "promoting bad behavior" and questioned whether "we really want to subsidize the losers' mortgages." He raised the specter of Cuban communism and called for a "Chicago tea party in July."[1] Santelli's remarks were picked up by the *Drudge Report* and other online self-styled conservative activists and gave name to an emergent protest movement.

By the eve of the 2010 midterm elections, the Tea Party movement had become a major force, credited with "upend(ing) the existing political order, reshaping the debate in Washington, defeating a number of prominent lawmakers and elevating a fresh cast of conservative stars."[2] Yet, even with millions of dollars pouring in from powerful national groups such as Freedom Works and Americans for Prosperity, a systematic attempt to document the size and scope of the movement by the *Washington Post* found "not so much a movement as a disparate band of vaguely connected gatherings that do surprisingly little to engage in the political process."[3] The *Post*'s months-long effort to track down all of the Tea Party groups in America suggested that "the breadth of the tea party may be inflated."

The *Post*'s attempt to "understand the network of individuals and organizations at the heart"[4] of the incipient movement, however, may be a case of looking for links in all the wrong places. In their study of the Tea Party, Theda Skocpol and Vanessa Williamson found "about 1000 groups spread across all 50 states" and noted that "some local Tea Parties are very large with online membership lists of 1000 people or more."[5] They estimate some 200,000 people nationwide to be members of active local Tea Parties.[6]

Skocpol and Williamson's work represents perhaps the most thorough extant academic exploration of the Tea Party movement's supporters and beliefs. Their multi-method research program combines data drawn from national and state-level surveys, in-depth interviews, interrogation of public records, news reports, statements made by elected officials and media figures flying the Tea Party banner, and analysis of the Tea Party presence on the Internet. Yet as they acknowledge, "We could not interview every Tea Partier, visit more than a small group of meetings, or regularly track many blogs."[7] We aim to supplement their work and the standing literature by training our analytic lens on the use of social media by Tea Party supporters, which, when combined with advanced content analysis software, actually does allow us to examine truly comprehensive and exhaustive streams of data.

To wit, a thriving Tea Party exists on Twitter, which, as Skocpol and Williamson note, is where the Tea Party first coalesced in the days after Santelli's rant.[8] Each day during the months leading up to the November 2, 2010, election, an average of nearly 11,000 messages per day included the hashtag "teaparty." Hashtags (the "#" symbol followed by descriptive text, e.g., #teaparty) are used to allow people looking for messages on a given topic to find them by searching for the corresponding hashtag. Figure 10.1 documents the number of #teaparty messages (or tweets) on Twitter between October 1 and November 7, 2010. The number of tweets peaks at better than 21,000 on Election Day.

Figure 10.1
Number of #Teaparty Tweets: October 1–November 6, 2010

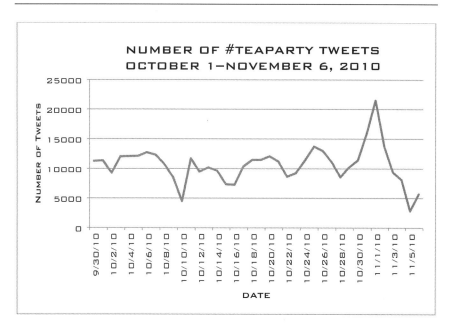

In his book *The True Believer: Thoughts on the Nature of Mass Movements*, Eric Hoffer describes "the militant man of words" who "prepares the ground for the rise of a mass movement."[9] For Hoffer, this is accomplished "1) by discrediting prevailing creeds and institutions and detaching them from the allegiance of the people; 2) by indirectly creating a hunger for faith in the hearts of those who cannot live without it, so that when the new faith is preached it finds an eager response among the disillusioned masses; 3) by furnishing the doctrine and the slogans of the new faith; 4) by undermining the convictions of the "better people"— those who can get along without faith—so that when the new fanaticism makes its appearance they are without the capacity to resist it. They see no sense in dying for convictions and principles, and yield to the new order without a fight."[10]

#Teaparty can be seen as a twenty-first-century incarnation of Hoffer's "true believer." We aim to substantiate this claim by analysis of nearly a year's worth of #teaparty messages on Twitter. The tweets and the counts in this report are based on a collection using Desktop Archivist, which is a Windows program that accesses the Twitter API every five minutes with a search query. The data was collected by G. R. Boynton of the University of Iowa, who graciously shared them with the author. Messages were collected between December 9, 2009, and July 2, 2010, and between September 6, 2010, and November 7, 2010.

Figure 10.2 documents the number of #teaparty tweets between mid-December, 2009, and June 30, 2010. The volume of messages remained below 10,000 per week until the week of Obama's State of the Union address. From that point forward, the weekly message count would fall below 20,000 on only three occasions. The two weeks immediately following the speech marked an initial early-spring peak (an average of roughly 34,000 #teaparty messages per week were sent during this period). The second major peak in #teaparty messages occurs following the passage of the healthcare bill (the Patient Protection and Affordable Care Act of 2009) on March 25 and during the run-up to the April 15 "Tax Day" protests organized by Tea Party members. The State of the Union address, healthcare bill, and "Tax Day" are powerful symbols of the prevailing system the true believer seeks to undermine. Indeed, Obama himself was consistently a major, if not the major, focus of #teaparty messages, as was his major nemesis in what might be called the "twitterverse," former Alaska Governor Sarah Palin.

Figure 10.3 indicates that #teaparty messages between mid-December 2009 and June 30, 2010, including references to Obama, follow the same pattern of #teaparty messages in general, peaking initially after the State of the Union and again after the passage of the healthcare bill. (Messages including *Barack*, *Obama*, *Barackobama*, or *BHO* were coded as referring to Obama). Palin references follow both in pattern and magnitude,

Figure 10.2
Number of #Teaparty Tweets: December 2009–June 2010

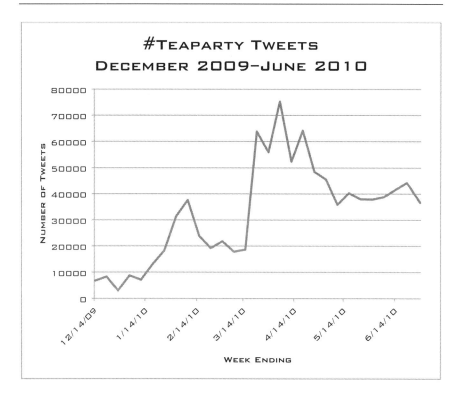

even eclipsing Obama references when #teaparty volume reached its peak. (Messages including the words *Sarah, Sarahpalin, Palin,* or *SarahpalinUSA* were coded as referring to Palin). Figure 10.3 also charts the number of #teaparty messages referencing then FOX media megastar Glenn Beck. (Messages including the words *Beck, Glenn, Glennbeck* or *Glennbec* were coded as referring to Beck). The Beck numbers generally follow the same twists of increase and decrease of #teaparty volume generally, though at a substantially lower level.

Figure 10.4 documents the percentage of all #teaparty messages referencing Obama, Palin, and Beck between mid-December 2009 and June 2010. Obama and Palin references largely move in tandem. As the share of #teaparty messages referencing Obama increases, so too does the share of messages referencing Palin, with two notable exceptions. Typically, approximately 15 percent of all #teaparty messages reference Obama. The share of all #teaparty messages referencing Obama peaked in late June when better than one in every four messages referenced Obama. By contrast, the peak share for #teaparty messages mentioning

Figure 10.3
#Teaparty References: October 1–November 6, 2010

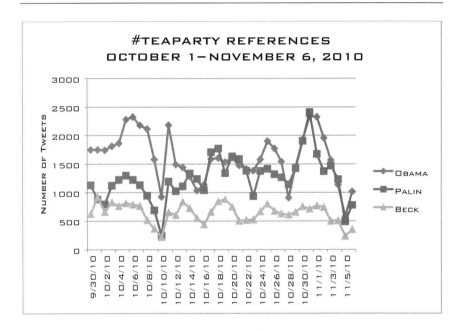

Figure 10.4
Share of #Teaparty Tweets December 2009–June 2010

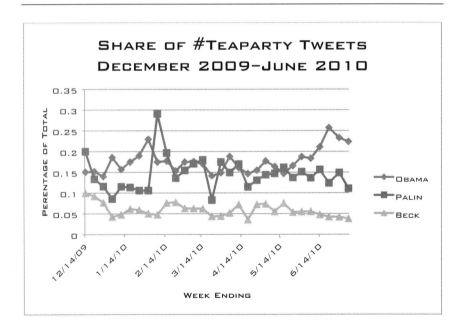

Palin (29%) occurred during the first full week of February, the week after Obama's early peak following the State of the Union address when 23 percent of all messages referenced Obama. The peak of Palin's share of references represents nearly triple the share of such references from the previous week, while at the same time the share of #teaparty messages referencing Obama falls from 23 to 17 percent.

A different pattern unfolded during the fall campaign. The data depicted in Figure 10.5 indicate that between September and November, the trendlines representing Obama and Palin references as a share of total #teaparty messages almost always move in different directions. As Obama references increase as a share of the total, Palin references decrease, and *vice versa*. Throughout this period, Obama references average 15 percent of total #teaparty messages while Palin references average 12 percent of total. Of the eight total week-to-week intervals, Obama and Palin references move in different directions seven times. This may well be due to the explicitly oppositional nature of electoral politics, particularly a midterm congressional election—often seen as a referendum on the performance of the incumbent president.

To explore more deeply the substance of #teaparty messages we must broaden our analytical lens. Hoffer suggests that "the faultfinding man

Figure 10.5
Share of #Teaparty Tweets: September–November 2010

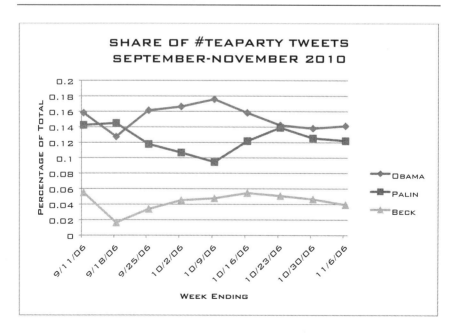

of words, by persistent ridicule and denunciation, shakes prevailing
beliefs and loyalties . . ."[11] One simple and available measure of this ridicule and denunciation may be the way different political figures are
referred to, specifically whether they are referred to solely by their last
name or whether they are referred to by their first name or by both their
first and last name. Last name only references may reflect a distancing of
sorts or an aversion to the figure in question.

Both Sarah Palin and Glenn Beck are more likely to be referred by either
their first name or their full name in #teaparty messages than Barack
Obama in the period between December 2009 and June 2010, as shown in
Figure 10.6. (Messages that included a first name or a first name and a last
name were coded as including a first name.) Here, Beck references are something of an outlier, with "Glenn" and "Glenn Beck" references consistently
exceeding those to "Beck" alone. For Beck, during December, first name
and full name references combined outnumber last name only references
by factors of four, three, and six in adjacent weeks. After December, the
number of first name and full name references are roughly equal to the number of last name only references for Beck. Neither Obama nor Palin ever
even come close to this ratio. In fact, the size of the Beck numbers may
obscure the notable differences between Obama and Palin. Throughout the
entire time period, at no point do first name or full name references for

Figure 10.6
#Teaparty First Name/Last Name Ratio: December 2009–June 2010

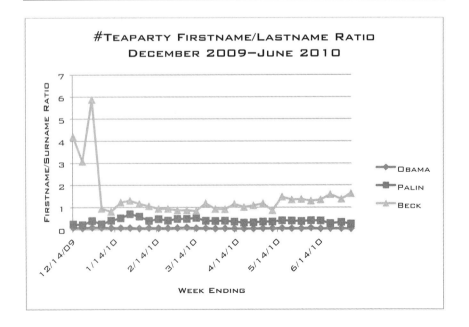

Obama account for as large a share of Obama references as first name or full name references to Palin. Overall, Palin's share of first name or full name references runs about three to four times higher than Obama's.

To further probe the substance of #teaparty references it may be useful to explore the occurrence and co-occurrence of particular words and phrases in #teaparty tweets. Provalis QDA Miner and WordStat content analysis software can generate such data. (The software will generate word counts or frequencies and exclude common words. For example, the first 10 words listed alphabetically beginning with the letter "a," that are excluded are: a, able, about, above, accord, accordingly, across, actually, after, and afterwards.) The volume of #teaparty messages peaked in the days before the November 2 election. Some 27,452 messages were sent in the two days immediately preceding the vote. The top five words appearing in #teaparty tweets during this period (with percentage of total tweets in parentheses) were *GOP* (25.2%), *Obama* (13.5%), *vote* (10.4%), *Palin* (8.3%) and *politics* (5.4%). For this analysis, other hashtags were excluded (e.g., #TCOT, #TLOT, etc.), except *GOP* which can serve both as a hashtag and a substantive word. Hashtags such as TCOT (top conservatives on Twitter) and TLOT (top libertarians on Twitter) are common enough to rank among the top 10 most common *words* had they been included. This also suggests the conclusion of the *Washington Post* analysis (Gardner 2010) that tea partiers "do surprisingly little to engage in the political process" may have been somewhat unwarranted.

The most frequently appearing words in this period speak to a politics polarized along ideological and partisan lines. Not only do Obama and Palin appear among the top five most frequent words, but the other political figures frequently mentioned are also of the polarizing sort: *Pelosi*, *Reid*, *O'Donnell*, *Paul*, and *Miller* are all among the top 100 most common words. Other words among the top 300 most common include assorted variations of the two major parties (e.g., *dems*, *Democrats*) and sundry ideological monikers, including socialism, conservative, liberal, left, and so on. Notably, neither *moderate* nor *centrist* appears among the top 300 most frequently appearing words during this period.

In the two days after the vote, the top five most frequent words in #teaparty messages were *GOP* (26.4%), *Obama* (13.4%), *election* (8.1%), *Palin* (6.7%), and *House* (4.2%). We can also look for co-occurrences, or words that appear together. While the five most frequently occurring words in the two days before and the two days after the election are largely identical, the co-occurrence pattern for the word *Obama* differs. In the two days before the election, the most common co-occurrences with *Obama* are: *GOP*, *dems*, *vote*, *dem*, and *America*. In the two days after the election, the five most common substantive words are *GOP*, *dems*, *million*, *cost*, and *trip*, reflecting a widely reported but erroneous claim that the president's trip to India was costing U.S. taxpayers $200 million a day.

By contrast, during the week leading up to the passage of the health-care bill, the top five most frequently occurring substantive words in #tea-party messages are *GOP* (23.4%), *Obama* (11.4%), *killthebill* (9.0%), *Obamacare* (6.9%), and *bill* (6.1%). During the final three days leading to the bill's passage, the top five words appearing in #teaparty tweets men-tioning Obama are *health, care, GOP, bill,* and *CNN*. During this same time period, the top five phrases (of two words or more) appearing in #teaparty tweets mentioning Obama are *health care, voted for Obamacare, vote 'em out in Nov, Glenn Beck,* and *Sarah Palin*.

Further insight into the tone and substance of #teaparty messages may be gleaned from a cursory "keyword-in-context" analysis. While there are too many references to Obama (more than 1,000 per day) to examine com-prehensively, we can simply glance at the first several messages to grasp at the general tenor. Here, one notes both relatively innocuous phrases like "[t]his needs to go viral Obama phrma deal," and "Obama funded Alin-sky School for Radicals, NO SUPRISE!," as well as more pointed commen-tary such as "we must lay bare the ugly core of Obama's evil designs," "HCR is just like Death Panels for the old, but this plan is for the DEATH OF AMERICA AND FREEDOM as we know it," and "The Coming Obama Gestapo And The War Against Christianity."

For Hoffer, one of the key tasks of the militant man of words is to pro-vide the doctrine and slogans of the new faith.[12] Twitter is incredibly well-suited to the task, and Sarah Palin's tweets alone have generated slo-gans and phrases that have spread like wildfire across the political dis-course. "Death panels," "refudiate," and "lamestream media," being among the most notable. While the genesis of the word *Obamacare* is less certain, its currency on #teaparty is demonstrable.

The data in Figure 10.7 indicate that from mid-December 2009 through early-March 2010, the number of #teaparty messages referencing "Obama-care" never rose above 500 per week. By mid-March, the number has jumped to nearly 1,000, a number that would increase by a factor of nearly five in the next week. Obamacare references would stay above 4,000 per week for three consecutive weeks before slowly declining to a more or less stable level of roughly 2,500 per week, better than five times the amount found early in 2010.

While the total volume of #teaparty messages did increase over this same period (see Figure 10.2), the percentage of all #teaparty tweets including "Obamacare" also rose during this period as documented in Figure 10.8. The share of #teaparty messages including "Obamacare" begins at about 3 percent in early-December and falls to less than 1 percent in mid-February. It then rises and exceeds 7 percent in the two weeks surrounding the passage of the healthcare bill. It then falls to roughly 5 percent and would continue to fluctuate in the range between 5 and 6 percent for the rest of the spring.

Figure 10.7
Obamacare References: December 2009–June 2010

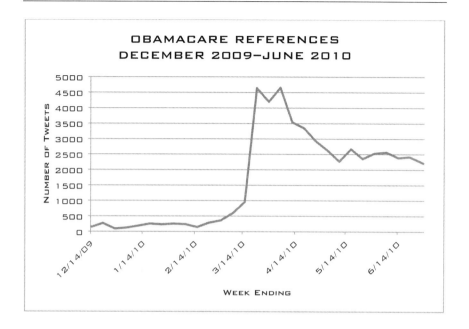

Figure 10.8
Obamacare Share of #Teaparty Messages: December 2009–June 2010

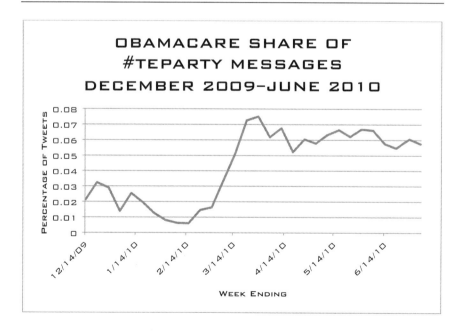

The five most common words co-occurring with Obamacare in the two days leading up to the vote on final passage of the healthcare bill in the U.S. senate were *Nov, voted, DNC, vote,* and *remember.* A casual keyword-in-context perusal of "Obamacare" finds comments such as "Obamacare & War Against Tyranny," "SHAME ON ALL WHO VOTED 4 obamacare YOU HAVE DEFIED THE WILL OF THE PEOPLE & you have hurt USA YOU WILL PAY at the polls," "Remember Bean, Melissa [D] from IL-8 voted for Obamacare—vote em out in Nov," and "ObamaCare is getting its ass sued off."

EXPLAINING THE TEA PARTY: PHILOSOPHY, POLITICS, POPULISM, AND IDENTITY

Observers of the Tea Party have identified several key elements of Tea Party discourse.[13] They include political philosophy (of both conservative and libertarian stripe), constitutionalism, populism, politics and political action, and issues of identity politics (including religion and ethnicity). To gauge the relative incidence of the different strains of Tea Party expression, we have used QDA Miner content analysis software and constructed dictionaries consisting of words and phrases consistent with each of these substantive foci.

Our coding scheme unfolds in three levels. The first or broadest level consists of coding language consistent with the broad categories identified as philosophy, politics, populism, and identity. We also deploy a separate category for conservative language.

The second level of our analysis subdivides these categories further. Philosophical language is coded as either libertarian or constitutional. The separate conservative language code is subdivided into political and social variants. Our politics code is comprised of five subdivisions: health care; Obama; Republican candidates, parties and leaders; Democratic candidates, parties, and leaders; and political action. We divide populism into political and economic subcategories. Identity is cleaved into separate political, religious, and ethnic/geographic subcategories.

Our third level of analysis consists of the actual words that make up each of the second-level categories. A full listing can be found in Appendix I.

Technical limitations with even state-of-the-art hardware and software preclude us from analyzing simultaneously the entire stream of messages we have created for this project, which spans nearly a full year. Accordingly, we will analyze approximately one- to two-month periods, focusing on three periods of intense activity: the run-up to the president's 2010 State of the Union address, the period surrounding the vote on final passage of the Patient Protection and Affordable Care Act, and the fall campaign season.

Winter of Discontent

Our first analytical period begins on December 9, 2009, and extends through February 27, 2010. Figure 10.9 compares the incidence of language consistent with our level-one dictionaries during this period.

By far, the largest category of Tea Party talk on Twitter during this period focused on politics. Nearly 60 percent of all messages included language in our politics dictionary (comprised of the subcategories of health care, Obama, GOP and Democratic parties and figures, and political action), roughly twice as large as the share of messages, including language from our populism dictionary, the second biggest category. Constitutional and libertarian philosophy language was found in about 10 percent of cases, about the same level as identity language. Least common among our categories was conservative language, found in roughly 5 percent of cases.

Our second-level dictionaries allow us to disaggregate the component parts of our politics dictionary. Figure 10.10 indicates that 40 percent of all cases included "politics" language involving Republicans. Next most common was Obama language (about 17% of all tweets), followed by

Figure 10.9
Substantive Focus of #Teaparty Language: December 9, 2009–February 27, 2010

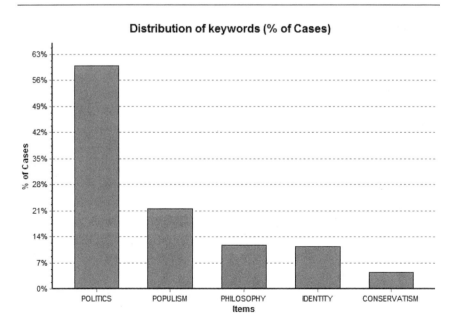

Figure 10.10
Substantive Focus of #Teaparty "Politics" Language: December 9, 2009–
February 27, 2010

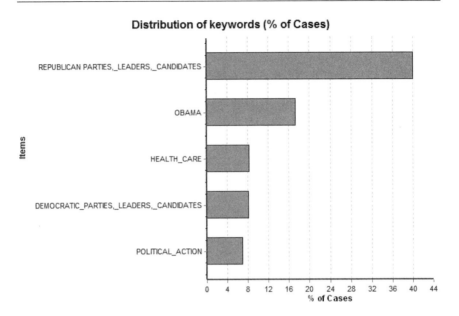

Distribution of keywords (% of Cases)

language of health care, Democratic figures, and political action, each found in about 7–8 percent of all #Teaparty Twitter messages during this period.

We can drill down deeper into the data to explore how changes in the level of Obama language affect the level of other language categories over time. Figure 10.11 plots the incidence of Obama, constitutional, libertarian, and (political) populist language by day during this time period. Increased Obama language appears to drive increases in libertarian and populist language but not increases in constitutional language.

Because increases in Obama language also tend to coincide with increases in language about Republicans, it is possible that it is the latter driving the increases in libertarian and particularly in populist language. Figure 10.12, however, suggests this is not the case. The trend line of political populist language is much more closely tied to the Obama line than to the Republican line.

Obamacare

The volume of activity in the #teaparty Twitter stream would reach its zenith surrounding the congressional action leading to the passage of the Patient Protection and Affordable Care Act on March 25, 2010.

Figure 10.11
#Teaparty Obama, Constitutional, Libertarian, and (Political) Populist
Language: December 9, 2009–February 27, 2010

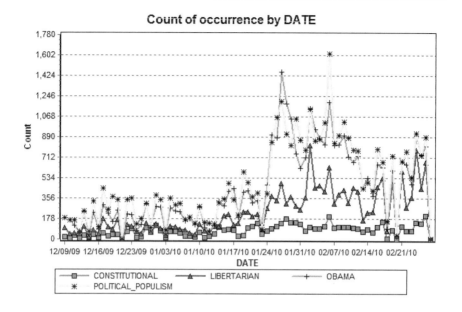

Figure 10.12
#Teaparty Obama, Republican, and (Political) Populism Language:
December 9, 2009–February 27, 2010

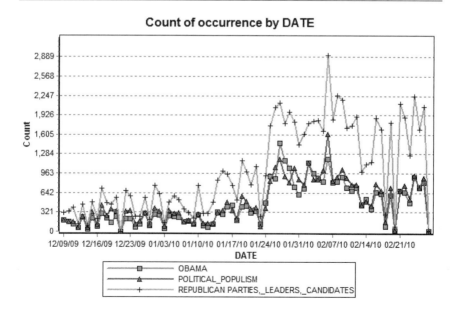

Figure 10.13
Substantive Focus of #Teaparty Language: February 28–April 4, 2010

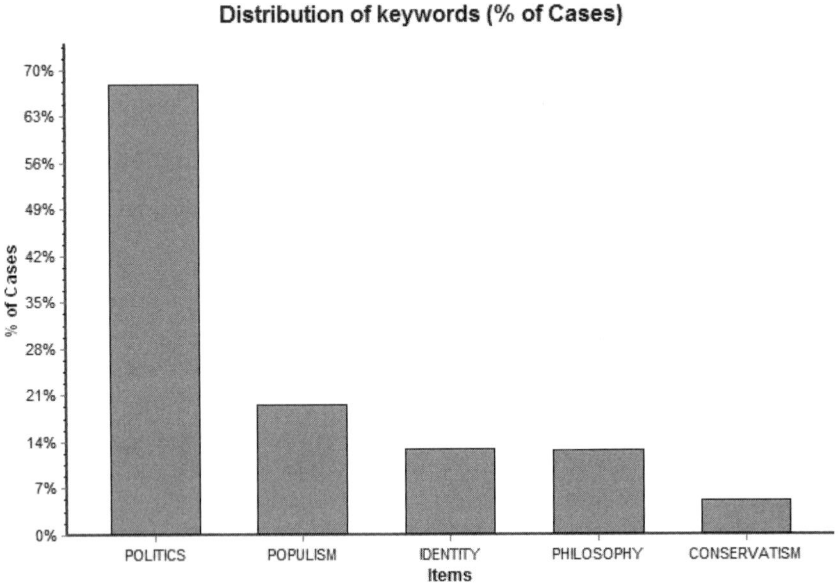

Distribution of keywords (% of Cases)

Figure 10.13 presents the percentage of cases in which language from each of our level-one dictionaries is found. There is little change from the pattern found during the earlier period, though politics language increases slightly, populist language ebbs somewhat, and identity language, which had been just behind philosophy language, moves just ahead of it.

Examination of our second-level dictionaries provides better purchase toward unpacking the substantive composition of the #teaparty Twitter stream during this period. Figure 10.14 provides the breakdown of the component parts of our politics category by percentage of cases. In contrast to the results from the earlier period (Figure 10.10), we find slightly less talk of Republicans and Obama, slightly more of Democrats, a discernable increase in political action language, and, unsurprisingly, a quadrupling of healthcare language.

Figure 10.15 indicates that as before, increased references to Obama are most closely tied to increased populist language. While the incidence of populist, libertarian, constitutional, and Obama references are fairly stable in the weeks leading up to passage of the bill, there is explosion of communication surrounding the final vote. Here, the incidence of constitutional and libertarian language roughly doubles. Yet, that increase pales in comparison to the rise of Obama references, which in turn is dwarfed by the outburst of populist language.

Figure 10.14
Substantive Focus of #Teaparty "Politics" Language: February 28–April 4, 2010

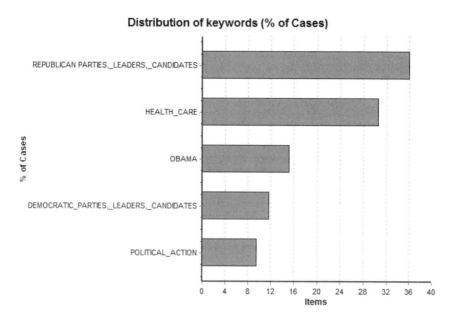

Distribution of keywords (% of Cases)

Figure 10.15
#Teaparty Obama, Constitutional, Libertarian, and (Political) Populism Language: February 28–April 4, 2010

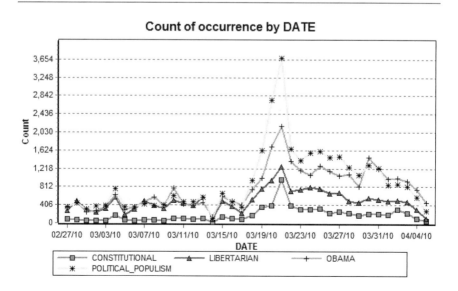

Count of occurrence by DATE

Our second-level dictionaries also allow us to explore the dynamics surrounding identity politics and the Tea Party. Figure 10.16 indicates a notable spike in language of ethnic/geographic identity just as the debate over "Obamacare" peaks. The incidence of such language would fall from peak levels but nonetheless remains elevated during the duration of this time period compared to what it had been previously.

On balance, our findings pertaining to the healthcare debate provide nuance to some widely held notions respecting the Tea Party. While its populist thread was dominant, there was also an increase in constitutional language as the Affordable Care Act neared final passage. We also found a concomitant distinct but minor rise in the language of ethnic/geographic identity.

The Midterms

The final time frame we will examine covers the final weeks of the midterm congressional election of 2010. Our data for this period begin with September 28 and end with October 29, the last Friday before Election Day. As before, we begin by analyzing the frequency of language in our level-one dictionaries.

As was the case in the two previous time periods examined, Figure 10.17 indicates that we find politics language most common, occurring in roughly 55 percent of all messages. Populist language is next most prevalent, found

Figure 10.16
#Teaparty Ethnic/Geographic Identity Language: February 28–April 4, 2010

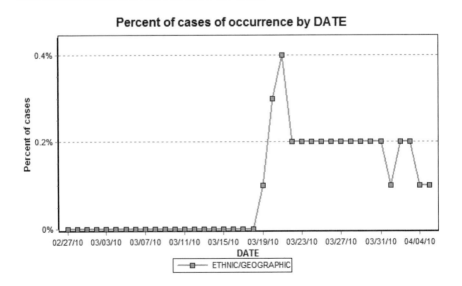

Figure 10.17
Substantive Focus of #Teaparty Language: September 28–October 29, 2010

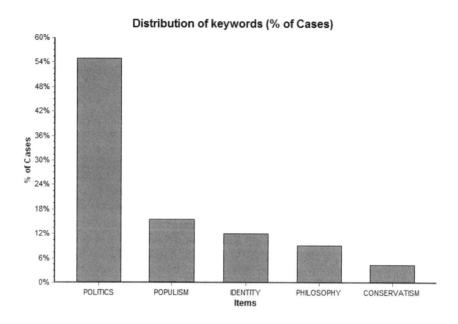

in almost 16 percent of cases. That level, however, reflects a slow downward trend in populist language over time. Identity language is next most frequent (in 12% of messages), reflecting an upward trend over time.

Exploring our level-two dictionaries allows us to more specifically follow the flow of Tea Party discourse on Twitter during the final month of the campaign. Figure 10.18 indicates that as in previous time frames, references to Republicans are most common, followed by references to Obama and Democrats, respectively. The references to Democratic figures represent an increase, however, from previous periods, and coincide with an increase in the language of political action (which grew in each successive time frame we have looked at). Notably, references to health care fall to just 3 percent of cases, far lower than the one-third of messages with healthcare language in the period surrounding the debate over the Affordable Care Act. Indeed a greater percentage of messages included healthcare language in the first time period we looked at (8%) than in the final month of the election, when just 3 percent of tweets included health care language.

Our level-two dictionaries also allow us to chart the relative incidence of populist, libertarian, and constitutional language over time during this period. Figure 10.19 shows Obama references and language of populism

Figure 10.18
Substantive Focus of #Teaparty "Politics" Language:
September 28–October 29, 2010

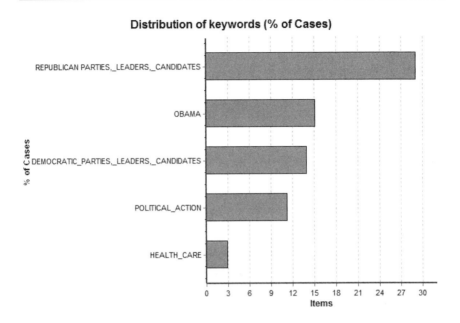

Distribution of keywords (% of Cases)

Figure 10.19
#Teaparty Obama, Constitutional, Libertarian, and Political Populism
Language: September 28–October 29, 2010

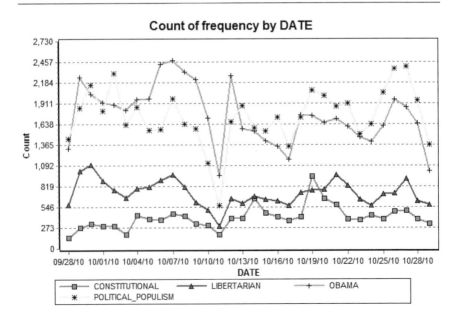

Count of frequency by DATE

loom large in Tea Party discourse for the entirety of the month leading up to Election Day. As before, our analysis suggests that populist language was considerably more prevalent than the language of either libertarian or constitutional philosophy during this time period.

CONCLUDING THOUGHTS: ASSESSING THE TEA PARTY AND SOCIAL MEDIA

The Tea Party movement proved to be the animating if not the overwhelming force in the 2010 midterm elections. The movement was an amalgamation of grassroots activists and seasoned party professionals. While as a movement it often appeared to elude efforts to define and track it, its life in the twitterverse was rich and revealing. We found evidence that #teaparty was home to the "militant man of words" described by Eric Hoffer in his book *The True Believer: Thoughts on the Nature of Mass Movements*. #Teaparty communication was rife with efforts to "discredit prevailing creeds and institutions." The "hunger for faith in the hearts of those who cannot live without it" was constantly stoked by those "furnishing the doctrine and slogans of the new faith."

Our analysis of the trend in #teaparty messages over time suggests that the Patient Protection and Affordable Care Act of 2009 carried great significance for the Tea Party movement. It created a spike in #teaparty messages after which the volume of such messages would never fall to the levels it had before the act's passage. For the tea partiers, Barack Obama's singular legislative accomplishment proved to be his singular liability.

We also found Tea Party discourse to be dominated by talk of everyday politics: candidates, parties, and leaders. Populism, far more than either conservatism or libertarianism, was readily apparent. While the whole Tea Party discourse on Twitter does not point to a cadre of constitutional scholars-in-residence, we did note arise in constitutional language during the time frame surrounding passage of the Affordable Care Act. While that debate would produce the largest volume of #teaparty traffic, with fully one-third of messages during that period on point, by the fall campaign for Congress only 3 percent of messages included healthcare language. Language of ethnic/geographic identity also increased over the three time periods we looked at.

This work suggests the utility of analyzing Twitter feeds as a valuable contribution to understanding the nature and flow of political thought and communication. It also points to the salience of the psychology of mass movements in the contemporary political environment.

APPENDIX I

Coding Framework

Level One	Level Two	Level Three
Philosophy	Constitutional	Constitution, constitutional, constitutionality, constitutional amendment, unconstitutional, rights, founding fathers, founders, framers, limited government, limited govt., Second Amendment, First Amendment, Fifth Amendment, Tenth Amendment, Ninth Amendment, Fourteenth Amendment, 1st Amendment 2nd Amendment, 4th Amendment, 5th Amendment 9th Amendment, 10th Amendment, 14th Amendment, 16th Amendment, Sixteenth Amendment, sovereignty, sovereign, enumerated, limited powers, enumerated powers, reserved powers, separations of powers, checks and balances, reserve clause, due process, equal protection, just compensation, "life, liberty, and property," free speech, freedom of speech, freedom of press, supreme court, Federalist, anti-federalist, federalism, Article I, Article II, Article III, Article IV, Article V, Article VI, executive, judiciary, commerce, Commerce Clause, commerce power, *Wickard vs. Filburn*, *Gonzales vs. Raich*, Wickard, Gonzales, taxing power, globalism, states' rights
	Libertarian	Liberty, libertarian, freedom, takings, tyranny, tyrannical, mandate, tax, taxes, taxing, taxpayer, fees, fee, regulation, regulations, market, markets, free-market, free-markets, small government, small govt., low taxes, individual, individual responsibility, zoning, eminent domain, tlot, burdensome, entrepreneur, government forcing, forced by government, Ron Paul, ronpaul
Politics	Health Care	Health care, individual mandate, Obamacare, repeal, death panels, abolish Medicare, Medicare, Medicaid, HMO, HCR, health care reform, kill the bill, killthebill, killbill, deathcare, health care bill, health bill, health care, health insurance, health, public option, bureaucratic takeover, socialized medicine

(continued)

NOTE: To conserve space, not all variants on individual names included in our analysis are included in this listing.

APPENDIX I   (Continued)

Level One	Level Two	Level Three
	Obama	Barack, Barack Obama, Obama, BHO, BO, birth certificate, community organizer, stimulus, porkulus, ARRA, teleprompter, Chicago-style, Chicago style, Chicago politics, White House, whitehouse, POTUS
	Democratic Parties, Leaders, Candidates	Democrats, D's, Democrat, Democratic, DNC, DCCC, DSCC, Biden, Pelosi, Nancy Pelosi, Reid, Harry Reid, Keith Olbermann, Rahm, Rahm Emmanuel, Emmanuel, Clinton, Hillary, Hilary, Landrieu, Barbara Boxer, Barbaraboxer
	Parties, Leaders, Candidates	GOP, Republicans, R's, Boehner, McConnell, Cantor, RNC, Brown, Scott Brown, scottbrown, Coakley, Rubio, Limbaugh, Rush, Rush Limbaugh, rushlimbaugh, Beck, Glenn Beck, glennbeck, Palin, Sarah Palin, Sarahpalin, Sarah, Mark Levin, Crapo, Mike Crapo, Mark Kirk, Kirk, Joe Wilson, Bachmann, michellebachmann, Cuccinelli, McCain, O'Donnell, christineo'donnell, Sharon Angle, sharonangle, Kelly Ayotte, kellyayotte, Scott Walker, scottwalker, Joe Walsh, joewalsh, Mike Lee, mikelee, Joe Miller, joemiller, Miller
	Political Action	Vote, votefor, call, meet, gather, demand, collect, ballot, referendum, donate, contribute, support, tell your friends, rally, march, assemble, convene, fund, tea party nation, tea party convention, Tax Day
Populism	Political Populism	Angry, anger, resent, resentment, elites, liberal elites, liberals, spending, unions, take our country back, I want my country back, take back, takeitback, handsoff, Washington, DC, D.C., government, handout, government hand-out, government hand-out, hand-outs, welfare, free-loaders, freeloaders, free-loader, freeloader, entitlement, dole, moochers, mooching, redistribution, hardworking, food stamps, criminals, Ivy League, Hollywood, Harvard, Yale, Princeton, politicians, deserving, undeserving, the media, liberal media, FOXNEWS, MSNBC, foxnews, grassroots, grass roots, we the people, wethepeople, the people, movement, thepeople, conspiracy, pro-tester, us, them, we, tea party rally, can you hear us now, social engineering, sell out

(continued)

APPENDIX I (Continued)

Level One	Level Two	Level Three
	Economic Populism	Wall Street, Wall St, bankers, banksters, banks, hedge fund, vulture capitalist, big business, billionaires, millionaires, billionaire, millionaire, plutocrats, plutocracy, corporations, corporate, bail-outs, bailouts, deficits, loopholes, loophole, debt, the rich, the wealthy, wealthy, the 1%, the one percent, the 1 percent, balanced budget, tax revolt, TARP, middle class, big-business, big business, bigbusiness, monied, moneyed, moneyman, moneymen, money man, money men
Conservatism	Political Conservatism	Tradition, order, duty, honor, country, respect, hierarchy, responsibility, obligation, patriotism, police, law and order, crime, punish, punished, punishment, criminal, lawbreaker, prison, penalty, law enforcement
	Social Conservatism	Abortion, gays, lesbians, gay marriage, pro-life, God, Church, religion, religious, Christian, Christianity, Christ, Jesus, evangelical, evangelicals, Bible, biblical, scripture, scriptures, values, family values, moral, morality, sanctity of life, traditional values, culture of life, traditional marriage, marriage, sacred, stem-cell, stem cell, worship, prayer, pray, born-again, sanctity of marriage, a man and a woman
Identity	Ethnic/ Geographic Identity	Black, NAACP, immigrants, immigration, illegals, illegal immigrants, undocumented, Mexican, Kenyan, African, blacks, Latino, Hispanic, white, Caucasian, protect our borders, border control, minorities, racial, racist, racism, aliens, black man, Mexican, Arab, Arabic, Chinese, Korean, Asian, European, Europe, Mexico, Kenya, Africa
	Religious Identity	Muslim, Muslims, Islam, Islamic, Islamics, Islamo-facist, Christian, fundamentalist, mosque, Jewish, Jew, synagogue, Sharia, Buddhist, Hindu, protestant, Lutheran, Baptist, Catholic, Mormon
	Political Identity	socialist, socialism, facism, facist, Nazi, Nazism, communist, communisim, liberalism, liberal, liberals, conservative, conservatives, Marxist, Marxism, conservative, conservatism, capitalism, capitalist

NOTES

1. CNBC, "Santelli's Tea Party," 2009, http://www.cnbc.com/id/15840232?video=1039849853.

2. Amy Gardner, "Gauging the Scope of the Tea Party Movement in America," *Washington Post*, October 24, 2010, http://www.washingtonpost.com/wp-dyn/content/article/2010/10/23/AR2010102304000.html?nav=emailpage.

3. Ibid.

4. Ibid.

5. Theda Skocpol and Vanessa Williamson, *The Tea Party and the Remaking of Republican Conservatism* (New York: Oxford University Press, 2012).

6. Ibid., 22.

7. Ibid., 17.

8. Ibid., 7.

9. Eric Hoffer, *The True Believer: Thoughts on the Nature of Mass Movements* (New York: Harper and Row, 1951), 139.

10. Ibid.

11. Ibid.

12. Ibid.

13. Skocpol and Williamson, *The Tea Party and the Remaking of Republican Conservatism*; Elizabeth Price Foley, *The Tea Party: Three Principles* (Cambridge: Cambridge University Press, 2012).

Chapter 11

Social Media versus the Madmen: Notes from the Frontlines of a Digital Insurgency

Bruce E. Drushel

On December 6, 2012, Tori Cardinale, whose house on Staten Island had been damaged by super storm Sandy six weeks before, posted a status update to her Facebook account.[1] The status update mentioned that her insurance agency had approved only an extremely low reimbursement for her extensive damages. She requested that other users report or share her message, so that her insurance company would be brought to justice via the media. Next to the text was a picture, presumably of her home, with plywood covering the front door, picture window, and garage door. Standing in front were two people holding a banner that read, "Thank you Allstate Homeowners Insurance ... approved for $165.35 in damages ... We are in 'Good Hands'!![2]

Within a week, the posting had been shared more than 84,000 times. As of January 2015, the total had grown to 87,256. At issue was whether damage caused by a fallen tree was the result of wind or flooding.[3] Wind damage would be covered by their homeowners policy, flooding would not.

According to an article posted in January 2013 by silive.com, the online version of the *Staten Island Advance* newspaper, Allstate claimed it had paid what its spokesperson called "significant dollars" toward the claim, though the company would not disclose the amount. The Cardinales had been seeking as much as $250,000, which apparently was more than what Allstate had paid to that point.[4]

The incident suggests more than just the potential of compelling personal struggles to "go viral"; it also suggests the potential for social media platforms to present a narrative that successfully competes with corporate marketing and promotional efforts. In Allstate's case, the marketing budget truly amounts to "significant dollars," estimated at $641.4 million.[5] Other examples abound, including blog entries belittling the ineptitude of Internet and cable company customer service, online horror stories of personal computers (and their replacements) that are dead-on-arrival, and devastatingly critical Twitter and Facebook reviews from early in a film's release weekend that are implicated when attendance for subsequent showings plummets.

Despite the fact that the vehicles that deliver them lack the slick production values of television commercials, print advertisements, or even online banner ads that are just a click away, these social media counter-narratives indeed may be more persuasive because, as Two-Step Flow Theory tells us, messages conveyed by those we know frequently are more trusted than those conveyed by media.

This chapter uses two well-established communication theories— Two-Step Flow Theory and Social Networking Theory—to examine the potential power of social media to defeat traditional marketing campaigns as well as potential strategies corporations might pursue in an effort to reduce their impact.

NOT IN GOOD HANDS BUT IN GOOD COMPANY

Cardinale's frustration with Allstate makes for a noteworthy, but hardly singular, story. In 2006, AOL received embarrassing and ill-timed publicity regarding its handling of customer requests to cancel their accounts. Weblog author Vincent Ferrari uploaded a five-minute audio excerpt of his encounter with an overly aggressive customer service representative who refused to allow him to end his relationship with the Internet service provider, in spite of his having asked to do so pointedly nearly 30 times in 21 minutes.[6] Requests for downloads of the clip grew exponentially to more than 300,000, so many that it both caused the host file server to crash and drew attention from the *New York Times*, the *New York Post*, and NBC News, as well as the video-sharing website YouTube. To make matters worse, coverage of the incident reminded the public that, two years before, AOL had signed agreements with both the Federal Trade Commission and the New York State attorney general's office to reform its cancellation practices.[7] Ferrari's post revealed an AOL reality that stood in sharp contrast to the customer-friendly web portal presented in AOL marketing which, as recently as 2003, was powered by a budget of close to $1 billion. Shortly after the incident, a corporate memo repudiated the practices and urged its employees to treat customers as though all of their calls would end up on the web.[8]

Just weeks before the Ferrari incident, a Comcast customer in Washington, DC, uploaded video to YouTube of a company technician who had come to his home to repair a faulty modem but was forced to call in to his employer's customer support number himself when the trouble proved intractable. In a scene that resonated with the experiences of many of Comcast's customers, the video showed that the technician had fallen asleep on the customer's sofa while waiting on hold for an hour. The customer added the rock ballad, "I Need Some Sleep," as background to the video clip. An estimated half-million people watched the one-minute clip.[9] Needless to say, the not-so-subtle message about Comcast customer support in the upload differed from those in Comcast's $1.6 billion annual marketing campaigns.

While each of these cases proved embarrassing for the corporations involved and provided both some solace for their aggrieved customers and entertainment for followers on social media, they pale in comparison to the damage believed inflicted on personal computer maker Dell at least in part by journalism professor and blogger Jeff Jarvis. Dell had been known as a direct-sales producer of low-cost customizable computer hardware and had taken first place in J. D. Power's first customer satisfaction surveys of the industry in 1991.[10] Under new CEO Kevin Rollins, Dell in 2004 began outsourcing its customer service functions, with disastrous results.[11] Beginning in June 2005, Jarvis made a series of well-publicized weblog entries detailing his experience with Dell customer service (referred to by Jarvis as "Dell Hell"), highlighted by a nonworking PC and a nonworking replacement. It took an e-mail message to Dell's chief marketing officer before he finally received a refund. In the meantime, Dell's customer satisfaction index began to decline, its quarterly profits plummeted 28 percent,[12] and its familiarity and favorability scores decreased, even as its advertising budget was increasing to upward of $744 million. The final humiliation occurred, ironically, a year to the day after Jarvis began his blog entries, when a Dell laptop caught fire at a conference in Japan.[13] Ultimately, Rollins was forced out as CEO, replaced by the return of company founder Michael Dell,[14] who championed initiatives designed to enable better communication with its customers.[15]

The Cardinale, Ferrari, Finkelstein, and Jarvis stories are compelling, not just because they are examples of mainstream awareness of content that originated in social media nor because they may be perceived as modern-day David against Goliath stories, but because they demonstrate the potential of a Facebook or Twitter message, weblog entry, or YouTube video with little or no associated marginal cost to negate the effects of corporate advertising budgets in the millions or even billions of dollars. Though these social media missives lacked both the reach and frequency of the corporate media campaigns, their viral dissemination likely enjoyed the credibility of a message endorsed by one friend to several, as opposed to the slick but impersonal efforts of a profit-making entity to burnish its own image.

THE FLOW OF INFORMATION

The tremendous growth in the use of social media and evidence of its greater ability than traditional media to persuade its users has renewed the interest of scholars from political science, advertising, and marketing in the Two-Step Flow Theory of communication, which was first described in the pioneering work of Elihu Katz and Paul Lazarsfeld in the 1950s.[16] Katz and Lazarsfeld hypothesized the existence in individuals' informal social networks of so-called opinion leaders who influenced others like themselves. But leaders were thought to differ from their followers in that they were socially more gregarious and more active and were more frequent media users.[17] Specifically, leaders were thought to occupy a strategic social location (with acquaintances both inside and outside of a social group) and were perceived by followers as competent and as people they would like to emulate.[18] The influence of opinion leaders was thought not to be overt and evidence suggested they could be passive in their leadership, though Two-Step Flow Theory seemed to address only active leaders.[19] According to Gabriel Weimann, leaders do more than merely draw the attention of others to an issue, product, or behavior—they recommend, model key behaviors, persuade, and even metaphorically infect unsuspecting followers with their message.[20] Psychologist Edwin Hollander has argued that leaders are best defined in terms of their ability to influence the attitudes and behavior of their followers.[21]

As tends to be the case with many long-lived theories that gain a measure of acceptance, Two-Step Flow Theory had critics who pointed to its shortcomings. Those include the implication that opinion leaders rely upon media only and that influence may involve a single step or more than two steps;[22] its reliance upon self-reports of attitudes and behaviors for empirical validation, its lack of methodological sophistication, the expense the study of specific media content involved, its tendency to underestimate the power of media relative to the power of leaders and followers, variations in its applicability due to the type of information and social conditions involved, and its failure to consider variables that are difficult to measure;[23] reliance by researchers upon its inconsistent definitions of mass media;[24] its failure to account for evidence that information regarding major news events tends to be spread directly by the media[25] or for evidence that opinions in matters of public affairs more often are shared than given;[26] and its failure to distinguish between people who acquire information sooner after its availability rather than later or between information-giving and persuasion on the part of opinion leaders.[27]

In general, Two-Step Flow Theory's social influence functions may be thought of as a special case of Social Network Theory (SNT), which addresses relationships and connectedness among individuals along social, economic, and political dimensions[28] and which first had been advanced at about the time of the early studies by Katz and Lazarsfeld.[29] In Social Network Theory, nodes consisting of individuals and organizations are interconnected by a series of ties, both strong and weak. Strong ties are based in deep and long-lasting friendships, while weak ties are less intense and frequently extend across heterogeneous social groupings.[30] Opinion leaders are thought to excel at forming both strong ties and weak ties. The former often are based upon homophily, or the tendency of individuals to be attracted to others like themselves;[31] the latter are used to introduce new ideas into groups. While followers tend to be influenced more by their strong ties, owing to the frequency and perceived importance of their contacts,[32] opinion leaders are more likely than their followers to be exposed to ideas outside of their immediate social networks via weaker ties, including those to appropriate media sources.[33]

Two-Step Flow Theory, developed as it was during the ascendency of television and in a period when other media, particularly newspapers and radio, had established themselves as dominant sources of both information and consumer impulse, seems to anticipate inevitable comparisons between the efficacy of mediated marketing and personal advice. From the outset, empirical tests of Two-Step Flow presented evidence that personal influence was more effective than media messages in the formation of attitudes and behaviors across a wide sweep of human activities and concerns from politics to fashion, though the media played important roles in information-gathering and legitimation.[34]

More recent studies continue to find audiences distrustful of both the traditional news media and advertising and showing a preference for friends, family, coworkers, and peers as information sources.[35] Conclusions regarding the value of emerging media, including online media generally and online social media specifically, are less certain, particularly since less is known about how online ties are formed.[36] One early study concluded that the particular online venue where the information is found as well as its source is important[37] (11) and that so-called word-of-mouth information was perceived as credible, relevant, and free of self-interests (7),[38] though another found face-to-face recommendations more effective than those from digital sources.[39]

Online sources may become valued in part through the sort of interactions in which they participate. Social Networking Theory potentially provides a measure of that value in the form of social capital which nodes, be they individuals or organizations, are thought to amass as a consequence of the number and strength of their ties. One study found that measures of social capital—including perceptions of trustworthiness, engagement, and knowledge—were related to frequent information exchange online, but not to other types of interactions, including those that were what the authors referred to as "social recreational."[40] This suggests that opinion leaders achieve their status through the accumulation of social capital, which owes to their focus on information exchange, rather than on less purposive interactions.

The notion that opinion leaders become opinion leaders, not spontaneously but through concerted effort, was echoed in a study of influence on Twitter, though the authors found the effort to focus on specific subject matter rather than type of exchange.[41] Based upon their work, Josh Pasek, Eian More, and Daniel Romer would agree on the connection between information exchange online and the gathering of social capital,[42] but would argue that the Two-Step Flow of information online among particularly civically engaged networks is much less linear, with media influence on opinion leaders playing less of a role and with multiple opinion leaders influencing followers in a manner that begins to resemble viral diffusion. They believe information flows in such a model could be far more extensive and that they could extend beyond the most engaged individuals.[43]

What opinion leaders have to say and how they say it may also be important. The more effective leaders seem to be those whose language is more profuse, diverse, assertive, and affective.[44] And mixing objective and highly subjective content in reviews of products and services appears to be less effective than either entirely objective or entirely subjective content.[45] But tenure within a network and the degree to which leaders took recommendations as well as made them also seem to be related to online opinion leadership.[46]

As *New York Times* reporter Randall Stross has noted, "Every piece of content on the web is essentially a recommendation to the public from the person who posted it."[47] Opinion leadership on Facebook thus poses unique challenges, since its recently introduced "like" button on third-party web pages facilitates recommendations from "friends" that are in turn posted to the user's Facebook page. Mere membership in one's social network does not necessarily make someone a good source, though human biases in favor of person-to-person information as opposed to recommendations from external sources tend to imbue "friends" with expert status. Perhaps not surprisingly, then, "friends" from online social networks are beginning to replace search engines as trusted sources and information is less an online destination than it is a product of social networks.

ASSESSING THE THREAT

The Two-Step Flow Theory and Social Network Theory, then, would seem to provide a potentially useful mechanism for assessing the threat to each of the four companies implicated in the case studies summarized earlier—Allstate, AOL, Dell, and Comcast—by the negative content posted to social media. For the threat actually to be realized, however, the literature suggests several conditions would need to be met.

First, the networks implicated would need to be sufficiently extensive that the content would reach an audience large enough to materially influence the reputations and fortunes of each company. Though more than 87,000 who "liked" Tori Cardinale's posts critical of Allstate were impressive by Facebook standards, a single nationwide airing of an Allstate television commercial in prime time easily would reach 10 times as many people, perhaps 100 times as many. The Comcast and AOL debacles each appeared to have had audiences in the hundreds of thousands, which are considerable, but which, again, represent a comparatively small portion of users of both social media and conventional media. No total audience estimates were reported in the Dell case, though one might assume them to be at least as large. In all four cases, however, the total audience grew when what had been exclusively social media stories were retold by more conventional media. And the total circulation for the content would have to include casual mentions among their viewers' off-line social networks. For businesses in competitive industry sectors, such as consumer electronics, residential insurance, and Internet portals, the effects would be more significant than for those with few rivals, such as residential broadband and video providers.

Second, the content itself would need to be compelling. The video of the sleeping Comcast service representative has appeal as entertainment; the Comcast, AOL, and Dell stories would resonate with viewers who had similarly frustrating and ultimately unsatisfactory experiences with customer service with consumer products or services companies. The Comcast experience would have the additional attraction of video; the AOL story had audio. The Dell weblogs and still images of the storm-ravaged home at the heart of the Allstate story were more static and to a lesser degree within the experience of those seeing them—and therefore likely less engaging. Even so, the extraordinary scenarios they describe may take on an almost mythic quality for those encountering them and may be just real enough to be cautionary. In any event, there is reason to believe those exposed to each of the stories were engaged with them, given the active response required for "likes," "shares," and download requests.

Finally, the sources of the critical accounts would have to be invested by their audiences with social capital in the form of perceptions that the information provided was important, relevant, and credible. Here, the evidence must remain at least to a degree speculative, since the task of tracing the paths from node to node within thousands of social networks would be formidable indeed. But taking to heart Stross's observation that social media messages about products and services essentially are personal recommendations from those who post them, it is no great leap of faith to assume that the "retweets" and "shares" represented in viral events come with at least the tacit belief of the intermediaries they are believable; to assume otherwise would be to accept the notion that members of a network value their participation above their own reputations. On balance, then, it seems the threat posed by incidents similar to those mentioned should not be underestimated.

THE POTENTIAL OF SOCIAL MEDIA

It bears repeating, then, that while the social scientific literature and proprietary industry research tend to favor the view that advertising in traditional media has significant limitations in its effectiveness, largely owing both to the overabundance of messages audiences receive and audience skepticism about product and service claims, the same is not to be said for purchase advice consumers receive from people they know whose opinions they trust. Social media amount to extensions of word-of-mouth communication but with far greater magnitude. Tools such as Twitter and Facebook allow companies to talk to customers and for customers to talk to each other. Companies cannot control the latter type of exchanges, but they can influence the conversations. Social media allow customers to talk to companies, too, but such communications tend to be used more for market research than for sales promotion.[48] It is not that companies fail to realize the value of social media to promotion but, rather, that they often fail to integrate them successfully.[49] The result is that, in the social media era, consumers have greater control over their decision making, with greater access to information and greater command over their consumption of media.[50]

A recent experiment suggests how companies may nevertheless impact conversations they cannot control: consumers with access to social media reviews of similar products at three different price levels could be influenced to buy the most expensive one, rather than gravitate to the mid-priced option, which was their tendency when no reviews were available. The results suggest companies can use social media to manipulate not only purchase choices but also a variety of other consumer behaviors.[51]

Needless to say, technologies that can be used to empower consumers also can be used to exploit them as well. The online ride sharing service

Uber, which has drawn criticism for allegedly unfair competition from taxi cab operators in cities internationally because it typically is not subject to the same regulations and municipal fees they are, recently mounted what the *New York Times* described as a "full marketing blitz" against New York Mayor Bill de Blasio's plans to limit the number of Uber licenses the city would award. The blitz included messages on the smartphone application customers use to reserve an Uber ride and supportive stories on its Twitter feed.[52]

More alarming is the potential harm should a trusted source maliciously post inaccurate content or negligently repost it from elsewhere. In one recent case, a rumor began on Twitter that a well-known local Cincinnati restauranteur had posted bail for a white University of Cincinnati police officer charged with killing an African American motorist during a routine traffic stop. In reality, the bail money had come from the officer's father. But before the tweet had been taken down and the rumor corrected in the mainstream media, it had prompted death threats against the restauranteur and bomb threats against one of his restaurants.[53]

GOING WITH THE (INFORMATION) FLOW

Despite evidence that social media are upending the usual rules governing the relationships between businesses and consumers, the real-world descendants of the "Mad Men" of cable television will outlast the nostalgic AMC television series: companies will not quickly abandon marketing methods they have found to be tried and true. The messages conveyed through traditional media advertising may lack the credibility of a "like" from a trusted friend or five-star ratings from peers real and perceived, but advertising may have value beyond its function of promotion to consumers. Publicly traded purveyors of consumer goods and services ultimately must serve two constituencies: buyers are important, of course, but investor perceptions frequently are of equal concern and companies must consider the impact of advertising on both. In their study of several industries, Amit Joshi and Dominique Hanssens found the stock market penalizes firms for significant deviations from optimal spending on traditional marketing either above or below the norm.[54] Thus, when Tori Cardinale's nemesis, Allstate, announced that, between 2013 and 2015, it would shift 20 percent of its advertising dollars to digital, bringing the share devoted to online efforts to roughly 33 percent, the change was significant even if it could not be traced directly to reaction to Cardinale's viral Facebook post.[55]

At Dell, the decision to more drastically shift resources to social media was motivated by a far different calculus. First, the threat to performance metrics by negative perceptions rooted in a poor social media image and fueled by coverage in traditional media was not potential but real. Second,

Dell's position in the market was faltering in spite of steady increases in spending on traditional advertising, not for want of them. Dell executives correctly saw the importance of authenticity, not sophistry, in its response it had to admit to its missteps and deal with them candidly. It suppressed the natural organizational impulse to speak and instead listened (to weblogs) and, even after taking to the "blogosphere" itself, continued to listen to consumers through IdeaStorm, a dedicated company website that allowed its customers to rank the company issues most important to them. Support for the transformation came from returned CEO Michael Dell himself and was sustained in spite of perceived cost.[56] Measures of buyer familiarity and favorability rebounded even as spending on traditional advertising plummeted from $729 million to $179 million in just six years.[57]

Dell archrival Apple appears to have learned from errors made by the former and, in a recent test of its social media crisis management skills, was faced with a potentially damaging incident involving one of its retail operations in Australia. In November 2015, Facebook and Twitter were abuzz with news that a group of black college students in Melbourne were barred by two uniformed security guards and a store staffer from entering an Apple store there because of fears they might "steal something." Though the store manager subsequently apologized after a school administrator accompanied the six students on a second visit, the reluctance of Apple Australia's corporate office to issue any sort of response was troubling to many and called into question the seriousness with which the company regarded the incident.[58] Exacerbating those concerns was the reticence of Apple's U.S. headquarters to file a required workforce diversity report with the Equal Employment Opportunity Commission, almost certainly because company officials knew it would reveal that 72 percent of its senior managers were white men and just 8 percent of its total workforce were black.[59] Eventually, the company's U.S. headquarters issued a more fulsome statement of its regret for the way the students were treated and reiterated its policy of equal treatment of its customers regardless of "race, age, gender, gender identity, ethnicity, religion or sexual orientation." It attributed the day's delay in issuing the statement to the need to look "into the details of the situation."[60]

Unlike companies such as Dell, Allstate, and AOL, whose warming to (or, in Dell's case, its passionate embrace of) social media was born of embarrassing incidents that went viral, the beginnings of changes in the film industry's promotion strategy arose from several instances in which social networks aided in films' successes. The first rumblings of the shift were felt in 2009 when Disney's much anticipated 3-D animated feature, *Up*, surpassed expert projections and earned $68 million in U.S. theaters in its first weekend. Studio audience tracking had suggested the film would not do well among adults without children; surprisingly, it did and

Disney executives attributed the phenomenon to a so-called Twitter effect, in which positive reviews at online social media sites by viewers of early screenings spurred others in their networks to see for themselves. The prospects of such reviews to either reinforce or defeat distributors' multimillion dollar promotion budgets led one analyst to predict that "the weekend box office has now shrunk to a single day: Friday"—meaning that traditional mediated messages to build audiences could be counted on to work as before only until the end of Friday evening early showings, after which most would-be audiences instead would be guided by messages on Twitter, Facebook, and weblogs.[61]

By July 2009, at least three other films appeared to be examples of the "Twitter effect": Warner Brothers' *The Hangover*, a film that lacked both the budget and known stars usually needed to compete with more formulaic Hollywood summer blockbusters but which exceeded even the most optimistic industry projections to earn $45 million its first weekend, and Sony Pictures' *Year One* and Universal Pictures' *Land of the Lost*, both of which were expected to be major successes, yet took in just $19 million each their first weekends. The only film thought to have been an exception to "Twitter effect" was *Transformers 2*, which received negative reviews both from traditional media critics and from social media but still was able to draw in large audiences, perhaps because the studio preemptively emphasized the attractiveness of the female lead in social media promotions.

Prior to its debut in the weekend of July 10, 2009, the box office performance of *Bruno* was expected to be a case study in the effects of social media messages on the success of a film. Indeed, the audience performance of *Bruno* not only appeared to provide the best evidence to date of the impact of social media networks on film box office revenues, but also was the first instance of the supposed "Twitter effect" to be widely reported to the general public. *Bruno* earned a respectable $30.4 million from July 10 to July 12, but its revenue dropped 39 percent from Friday to Saturday which, according to a *Los Angeles Time* weblog on the film industry, was a signal of negative "buzz" that would lead to a short run for the film and make it doubtful it would equal the revenues of star Sacha Baron Cohen's previous film, *Borat*.[62] Writing in *Time* magazine on the day the weekend's numbers were released, film critic Richard Corliss argued, "Instant-messaging can make or break a film within 24 hours. Friday is the new weekend." Specifically, Corliss believed negative buzz regarding the film's representations of gay men and its last-minute removal of a scene concerning singer Michael Jackson perceived in poor taste following the star's untimely death had resulted in audiences responding to *Bruno*, a comedy, as they would to a horror film: hardcore fans would attend the first screenings and others would be scared away.[63]

Major films can cost between $40 million and $200 million to market globally, up to 70 percent of their gross revenue, fully half of which is spent on television. According to a recent study by Twitter and Nielsen, 87 percent of Twitter users over the age of 13 said tweets influenced their movie choices. It also showed that 62 percent of moviegoers used the Internet or mobile apps to learn about films. Even so and in spite of evidence of the effects of social media on box office sales, studios rarely spend more than $10 million each on digital marketing.[64]

In addition to shifts in the amounts allocated to online versus traditional media promotion, further refinement may be needed in how the online portion is spent. Currently, a significant amount is spent on official film websites which, at a time when audiences can access synopses on Internet Movie Database (IMDb) and trailers on YouTube, no longer offer unique selling points. According to Katie Khan, head of digital strategies at Paramount Pictures UK, websites foster one-way conversation with film fans, while social media promote a dialogue. Therefore, films need a well-"liked" Facebook page, a dedicated Twitter following, and a Tumblr account with at least a dozen animated GIFs of characters. Official film social media feeds, frequently run by student interns, generate thousands of meaningful interactions, leading one analyst to conclude that 140 characters are more effective in marketing than 1,400 lines of code.[65] Indeed, promotional trailers for new films and display ads have begun to feature films' Twitter hashtags alongside their website URLs; however, references to Facebook pages or other social media venues seldom are made.

Cameron Crowe's 2015 film *Aloha* provided a glimpse at possibilities for the tactical use of social media platforms, particularly for releases for which the advance "buzz" was less than positive. In spite of Crowe's generally well-regarded reputation as the director of films such as *Fast Times at Ridgemont High*, *Jerry McGuire*, and *Almost Famous* and a cast that included such well-known actors as Bradley Cooper, Emma Stone, Rachel McAdams, Bill Murray, and Alec Baldwin, the film was expected to fare poorly at the box office and was almost universally panned by critics. Among the elements of the social media campaign were behind-the-scenes features on YouTube, a session on IMDb two weeks before the premiere in which users of Facebook and Twitter were encouraged to submit questions to Crowe,[66] and, just days before the premiere, another YouTube feature intended to counter complaints in both social and traditional media that the film misrepresented its Hawaii location as populated predominately by Caucasians.[67]

Film audiences differ in their degree of enthusiasm and activism regarding the films they see and, likewise, one might expect online social networks to comprise members with varying levels of participation in conversations about film. According to researchers Charlene Li and Josh Bernoff, opinion leadership in the age of social media is multifaceted and in some cases more subtle than might be imagined. Of the seven distinct types of social technology behavior they describe, four particularly have the potential to influence consumers, including film audiences: creators, conversationalists, critics, and collectors (joiners, spectators, and inactives seem less likely to.) The distinctions among the four types mainly are a matter of degree of engagement. While collectors may "like" a Facebook page, for instance, critics post ratings and comment on another user's weblog, conversationalists post updates on Twitter, and creators write articles or weblogs or upload video or audio to sites.[68]

Of course, Twitter feeds and Facebook pages run by the studios amount to just one set of voices in the conversation about a film; the danger of contrary voices drowning out the positive official line still exists. To guard against opinion leadership that runs afoul of promotional messages by film distributors, one industry observer recommends distributors provide advance screenings to audiences, either at theaters or through video-on-demand (VOD), that they encourage audiences to share their feedback online (perhaps through the official social media feeds), and that studios offer "rewards" to encourage users to talk enthusiastically about a film.[69]

GOING FORWARD: LESSONS LEARNED

The case studies mentioned in this chapter recounting damning critiques of a broad range of companies and their products and services that spread virally through social media until they either materially damaged the companies or caught the attention of executives who feared for their reputations provide at the very least anecdotal evidence of the efficacy of the Two-Step Flow Theory specifically and Social Networking Theory more generally. Individuals on social media platforms that form the basis of social networks who are perceived as knowledgeable, credible, and homophilous may indeed have the capability to significantly shift the public conversation about products and services that are promoted through traditional channels and to do so either positively or negatively.

While differences in particular circumstances surrounding companies and industries make more specific generalizations difficult, there do appear to be three commonalities among organizations that have successfully transformed their marketing approaches to acknowledge the existence and formidability of social media.

First, companies seeking to leverage the power of social media will visualize social networks as an ecosystem.[70] They will attempt to create communities of like-minded individuals for interaction, perhaps with contributions from employees.[71] If employees are part of these communities, it is important from the standpoint of the long-term viability of the effort that they be identified as such; moles, if they are uncovered (and probably would be) would be poisonous to any effort to foster candid and credible conversations, because they would be perceived more akin to corporate shills than members of a peer network. They will use social media tools such as blogs to encourage feedback, creating a greater sense of engagement, and combine traditional promotional tools such as contests with social media-based tools.[72]

Second, they will communicate their messages through stories that are compelling—either someone else's[73] or their own.[74] A quick scan at any given moment of one's Facebook timeline reveals that the items that have been shared most widely are those that focus on an individual or small group and the events and issues that impact them. The content audiences enjoy in entertainment media frequently are personal stories executed in larger-than-life form. And even the best of traditional advertising must begin with a story.

And third, they will not be afraid to be outrageous[75] or unique.[76] If traditional advertising platforms such as television commercials have been rendered less effective by "clutter," social media tools will be obscured by the noise of millions of interactions on thousands of topics. To be seen and heard is to be spread virally and that requires a message and execution that stand apart in an environment in which others will be trying to do the same.

NOTES

1. Tori Cardinale, "Timeline Photos," *Facebook,* December 24, 2012, https://www.facebook.com/#!/photo.php?fbid=4418418816299&set=a.4418418776298.227657.1163750306&type=1&theater.

2. Ibid.

3. Ibid.

4. Mark D. Stein, "Post-Sandy Insurance Claims Cause Confusion and Anger among Staten Island Residents," *Staten Island Advance*, January 6, 2013, http://www.silive.com/southshore/index.ssf/2013/01/post-sandy_insurance_claims_ca.html.

5. Suzanne Vranica, "Allstate Moving TV Dollars to Digital," *Wall Street Journal*, September 30, 2014, http://blogs.wsj.com/cmo/2014/09/30/allstate-moving-tv-dollars-to-digital/.

6. W. Glynn Mangold and David J. Faulds, "Social Media: The New Hybrid Element of the Promotional Mix," *Business Horizons* 57 (2009): 357–365.

7. Randall Stross, "AOL Said, 'If You Leave Me I'll Do Something Crazy." *New York Times*, July 2, 2006, http://www.nytimes.com/2006/07/02/business/yourmoney/02digi.html?pagewanted=all.

8. Emily Yellin, *Your Call Is (Not That) Important to Us: Customer Service and What It Reveals about Our Word and Our Lives* (New York: Free Press) (2009): 45.

9. Ken Belson, "Your Call Is Important to Us. Please Stay Awake," *New York Times*, June 26, 2006, http://www.nytimes.com/2006/06/26/technology/26comcast.html.

10. Jim Bartimo, "Marketing and Media," *The Wall Street Journal*, May 14, 1991, 6.

11. James R. Gregory, "Michael Dell's Plans to Take His Company Private 'Right on Schedule," *DailyDog*, February 28, 2013, https://www.bulldogreporter.com/dailydog/article/michael-dells-plans-take-his-company-private-right-schedule.

12. Charlene Li and Josh Bernoff, *Groundswell*, rev. ed. (Boston, MA: Forrester Research, Inc., 2011), 223–224.

13. Ibid., 225.

14. James R. Gregory.

15. Charlene Li and Josh Bernoff, 229.

16. Matthew C. Nisbet and John E. Kotcher, "A Two-Step Influence? Opinion Leader Campaigns on Climate Change," *Science Communication* 30, no. 3 (2009): 331–332.

17. Elihu Katz and Paul F. Lazarsfeld, *Personal Influence: The Part Played by People in the Flow of Mass Communications* (Glencoe, IL: The Free Press, 1955).

18. Elihu Katz, "The Two-Step Flow of Communication: An Up-To-Date Report on an Hypothesis," *Public Opinion Quarterly* 21 (1957): 61–78.

19. E. Rogers and F. Shoemaker, *Communication of Innovations* (New York: The Free Press, 1971): 206.

20. Gabriel Weimann, *The Influentials: People Who Influence People* (Albany, NY: State University of New York Press, 1994).

21. Edwin. P. Hollander, "Emergent Leadership and Social Influence," in *Leadership and Interpersonal Behavior,* eds. L. Petrullo and B. M. Bass (New York: Holt, Rinehart and Winston, 1961), 30–47.

22. Werner J. Severin and James W. Tankard Jr., *Communication Theories: Origins, Methods, Uses* (New York: Hastings House, 1979), 206.

23. Stanley J. Baran and Dennis K. Davis, *Mass Communication Theory: Foundations, Ferment, and Future* (Belmont, CA: Wadsworth, 1995), 120–121.

24. N. Lin, *The Study of Human Communication* (Indianapolis, IN: Bobbs-Merrill, 1971), 204.

25. B. Westley, "Communication and Social Change," *American Behavioral Scientist* 14 (1971): 726.

26. V. Troldahl and R. Van Dam, "Face-to-Face Communication about Major Topics in the News." *Public Opinion Quarterly* 42 (1965–1966): 403–412.

27. E. M. Rogers and F. F. Shoemaker, *Communication of Innovations: A Cross-Cultural Approach* (New York: Free Press), 208, 259, 348.

28. Mark Granovetter, "The Strength of Weak Ties," *American Journal of Sociology* 78 (1973).

29. Linton Freeman, *The Development of Social Network Analysis* (Vancouver, BC: Empirical Press, 2006).

30. Mark Granovetter.

31. C. Fisher, *To Dwell among Friends: Personal Networks in Town and City* (Chicago, IL: University of Chicago Press, 1982).

32. Jo Brown, Amanda J. Broderick, and Nick Lee, "Word of Mouth Communication within Online Communities: Conceptualizing the Online Social Network," *Journal of Interative Marketing* 21, no. 3 (2007, Summer): 5.

33. Werner J. Severin and James W. Tankard, Jr., 205.

34. Ibid., 204–205.

35. E. B. Keller and J. L. Berry, *The Influentials: One American in Ten Tells the Other Nine How to Vote, Where to Eat, and What to Buy* (New York: Simon & Schuster, 2003).

36. Jo Brown, Amanda J. Broderick, and Nick Lee, 15.

37. Ibid., 11.

38. Ibid., 7.

39. E. B. Keller and J. L. Berry.

40. D. V. Shah, N. Kwak, and R. L. Holbert, "'Connecting' and 'Disconnecting' with Civic Life: Patterns of Internet Use and the Production of Social Capital," *Political Communication* 18 (2001): 141–162.

41. Meeyoung Cha, Hamed Haddadi, Fabricio Benevenuto, and Krishna P. Gummadi, "Measuring User Influence in Twitter: The Million Follower Fallacy," *Proceedings of the Fourth International AAAI Conference on Weblogs and Social Media* (2010): 17.

42. Josh Pasek, Eian More, and Daniel Romer, "Realizing the Social Internet? Online Social Networking Meets Offline Social Capital," *Journal of Information Technology and Politics* 6, nos. 3/4 (2009, July): 207.

43. Ibid., 202.

44. David Huffaker, "Dimensions of Leadership and Social Influence in Online Communities," *Human Communication Research* 36 (2010): 609.

45. Anindya Ghose and Panagiotis G. Ipeirotis, "Estimating the Helpfulness and Economic Impact of Product Reviews: Mining Text and Reviewer Characteristics," *IEEE Transactions on Knowledge and Data Engineering* (September 27, 2010).

46. David Huffaker, 609.

47. Randall Stross, "World's Largest Social Network: The Open Web," *New York Times*, May 16, 2010, BU3.

48. W. Glynn Mangold and David J. Faulds, "Social Media: The New Hybrid Element of the Promotional Mix," *Business Horizons* 57 (2009): 358–359.

49. Richard Hanna, Andrew Rohm, and Victoria L. Crittenden, "We're All Connected: The Power of the Social Media Ecosystem," *Business Horizons* 54 (2011): 271–272.

50. C. Vollmer and G. Precourt, *Always On: Advertising, Marketing, and Media in an Era of Consumer Control* (New York: McGraw-Hill, 2008).

51. Matt Richtel, "There's Power in All Those User Reviews," *New York Times*, December 8, 2013, BU-3.

52. Lauren Johnson, "Uber Takes over New York Times Homepage with Large Ad Calling Out the Mayor: Plays Up Newspaper's 'Bad Idea' Editorial," *Adweek*, July 22, 2015, http://www.adweek.com/news/technology/uber-takes-over-new-york-times-homepage-fight-proposed-bill-166050.

53. Sharon Coolidge, "Jeff Ruby Says He Did Not Post Tensing's Bail, Contrary to Rumors," *Cincinnati Enquirer* (August 1, 2015): 17A.

54. Amit Joshi and Dominique M. Hanssens, "The Direct and Indirect Effects of Advertising Spending on FirmValue," *Journal of Marketing* 74 (January 2010): 31.

55. Suzanne Vranica.

56. Charlene Li and Josh Bernoff, 229.

57. James R. Gregory.

58. Melissa Davey, "Apple Store Accused of Racial Profiling after Video Shows Staff Ejecting Black Students," *The Guardian*, November 11, 2015, http://

www.theguardian.com/technology/2015/nov/12/apple-store-in-melbourne
-accused-of-racism-after-video-shows-staff-ejecting-african-students.

59. Rupert Neate, "Apple's Senior Executives Are 70% White Men, Diversity Filing Reveals," *The Guardian*, August 13, 2015, http://www.theguardian.com/technology/2015/aug/13/apple-diversity-report-white-men.

60. Melissa Davey, "Apple Apologises after Saying Black Students 'Might Steal Something,'" *The Guardian*, November 12, 2015, http://www.theguardian.com/technology/2015/nov/13/apple-apologises-after-saying-black-students-might-steal-something.

61. Sharon Waxman, "Social Networking Making Friday the Only Day that Counts: Twitter, Facebook Have Changed What 'Word-of-Mouth' Really Means," *The Wrap*, July 9, 2009, http://www.thewrap.com/movies/article/social-networking-making-friday-only-day-counts-4229?page=1,0.

62. Ben Fritz, "'Bruno' Starts off Strong on the Box-Office Runway, Then Stumbles," *Los Angeles Times*, July 12, 2009, http://latimesblogs.latimes.com/entertainmentnewsbuzz/2009/07/bruno-starts-off-strong-on-the-box-office-runway-then-stumbles.html.

63. Richard Corliss, "Box-Office Weekend: Brüno a One-Day Wonder?" *Time*, July 13, 2009, http://www.time.com/time/arts/article/0,8599,1910059,00.html.

64. Pamela McClintock, "$200 Million and Rising: Hollywood Struggles with Soaring Marketing Costs," *The Hollywood Reporter*, July 31, 2014, http://www.hollywoodreporter.com/news/200-million-rising-hollywood-struggles-721818.

65. Ali Gray, "How Twitter Killed the Official Movie Website," *The Guardian*, June 16, 2014, http://www.theguardian.com/film/filmblog/2014/jun/16/twitter-movie-website-hashtag-film-social-media.

66. Brielle Jaekel, "IMDb Holds Twitter Q&A to Promote Aloha with Director Cameron Crowe," *Mobile Marketer*, May 14, 2015, http://www.mobilemarketer.com/cms/news/social-networks/20435.html.

67. Christopher Rosen, "Sony Defends 'Aloha' after White-Washing Claims," *Entertainment Weekly*, May 26, 2015, http://www.ew.com/article/2015/05/26/aloha-white-washing-sony.

68. Charlene Li and Josh Bernoff, 43–45.

69. Chris Thilk, "Even Tom Cruise Couldn't Beat This Summer's Hollywood Memes," *Advertising Age On-Line*, June 29, 2010, http://adage.com/madisonandvine/article?article_id=144726.

70. Richard Hanna, Andrew Rohm, Victoria L. Crittenden, 271.

71. W. Glynn Mangold and David J. Faulds, 361.

72. Ibid., 362.

73. Ibid., 364.

74. Richard Hanna, Andrew Rohm, Victoria L. Crittenden, 271–272.

75. W. Glynn Mangold and David J. Faulds, 363.

76. Richard Hanna, Andrew Rohm, Victoria L. Crittenden, 272.

Chapter 12

#NothingButTheTruth: Using Social Media to Educate the Public about Courts

Jason Zenor

Prior to mass electronic communication, courts were often an entertaining pastime for folks. The trials offered the same tropes we find in visual storytelling today, such as intrigue, gossip, scandal, and sensationalism. The reasons for going to court may have been entertainment, but while there, the citizenry could also learn how a pivotal branch of government functioned.

But with the advent of radio and television, visiting courts did not seem to hold the same captivation, thus public attendance dropped. In the twentieth century, people mostly learned about the court system through truncated stories on media channels.[1] Consequently, as this time there were great concerns about how the media portrayed the courts: was there something lost through the mediation? Did the media present the truth? Could it educate the public?[2]

For most of the twentieth century, cameras were not allowed in the courtroom. Today, many states have adopted cameras in the courtroom and the federal courts are currently testing the effects of allowing them.[3] But, the U.S. Supreme Court is still steadfast in its stance not to allow cameras in its court room.[4] Although many state courtrooms allow cameras and audio transcripts are available in federal courts, for most people, their experience with the courts still only comes through limited news reports and televised dramas.

Thirty years ago, if the news media chose to cover something, then the public probably saw it. For example, as late as 1980, there were only three national television networks that garnered 90 percent of the viewing audience.[5] But today, things are different. Audiences are fragmented. The millennial generation does not read newspapers or watch television news. Many people today get their information from social media and apps that are very personalized and allow for users to bypass any news that is not to their liking.[6]

As far of court coverage, some cases will receive a great deal of attention. Trials involving celebrities will be in the headlines. Cases on hot button issues such as affirmative action or gay marriage will be newsworthy, as will sensational cases that include murder and sex. But in this digital era, there are too many other entertaining options that capture people's attention. Consequently, complex cases about important issues, such as voting rights or investor fraud or government surveillance, are often ignored.[7] This lack of attention seems like an impossible problem. How can the judiciary, which is the least entertaining and often most complex branch of government, compete for the attention of the citizenry in the digital age?

This chapter argues that courts need to change their traditional fear of technology. Courts must now adopt new technologies to circumvent the gatekeepers and go straight to the citizenry to help educate them about the court system. First, this chapter outlines why this is important by detailing the average American's ignorance concerning the courts. Second, the chapter touches upon how government agencies are using social media and other new technology. Next, the chapter examines the judiciary's frayed relationship with new technology because of perceived harms. Finally, the chapter examines the legal obligations that courts have to be open to the public and how this extends to using tools to inform the public directly.

THE UNINFORMED PUBLIC

There is an appetite for television programming that portrays the American judicial system.[8] *Judge Judy, Judge Joe Brown, Hot Bench, Boston Legal, The Practice, Damages,* and *Law & Order* are just a few examples of television programs centered on courtrooms. They are also examples of how this genre is a very lucrative venture for broadcasters. 24/7 news stations also receive some of their highest ratings when there is a high-profile trial being litigated.[9] Americans are very familiar with the mediated courtroom and judges. They are very familiar with the law as shown to them through the scripted drama and cable news. But, the question is whether the audience is aware of the degree to which it is sensationalized.[10]

Research shows that the more people watch television, the more they believe that it reflects reality.[11] Consequently, a significant amount of what the public knows about courtrooms and the judicial system comes from their exposure through dramatized television.[12] But if this is the case, then Hollywood is doing a poor job. The National Center for State Courts found that only 21 percent of those polled could name all three branches of government. In 2011, only 41 percent of people could name the vice president. The public's low awareness of basic civics is disconcerting, but, when it comes to knowledge of the judiciary, it gets worse. Nearly two-thirds of Americans cannot name a single member of the U.S. Supreme Court and only 1 percent can name all nine.[13] Only 20 percent can name the chief justice of the United States.[14]

This lack of knowledge and understanding does matter as it translates to opinions and judgment on the judiciary. "Better-informed citizens tend to have more confidence in their [] courts, are more likely to see judges' decisions as fair, and more highly value an independent judiciary."[15] But, only 36 percent of Americans approve of the job that the U.S. Supreme Court is doing.[16] Only 13 percent of Americans have confidence in the state courts.[17] Despite drastic budget cuts, only 17 percent of Americans believe that courts are underfunded.[18] This lack of knowledge also affects people's everyday lives. Those who do not trust or understand the judiciary are less likely to use it. Studies show that people who learn positive information about any government agency or program, even if from the media, are more likely to use it.[19]

Many people will argue that it is not the media's job to educate as that is the role of schools. But school budget cuts and the focus on math and science testing has made it easy for schools to cut civics and history classes.[20] If the schools are not educating the public on the judicial system, then maybe the news media is in the best position to do so. But in the digital age, it is next to impossible for the news media to mainstream the public's knowledge and opinions. The new media environment means that the audience is fragmented and people are not watching the same news.[21] Those who are getting news are often getting only headlines on digital media platforms. Those who are watching television news are watching partisan cable news that does not report on the objective workings of the court.[22]

Even if the traditional news media covered the courts, many people would not see it as they are spending time with other media platforms. Today, people spend three hours a day with social media, and this is even higher among millennials.[23] This may seem like a threat to courts and other government agencies as people can basically avoid coverage on public affairs. But, the reality may be different as social media users are consuming news through their feeds and will often seek out further information directly from the source if they find it to be important.[24] This means that social media may be a great opportunity for the judicial system to bypass the gatekeepers and go straight to the public, which it serves.

OPEN GOVERNMENT AND SOCIAL MEDIA

People now turn to social media to learn about products, brands, and services,[25] including government services and information.[26] If the opinions of the courts are going to improve, then it is going to have to be the courts that start the information campaign. Moreover, the new political expectations of the digital environment are that the government, including courts, will be open and transparent, including adopting new technologies to create a discussion with the public.[27] As Garrett Graff, editor of *Washington Magazine*, argues:

> [Courts] must not only learn how to communicate with new tools; they must also envision new means of judicial engagement with the public through the new social media that can further advance the legitimacy of courts in a democratic society.[28]

The other branches of government have also begun to slowly adopt social media as a strategy to improve services through digital means (also known as e-government). Social media allows for government to be more collaborative, participatory, and transparent.[29] It does this by spreading information and creating social ties through the sharing of text, documents, images, and videos.[30] It also allows for citizens to have a voice.[31] These social networks can give a face to what is often seen as a cold bureaucracy.[32]

Many government agencies view these social networks as the most effective way in which to communicate with the public.[33] This has been most effective in the management of natural disasters.[34] Agencies such as FEMA and the CDC have used social media to alert and inform the public that may have missed such information if broadcasted on traditional media.[35]

Government agencies approach social media through three strategies: push, pull, and networking.[36] The push strategy uses social media to inform the public, whereas the pull strategy uses social media to draw audience to other sites, both online and in person. A networking strategy uses social media as two-way communication allowing citizens to become active participants in the government by having a voice in developing policy.[37]

JUDICIAL BRANCH AND SOCIAL MEDIA

According to the National Center for State Courts, 29 state court systems, the District of Columbia, Guam, and Puerto Rico use some form of social media to communicate with its constituencies.[38] Thirty-one state high courts have a Twitter account,[39] and 16 state high courts have a Facebook account (15 of which also have a Twitter account).[40] Twenty state high courts have a YouTube account[41] (for five of those states it is the only social media it utilizes).[42] There are nine state high courts that have accounts with all three social media sites.[43] In addition, 25 percent of federal courts use some social media account.[44]

The courts use these sites in many different ways. They use these sites not only to send text but also publish documents and videos and create blogs. The courts also use social media for community outreach. This includes guiding constituents on how to access court services, publicizing events, and publicizing volunteer opportunities. They also use social media to provide training for employees and the greater legal community. The courts use social media to publish information to news media and other government agencies. Arguably, the most important use of social media is helping to assist the increasing number of litigants who are representing themselves (and do not have any legal training).[45]

The number of courts using social media seems fairly high, but still, more than half of the state judiciaries have no presence on social media. If we consider that close to three quarters of the people in the United States have a social media account and that the millennial generation is almost exclusively getting their information from digital formats, then these numbers do not seem so impressive. The question is why have the courts moved so slowly to adopt this impactful tool.

THE TROUBLED HISTORY OF COURTS AND NEW TECHNOLOGY

Legal institutions are notorious for their slow evolution. This is the polar opposite of communication technology that changes at blazing speeds. The judiciary is an institution that is unidirectional, impersonal, and rooted in lengthy, dry texts.[46] Whereas social media technology is decentralized, democratized, intimate, and based in short bursts of multimedia immersion.[47] The two worlds are polar opposites. For example, the idea that the U.S. Supreme Court justices will adopt social media anytime soon is wishful thinking. Today, most of the justices of the U.S. Supreme Court do not even use e-mail, a technology that has been around for a quarter of a century.[48] Justice Kagan, who in her 50s, making her one of the younger members of the court, commented on the high court's ambivalence toward technology: "The justices are not necessarily the most technologically sophisticated people . . . [this may] sound quaint and endearing, until you remember that these are the people charged with interpreting the law of the land on issues like online privacy and digital surveillance."[49]

As with any new technology, there are pros and cons and in the short history of the technology in the court systems, there are examples of both. Courts are charged with ensuring a fair trial and any outside influence that may interfere with that charge is treated as a fundamental threat. There have been some abuses of social media in courts that has perpetuated the fear of it. Some of the uses are just new approaches, but not unethical, such as attorneys using it to research and impeach witnesses.[50] Some of the uses are questionable, such as attorneys using it to research jurors and jury pools.[51] Some of the uses have been an outright violation of court rules, such as outside communication between attorneys and jurors or attorneys and judges during a trial. For example, in one case, jurors went online and researched the defendants and witnesses and found information that was not admissible in court.[52] In another case, it was discovered that some jurors were Facebook's friends with the victim's mother.[53] These types of actions can lead to a mistrial and is an obstruction to the administration of the judicial system.

As a result of these abuses, many jurisdictions have created jury instructions explicitly addressing social media use.[54] In some states, violating these instructions could lead to a charge of contempt, which could lead to jail time. In a few other cases, courts have had to issue gag orders or sequestration of jurors.[55] Despite a few infamous cases of misuse, recent studies indicate that social media abuse is not actually a common problem in courts.[56]

This fear of social media in the court has extended to outside the court. Many judges will not open a social media account in order to avoid any assumed impropriety. But some judges, especially those who are elected, do have a social media account and are very active.[57] For example, Justice Don Willett of the Texas Supreme Court has over 7,000 followers on Twitter and has sent out over 10,000 tweets. Willett argues that "people find it rare and refreshing for a Supreme Court Justice to step out from behind the bench and demystify things. Folks are surprised that stiff judges can be comedic, authentic and informative."[58]

Another concern with adopting any new technology is the knowledge gap. Courts are concerned that everyone gets a fair shake in the system. Unfortunately, there is always a gap between the have and have-nots. Social media seems fairly ubiquitous. But still today, only 80 percent of people in the United States have regular access to the Internet (wire and wireless). This means that roughly one in five people will be accessing the information that courts provide online.[59] If courts move to all electronic systems (filing, paying fines, accessing records, calendars, etc.), then there will still be a good amount of people left behind, many of whom are elderly and immigrants who are more likely to be involved in the judicial system. This type of gap has always been a concern for courts as it perpetuates the belief that "justice only belongs to those who can afford it." As more technology is adopted, then those who cannot afford such services may be behind in our adversarial system.

OPEN COURTS AND INFORMED CITIZENRY

The chief concern of the First Amendment is to protect the free flow of information, to the people, concerning issues of public interest.[60] "Secrecy in government is fundamentally anti-democratic."[61] When our government shrouds itself in secrecy, it "provides no real security for our Republic." [62] Open debate of public issues is vital to our national health and thus, information should be open and uninhibited.[63] Openness increases people's trust in their government.[64] "People in an open society do not demand infallibility from their institutions, but it is difficult for them to accept what they are prohibited from observing."[65]

Access to courts serves as a check on that institution's power. It prevents things like perjury and biased judges. In the end, transparency in courts can help prevent parties from having to pay inordinate damages if they are not truly liable. It may help ensure that the guilty go to jail and that innocent people do not.[66] Transparency plays a significant role in the judicial process by promoting public scrutiny, public respect, and public participation.[67]

More courts should use social media accounts to promote transparency and public participation in the judicial system. Courts could utilize the technology in many productive ways. Courts could use the social media accounts to publish their decisions, this could be in the form of links to PDFs or video and audio recordings of proceedings. They could also publish information such as calendars, bar exam information, links to forms and instructions on how to proceed in court (including guidelines on how to represent oneself in court).

But, social media accounts can also be used to educate the public about how the justice system operates. After U.S. Supreme Court Justice Sandra Day O'Connor retired, she helped to create Our Courts America, a nonpartisan, not-for-profit organization that attempts to educate the public on the importance of a "well-funded, effective and impartial courts."[68] The site provides multimedia educational programs aimed at school-age audience, with the objective of having judges come in contact with young people. Our Courts America has teamed up with other advocacy groups such as Least Understood Branch Project (a project of the American Bar Association), Center for Civic Education, iCivics Constitutional Rights Foundation, and many state bar associations to fill the void in formal education. State courts could do similar work through social media accounts by creating their own educational material or republishing the works of educational nonprofits.

Social media accounts can be used to spread information, but they can also be used to collect information to better serve constituents. Courts can send out links to surveys that measure the effectiveness of customer service and the public's opinions on the court's transparency and accessibility. Courts could also use analytics collected by companies like Google and Twitter to assess who the courts serve. Furthermore, when controversies arise around the courts (unpopular opinions or decisions), the judiciary can utilize social media to help repair the public's belief in justice and impartiality.

Ultimately, courts that utilize social media accounts should be objective and nonpartisan in their posts, even for judges who are elected. Any news or cases that they post should not have further commentary (outside the inherent ideology in any appellate court opinion). Ultimately, when it comes to communication through social media, members of the judicial branch must be judicious in their postings as they are "the subject of public scrutiny that might be viewed as burdensome if applied to other citizens."[69]

CONCLUSION

The Model Code of Judicial Conducts states that judges must "respect and honor the judicial office as a public trust and strive to maintain and enhance confidence in the legal system."[70] As U.S. Supreme Court Justice Frankfurter said, "[T]he public confidence in the judiciary hinges on the public's perception of it." But when he said this 60 years ago, the perception hinged upon the media's portrayal of the courts. But this is not the case today as people no longer trust the news and often avoid it. People get their news from each other on social media—what is shared with them from people whom they know. Moreover, the "media" is no longer the sole framer of public perception. Today user-generated content on social media allows for anyone with the voice (and a message that people want to hear) to shape the public, albeit smaller more fragmented publics. Thus, courts can bypass the traditional media and speak directly to constituents. But, for most courts, they do not implement any social media strategy. The reasons are multiple: lack of social media officer, a fear of new media, a belief that they are above public relations, and that it is simply not their role.

But, today, maybe more so than ever, it should be the court's role. With the fragmented audience only confronting the judicial system through the random high-profile case or through heavily dramatized legal serials, there is a lot of misinformation that has led to a lot of distrust or ignorance. This "affects the public's belief in our justice system, and ultimately, their faith in our democracy."[71] Thus, we have a citizenry that is dangerously uninformed about this very significant branch of government.

Chief Justice Berger said, "It is not unrealistic even in this day to believe that public inclusion affords citizens a form of legal education and hopefully promotes confidence in the fair administration of justice." He said this 40 years ago and was speaking about press access to the courts. At that time, as people no longer had time or interest to observe courts, it was the press that was the surrogate. Yet, today in the digital age, his statement seems to ring truer, even though there is no longer a clear press serving as a surrogate. Today everyone is his or her own press—this can include the courts, if only they are willing to do so. But the judicial branch needs to take a page from its political brethren in the executive and legislative branches and utilize this technology to get out a message and serve its constituents. "Technology creates many opportunities for courts. The opportunity to improve customer services is here now, and courts should consider taking that opportunity."[72]

NOTES

1. "In earlier times, both in England and America, attendance at court was a common mode of 'passing the time.' With the press, cinema, and electronic media now supplying the representations or reality of the real life drama once available only in the courtroom, attendance at court is no longer a widespread pastime," *Richmond Newspapers, Inc. v. Virginia,* 448 U.S. 555, 572 (1980).

2. Connie McNeely, "Perception of the Criminal Justice System: Television Imagery and Public Knowledge in the United States," *Journal of Criminal Justice and Popular Culture* 3, no. 1 (1995): 1–20.

3. "Cameras in Courtrooms," *Reporters' Committee for Freedom of the Press*, 2013, http://www.rcfp.org/browse-media-law-resources/digital-journalists-legal -guide/cameras-courtrooms.

4. "Justices' Comments Cast More Doubts on Supreme Court Camera," *National Constitution Center,* February 4, 2014, http://blog.constitutioncenter .org/2015/02/justices-comments-cast-more-doubts-on-supreme-court-cameras.

5. Douglas Hindman and Kenneth Wiegand, "The Big Three's Prime-Time Decline: A Technological and Social Context," *Journal of Broadcasting & Electronic Media* 52, no. 1 (2008): 119–135.

6. Paula Pointdexter, *Millennials, News and Social Media: Is News Engagement a Thing of the Past?* (New York: Peter Lang Publishing, 2012).

7. Seth Motel, "What Kinds of Supreme Court Cases Interest Americans? Not Campaign Finance," *Pew Research,* April 10, 2014, http://www.pewresearch.org/ fact-tank/2014/04/10/what-kinds-of-supreme-court-cases-interest-americans -not-campaign-finance.

8. Henry F. Fredella and Brandon Burke, "From the Legal Literature," *Criminal Law Bulletin* 43, no. 5 (September–October 2007).

9. Jeffrey Johnson, "The Entertainment Value of a Trial: How Media Access to the Courtroom is Changing the American Judicial Process," *Villanova Sports & Entertainment Law Journal* 10 (2003): 133.

10. Angelique Paul, "Turning the Camera on Court TV: Does Televising Trial Teach Us Anything about the Real Law?" *Ohio State Law Journal* 58, no. 2 (1997): 656–693.

11. George Gerbner and Larry Gross, "Living with Television: The Violence Profile," *Journal of Communication* 26 (1972): 17–40.

12. Valerie Hans and Juliet Dee, "Media Coverage of the Law," *American Behavioral Scientist* 35, no. 2 (1991): 138.

13. Doug Mataconis, "Two-Thirds of Americans Can't Name a Single Member of the Supreme Court," *Outside the Beltway,* August 12, 2012, http://www.outsidethe beltway.com/two-thirds-of-americans-cant-name-a-single-member-of-the -supreme-court/.

14. Larry Downing, "Nearly Two-Thirds of Americans Can't Name a Single Supreme Court Justice, Can You?" *NBC News,* August 22, 2012, http:// usnews.nbcnews.com/_news/2012/08/22/13413900-nearly-two-thirds-of-americans -cant-name-a-single-supreme-court-justice-can-you?lite.

15. James Podger, "Survey: Many American Today Would Get 'F' in Civics," *ABA Journal,* May 8, 2009, http://www.abajournal.com/news/article/survey _many_americans_today_would_get_f_in_civics.

16. "Supreme Court Update," *Rasmussen Reports,* July 24, 2015, http:// www.rasmussenreports.com/public_content/politics/mood_of_america/ supreme_court_update.

17. "The Challenge," *Our Courts America,* 2014, http://ourcourts.org/ the-challenge/.

18. National Center for State Courts, "Funding Justice: Strategies and Messages for Restoring Court Funding," 2013, http://www.justiceatstake.org/media/cms/ Funding_Justice_Online2012_D28F63CA32368.pdf.

19. Lynda Kaid, Mitchell McKinney, & John Tedesco, "Political Information Efficacy and Young Voters," *American Behavioral Scientist* 50 (2007): 1103.

20. Jen Kalaidis, "Bring Back Social Studies," *The Atlantic,* September 23, 2013, http://www.theatlantic.com/education/archive/2013/09/bring-back-social -studies/279891.

21. David Tewksbury, "The Seed of Audience Fragmentation: Specialization in the Use of Online News Sites," *Journal of Broadcasting & Electronic Media* 49, no. 3 (2005): 332–348.

22. "Press Release: Judiciary Uses Social Media to Keep Court Users Informed," *New Jersey Courts Judicial Branch,* August 18, 2009, http://www.judiciary .state.nj.us/pressrel/2009/pr090818a.

23. "Social Networking Eats Up 3+ Hours Per Day for the Average American User," *Marketing Charts,* January 9, 2013, http://www.marketingcharts.com/ online/social-networking-eats-up-3-hours-per-day-for-the-average-american -user-26049.

24. American Press Institute, "How Millennials Get Their News: Insights into the Habits of America's First Digital Generation," American Press Institute, March 16, 2015, http://www.americanpressinstitute.org/publications/reports/ survey-research/millennials-news.

25. "Social Media Explosion," *CQ Researcher* 4 (January 25, 2013): 88, http://ils.unc.edu/courses/2013_spring/inls200_002/Readings/CQResearcher_Social Media.pdf.

26. Jan Jacobowitz & Danielle Singer, "The Social Media Frontier: Exploring a New Mandate of Competence in the Practice of Law," *University of Miami Law Review* 68 (2014): 472.

27. Norman Meyer, "Social Media and the Courts: Innovative Tools or Dangerous Fad? A Practical Guide for Court Administrators," *International Journal for Court Administration* 6, no. 1 (June 2014): 5.

28. Garrett Graff, "Courts Are Conversations: An Argument for Increased Engagement by Court Leaders," *National Center for State Courts,* 2012, http://www.ncsc.org/services-and-experts/court-leadership/harvard-executive-session/courts-are-conversations-an-argument-forincreased-engagement-by-court-leaders.aspx.

29. John Carlo Bertot, Pau Jaeger, and Derek Hansen, "The Impact of Policies on Government Social Media Usage: Issues, Challenges, and Recommendations," *Government Information Quarterly* 29, no. 1 (2012): 30–40.

30. Video sharing services such as YouTube allow for the government to publish training material for self-services. Gohar Feroz Khan, "Models for Social Media-Based Government," *Asia Pacific Journal f Information Systems* 25, no. 1 (2015): 1–20.

31. Bertot, Jaeger, and Hansen, "The Impact of Policies on Government Social Media Usage: Issues, Challenges, and Recommendations," 30–40.

32. Minjeong Kim & Han Woo Park, "Measuring Twitter-based Political Participation and Deliberation in the South Korean Context by Using Social Network and Triple Helix Indicators," *Scientometrics* 90 (2012): 121–140.

33. Gohar Feroz Khan, Ho Young Yoon, and Han Woo Park, "Social Media Communication Strategies of Government Agencies: Twitter Use in Korea and the USA," *Asian Journal of Communication* 24, no. 1 (2014): 60–78.

34. Michael Magro, "A Review of Social Media Use in E-Government," *Administrative Sciences* 2, no. 2 (2012): 148–161.

35. Bertot, Jaeger, and Hansen, "The Impact of Policies on Government Social Media Usage: Issues, Challenges, and Recommendations," 30–40.

36. Ines Mergel, "Government 2.0 Revisited: Social Strategies in the Public Sector," *American Society for Public Administration* 33, no. 3 (2010): 7–10.

37. Khan, Yoon, and Park, "Social Media Communication Strategies of Government Agencies: Twitter Use in Korea and the USA," 60–78.

38. The federal judiciary has a YouTube channel. Also four federal U.S. bankruptcy courts have a Facebook page: District Hawaii, Southern District of Mississippi, District of New Mexico, and District of Rhode Island. "Social Media and the Courts: State Links," *National Center for State Courts,* http://www.ncsc.org/Topics/Media/Social-Media-and-the-Courts/State-Links.aspx?cat=Social Media and the Courts.

39. The states are Arizona, California, Connecticut, District of Columbia, Florida, Georgia, Guam, Hawaii, Idaho, Illinois, Indiana, Iowa, Kentucky, Maine, Massachusetts, Michigan, Montana, New Hampshire, New Jersey, New York, Ohio, Pennsylvania, Puerto Rico, Rhode Island, South Dakota, Tennessee, Texas, Utah, Vermont, Washington, and West Virginia. "AOC and High Courts," *National*

Center for State Courts, http://www.ncsc.org/Topics/Media/Social-Media-and-the
-Courts/Social-Media/aoc-and-high-courts.

40. The states are Arizona, Colorado, District of Columbia, Georgia, Hawaii, Kentucky, Michigan, Montana, New Jersey, Ohio, Puerto Rico, South Dakota, Texas, Utah, Vermont, and Washington. Ibid.

41. The states are Alaska, Connecticut, California, Colorado, Delaware, District of Columbia, Hawaii, Indiana, Massachusetts, Michigan, Minnesota, Mississippi, New Jersey, Ohio, Oregon, Puerto Rico, South Dakota, Utah, Vermont, and Washington. Ibid.

42. The five states are Alaska, Delaware, Minnesota, Mississippi and Oregon. Ibid.

43. The nine states are the District of Columbia, Hawaii, Michigan, New Jersey, Ohio, Puerto Rico, South Dakota, Utah, Vermont, and Washington. Five states also have a Flickr account: California, Indiana, Kentucky, Tennessee, and West Virginia. Ibid.

44. Norman Meyer, "Social Media and the Courts: Innovative Tools or Dangerous Fad? A Practical Guide for Court Administrators," *International Journal for Court Administration* 6, no. 1 (June 2014): 7.

45. Ibid.

46. Ibid., 5.

47. Ibid.

48. Will Oremus, "Kagan Admits Supreme Court Justices Haven't Quite Figured Out Email Yet," *Slate,* August 20, 2013, http://www.slate.com/blogs/future _tense/2013/08/20/elena_kagan_supreme_court_justices_haven_t_gotten_to _email_use_paper_memos.html.

49. Ibid.

50. Seth Muse, "Ethics of Using Social Media during Case Investigation and Discovery," *American Bar Association*, June 13, 2012, http://apps.americanbar.org/ litigation/committees/pretrial/email/spring2012/spring2012-0612-ethics-using -social-media-during-case-investigation-discovery.html.

51. Brian Grow, "Internet v. Courts: Googling for the Perfect Juror," *Reuters*, February 17, 2011.

52. *Wilgus v. F/V Sirius, Inc.*, 665 F. Supp. 2d 23 (D. Me, 2009): 24.

53. *Sluss v. Commonwealth of Kentucky*, 381 S.W.3d 215 (Ky. 2012).

54. Andrew Flake, "Juror Use of Social Media: Closing the Evidentiary Back Door," *American Bar Association*, November 1, 2013, http://apps.americanbar.org/ litigation/committees/trialevidence/articles/fall2013-1113-juror-use-social -media-closing-evidentiary-back-door.html.

55. Emily Janoski-Haehlen, "The Courts Are All-a-Twitter: The Implications of Social Media Use in the Courts," *Valparaiso University Law Review* 46 (2011): 51.

56. In one study of 508 judges, only 30 reported an abuse of social media in at least one of their cases. Federal Judicial Center, "Jurors' Use of Social Media during Trials and Deliberations: A Report to the Judicial Conference Committee on Court Administration and Case Management," May 1, 2014, http://www2 .fjc.gov/content/jurors-use-social-media-during-trials-and-deliberations-report -judicial-conference-committ-0.

57. John Browning, "Why Can't We Be Friends? Judges' Use of Social Media," *University of Miami Law Review* 68 (2014): 487–534.

58. "Interview with Justice Don Willett of the Supreme Court of Texas," *Declarations: The Coverage Opinions*, May 7, 2014, http://www.coverageopinions.info/Vol3Issue8/Declara tions.html.

59. Adi Robertson, "Only 2 Percent of Americans Can't Get Internet Access, but 20 Percent Choose Not To," *Verge*, August 26, 2013, http://www.theverge.com/2013/8/26/4660008/pew-study-finds-30-percent-americans-have-no-home-broadband.

60. *Garrison v. Louisiana,* 379 U.S. 64, (1964): 85.

61. *United States v. New York Times,* 403 U.S. 713, (1971): 724.

62. Ibid., 719.

63. *New York Times Co. v. Sullivan,* 376 U.S. 254 (1965): 269–270. There is a "profound national commitment to the principle that debate on public issues should be uninhibited, robust, and wide-open, and that it may well include vehement, caustic, and sometimes unpleasantly sharp attacks on government and public officials." Ibid.

64. "Openness enhances both the basic fairness of the criminal trial and the appearance of fairness so essential to public confidence in the system," *Press-Enterprise Co. v. Superior Court,* 464 U.S. 501 (1984): 508.

65. *Richmond Newspapers, Inc. v. Virginia,* 448 U.S. 555 (1980): 572.

66. Ibid., 567–568.

67. *Globe Newspaper v. Superior Court,* 457 U.S. 596 (1982): 606.

68. Our Courts America, "Our Approach," 2014, http://ourcourts.org/our-approach.

69. American Bar Association, *Model Code of Judicial Conduct*: Rule 1.2, Comment 2, 2011, http://www.americanbar.org/content/dam/aba/migrated/judicialethics/ABA_MCJC_approved.authcheckdam.pdf.

70. Ibid., Preamble.

71. American Bar Association, "Public Perceptions of Lawyers: Consumer Research Findings," (2002): 24.

72. "Future Trends in State Courts 2007," *National Center for State Courts* (2007): 24.

Chapter 13

Chinese Netizens Set China's Public Agenda via Social Media

Yu Zhang

INTRODUCTION

Studies have established that, while the Chinese Communist Party (CCP) still defines, frames, and dictates what China's state media can or cannot publish on critical issues and events, it can no longer control or prevent public discussion of issues and events of major social consequences and political significance[1] due to social media. Despite, and perhaps because of Chinese government's blocking of access to the global social media such as Twitter and Facebook, Chinese indigenous social media such as Weibo (微博, microblog) and WeChat (微信, messaging) were born to provide an alternative service. Weibo was first launched in 2009 by Sina.com, one of China's biggest online service providers. Other major Chinese online providers, such as Netease, Tencent, and Sohu, have followed and launched their own Weibo.[2] WeChat is a product from China's Tencent (腾讯) corporation.

In recent years, insignificant tweets, images, or incidents from these social media entities have started virtual fires that set a national agenda for the Chinese media and the public. In some cases, ordinary citizens were able to divert public attention and discussion toward the direction where the public wanted to go instead of where the state wanted to lead the public. Digital activism and civic engagement on social media not only reflect the rising individualism in Chinese society but also set the public agenda, which has profoundly and effectively transformed the relations between individuals and government. The pursuit of individual and public interest as concerned netizens, and their rights-assertion activities, helps promote their agenda. Social media help define, refine, and grow citizen–government relation as well as public agenda. A right-to-know sense by citizens challenges the Chinese political tradition that bestows the state with absolute authority.[3] The growing digital activism offers fresh perspectives on the relationship between self and others, individual and collectives, private and public, as well as spatial boundaries in broader contemporary Chinese society.[4]

THE BI FUJIAN INCIDENT

A Chinese celebrity TV host's impromptu parody of a Chinese classic revolutionary song had gone viral on social media in spring 2015. Bi Fujian, a host of the world's most-watched annual television event, the Chinese New Year Gala on China's national television station CCTV, was making fun of *The Taking of Tiger Mountain*, an oldies from a 1958 revolutionary opera, on April 6, 2015, at a restaurant table with several laughing companions.[5] The song lauds the CCP leader Mao Zedong and the People's Liberation Army during the civil war with the Nationalists in the late 1940s.[6]

In the video, Bi ridiculed the song's exaggerated sentiment and patriotism. After the lyric "we wear a red star on our heads, red flags on both sides," Bi joked, "What kind of dress is that?" He then called Mao an expletive, saying he had "really hurt us bitterly."[7] The video was released by an unknown person and quickly ignited a national debate on social media. CCTV fired Bi Fujian days later. This case demonstrated the tremendous power of social media and proved that what can be discussed by the Chinese public can no longer be precooked only by the state media in an era of social media.

This chapter attempts to use this case and other cases to illustrate that the Chinese government's agenda-setting power is increasingly balanced and shared by ordinary Chinese netizens, who are armed with social media. As a result, social media have significantly weakened the Chinese information censorship, forcing the government to rethink its strategy. This chapter argues that, as a formidable force, social media compete with the state media to set the agenda in favor of ordinary citizens, who increasingly leverage the "courts" of social media to deliver justice. It finds that a seemingly trivial incident can be magnified by the social media, which increasingly functions as a pressure valve in the Chinese society and empower ordinary citizens to raise questions loudly and get faster and better responses for those questions.

RETHINKING AGENDA-SETTING THEORY

Agenda-setting theory emphasizes media's role as a central gatekeeper to construct the social reality in the public's mind and that the media can transfer the salience of issues on media agenda to the public agenda.[8] By concentrating on a particular topic, the media "help" the public find which issues and topics are important based on the fact that it is reported on or not. This theory dictates that the frequency of certain content appearing in mass media helps the public frame or perceive certain issues as important or not. However, empirical studies[9] show that digital communication has reduced the ability of the Chinese authorities to dictate media content on Chinese public.[10] Thus, agenda setting enters a new age of limited media effects in China while social media, on the other hand, play a role in setting public agenda in the Chinese society.

Agenda setting, as a form of soft power, is superior to the draconian censorship when it comes to thought control. It can seep through people's minds and hearts to influence. Chinese authorities realize that a more sophisticated way to exert state influence over public discourse is to allow selective dissent. For example, Chinese President Xi Jinping's anticorruption campaign encourages media to report high-level CCP corruption in an attempt to convince the public that the Party is serious in curbing corruption. This position serves to both dampen online rumors about a specific case and to take a preemptive strike against any criticisms. In this capacity, despite its temporary reputational costs, this proactive approach enhances the Party's long-term reputation and thus influences the public in a positive way.[11]

As a battleground between authorities and citizens in competing for agenda setting for the Chinese public, social media have turned ordinary citizens into amateur reporters and news moderators. Social media's unique, sweeping, immediate, and powerful effect on the Chinese society often leads to deeper and wider investigation and discussion of the reported issues.[12] As the Bi Fujian case indicated, while agenda setting was previously a privilege of only the state or the elite, it is no longer necessarily so. The interactive and decentralized nature of social media has empowered citizens, whose priorities, interests, and concerns were routinely ignored by the state media, to appeal their issues directly to the masses via social media, thus bypassing the hierarchical state media.[13]

Chaffee and Metzger have argued that the agenda setting have been increasingly shifting from what issues the media tell people to think about to what issues people tell the media they want to think about.[14] The Bi video incident has powerfully illustrated how an ordinary netizen can sway the agenda of the public and of the media toward what the public want to talk about. In this case, Chinese netizens have collectively determined that this case is important for public discussion and debate. In this sense, they are no longer merely information consumers of state media but information producers as well.

While this case has embarrassed the Party, it has also converged the public interest and the state interest. Not only did the incident quickly attract the attention of those with a resurgent loyalty to Mao Zedong and his policies, the mocking from a host of CCP's top media mouthpiece against the founder of the Party and PRC is also unacceptable to many Chinese citizens. For other Chinese, the national criticism of Bi feels like a dejavu or a return of the Cultural Revolution, when friends, neighbors, and even family members were encouraged to betray one another for devotion to Mao's ideals. "During the Cultural Revolution, wives would report what their husbands said under the sheets; sons would report what mothers said at the dinner table," as one Weibo post said.[15]

TOWARD AN AUTHORITY-CITIZEN INFORMATION SHARING PLATFORM

The social media platform and its marketplace of opinions give commoners an equal opportunity to communicate to the public as members of the ruling class can on the same platform. For the first time ordinary citizens can argue, criticize, and mock authority online in a way they never could offline.[16] In addition, social media can potentially turn everyone into anybody, such as a villain or a hero. In this sense, netizen discourse and their collective agenda not only become an invaluable reality of Chinese people's lives but can also shape their future.

China's netizens aim not only to criticize and shame the privileged, the corrupt, and the hypocritical, but they also renew, recreate, and regenerate understanding about issues and public agenda, and embracing agenda that matter to the ordinary citizens. Under this circumstance, an equal and open concept of discourse agenda can force or attract the authorities, the elites, and the populace to a dialogue and reconstruct public discourse together. China's netizen discourse illustrates the power of the populace to create its own discourse culture, which is liberating, natural, and creatively playful. Besides building an agenda, Chinese netizens also deconstruct or upset the agenda from the authorities and elites. As the Bi Fujian case has indicated, this sudden "video incident" agenda served to influence and force official agenda to be open and transparent and democratic in responding to the "misconduct" of one of their own elites.

Domestic and international voices and pressures for political reform and demand for social justice are overwhelming the Chinese authorities. The Chinese leaders, while continuing to view economic development as their first priority, now pay substantial attention to social inequality, economic disparities, and public dissatisfactions.[17] They have warned officials to be receptive to citizen opinions and to address their immediate grievances as required by the walking the Mass Line campaign that attempted to build closer relation between the masses and the Party.[18] The CCP's ultimate appeal, at home and abroad, while still resting largely on the country's economic success, now increasingly depends on making real progress in the areas of freedom of speech and political reform.

Freedom of speech is, understandably, voraciously pursued and exercised on social media by the Chinese public who previously had no outlet for critical public discourse. On the other hand, the Chinese leadership needs a certain level of information and supervision openness in pushing for more opportunities and resources to the long-neglected, disadvantaged, and marginalized populations and regions. The Party is consolidating its power by being increasingly responsive to public demands. As an increasingly responsive authoritarianism,[19] the CCP regime needs and allows citizens to vent many of their frustration on social media.

Zhongdang Pan argued that competition and fight for the articulation between the state media and citizens is common and that articulation allows citizens to sustain, repair, or fortify as well as amend, resist, or erode an otherwise unjust agenda.[20] Social media's democratizing appeal to advance an agenda or a point of view, or simply coordinate some oppositional discourse or collective actions, is irresistible, according to Pan. Within the state-society framework, vitalized netizens have creatively resisted the authoritarian state to articulate their own agenda or interests. To netizens, the opportunity to express is also an opportunity to impress and to make that voice matter. Viewed in this light, the persistent inequality and injustice in political and civic participation are alleviated with the help of Weibo, WeChat, and other social media.

As a public square for expression, understandably, this platform is increasingly shared by both citizens and authorities. Citizens' insights, complaints, and grievances on public policy and political issues often engender social action, as they publicize social problems, analyze public events, and criticize government corruption and even the taboos and forbidden subjects. In contrast to the hierarchical structure of public and political life, online lives are more egalitarian and spirited, providing an even dialogue between authority and the populace. This atmosphere of dialogue helps facilitate and produce discourse, agenda, critics, and neologisms, which in turn create enjoyment and more freedom than off-line life can provide.

DIGITAL ACTIVISM

The rising tide of activism and discourses on social media challenge the legitimacy of the CCP's political power, especially on issues that matter to the public such as livelihood, environment, and social justice. To contain such challenge, the Chinese government not only has invested enormous technological and human resources on censorship but also attempts to influence public opinion. In general, the government has leveraged Weibo and WeChat to mobilize Chinese citizens to advance Party causes and discourses such as the China Dream, the Mass Line, and anticorruption to ensure that the Party not only stays in power but is well liked as well. Specific examples include state Weibo accounts praising Xi Jinping's December 2014 unexpected visit to a local restaurant in Beijing, where he stood in line to order his meal, paid, ate, and chatted with other diners.[21] Xi was also lauded for braving the smog-ridden Beijing air without a face mask.

Despite insisting on continuous censorship, the Chinese authorities also see digital activism and civic engagement serve as a safety valve[22] in the Chinese society for people to vent frustration, thus reducing some steaming pressures in the nation. In Bi's case, the social media's stormy discussion not only magnified and added fuel to the debates between conservatives and reformers but also helped the public vent their frustration about hypocrisy of the establishment in today's Chinese society. However, it also forces onto the national agenda the reconsideration of what constitutes private speech and what is not. Previously, most people felt that they could talk freely among friends or at a dinner table. However, this case reminds the public that the pervasiveness of technology such as smartphones and social media can threaten the cozy social oasis as much as state censorship. In this case, it ended Bi's career with the prestigious CCTV.

On the other hand, the Party is also wary of any challenging, competing, and dissenting discourses on social media that might upset its agenda even as it encourages the public to vocalize concerns about government in an attempt to release the explosive social pressures accumulated over the years. While the state did not find the Bi incident as menacing, it did find some other similar cases as threatening to the Party's legitimacy. For example, in early 2015, the Cyberspace Administration shut down 133 public WeChat accounts for disseminating "distorted" views of history.[23] Some WeChat users claim "inside secrets" or use "hot topic" as fodder for conversation. For example, they questioned how Qiu Shaoyun, a Chinese soldier, who died fighting U.S. troops in Korea in 1951 could lay motionless as the government has claimed, when the fire set off by an enemy bomb engulfed him.[24] The state media had claimed that Qiu, who did not want to expose his comrades laying near him, endured unbearable pains and died without moving. Some people have said that it is humanly impossible not to move when fire was burning him. Such a challenging version would have never made it to the traditional media. But the social media have set a virtual fire on an old story and put the issue up for public agenda discussion.

China's geographic size and massive population can no longer prohibit an activist from connecting with like-minded activists elsewhere. Social media allow them to easily connect with and support each other, thus magnifying their causes among netizens, which often helps produce a mass online campaign. A grassroots coalition of interested netizens,[25] who leverage the social media to collectively advocate for issues that matter to them, is a potent force to set a public agenda. As a result, powerful opinion discourse often quickly forms and forces the government to address their concerns. The public agenda, the media agenda, and the policy agenda often converge as a result of these civic engagements. Public opinion and discourse from Weibo and WeChat have emerged as a competitive, agenda-setting force to make certain social and political issues more salient. Their voices have often become too loud to ignore. Their postings and discourse have influenced or changed the agenda of state media and the government.

CCP's communication power has focused on its ability to influence political preferences through setting agenda for the nation. However, netizens can upset that agenda. For example, the state's "harmonious society" slogan has been sarcastically twisted by netizens into "being harmonized," which implies being forced into accepting the state's indoctrination. Over time, opposite interpretation has neutralized and limited the state's ability to indoctrinate. As mentioned previously, netizens' humorous adaptation of state discourse have emboldened them to challenge widespread political injustices, which ultimately helps level the playing field between state and citizens over time. The omnipotence of the ubiquitous social media and their users shows that if enough netizens yell together, the government and the public will not only hear it, but they are also likely to do something about it.

"COURT" OF SOCIAL MEDIA

Social media have allowed the Chinese public to become more outspoken and engaging in social, public, and state affairs while letting the government leverage public opinion on social media to solve thorny social issues. It has driven the co-governance and mutual supervision between the state and citizens on state affairs[26] and empowers a consensus seeking between the government and the public. For example, Chinese citizens' growing consciousness in monitoring government performance and holding officials accountable is motivating the public to identify corrupt officials, expose their misconducts, and amplify the abuse of power.[27]

The Chinese government increasingly leverages digital activism to measure public opinion, test-drive policies, and respond to citizens' concerns. This gives social media an opportunity to help formulate the co-governing agreement between the Chinese authorities and the masses. Seizing this opportunity, Chinese citizens demand local government agencies to enforce social justice, punish corrupt officials, and improve their performance. This forces authorities to widen, deepen, and speed up the anticorruption fight. In this sense, social media have linked the public who feed information and the CCP's disciplinary mechanisms, who seek and use those information to fight corruption. To a certain degree, the Chinese citizens, the Party, and social media are all partners in this campaign.

Since in-depth information on controversial cases and sensitive issues are not always pursued or provided by the state media, Chinese netizens themselves have to find, feed, and spread the related information and perspectives on these issues via social media. For example, Yang Dacai, a Shaanxi provincial official, was often photographed wearing luxurious and brand-name watches, thus gaining him the nickname Brother Watch. In August 2012 when visiting the site of a serious traffic accident that killed 36 people, Yang was photographed smiling. His demeanor triggered heated reactions on Weibo and resulted more pictures of him wearing various luxurious watches on many occasions. The online outrage soon led to an official probe and his dismissal.[28] In September 2013, Yang was sentenced to 14 years in prison for bribery and possession of assets of unclear origin.[29]

In another case, the Chinese public were furious over a school principal who spent the night in a hotel room with four underage girls in southern China's Hainan province in early 2013. Citizens posted on Weibo photographs of themselves with the handheld message: Principal, get a room with me, leave the young students alone.[30] The online public reaction resulted in the quick firing, prosecution, and sentencing of the principal to 13 years in prison.[31] Since censorship has trained and conditioned Chinese citizens to become sensitive to official information, misinformation, or disinformation, alternative sources of information from Weibo and WeChat and their transparent and interactive platforms of information have provided valuable services to China's citizens, although the information they carry has often become political quicks and that can undermine the carefully crafted veneer of social harmony.[32]

As the Bi Fujian case and the aforementioned other cases have indicated, public discussion of an otherwise ordinary event or incident often snowballs into potent national dialogues. In another case, after a Chinese teenager scratched Ding Jinhao visited here on a temple wall in the ancient city Luxor in May 2013, a posted photo by another Chinese tourist triggered an online storm, which attacked Ding and his act. The 15-year-old boy was quickly identified, prompting his parents to publicly apologize to the nation for damaging the image of the Chinese people.[33] Cases like these have demonstrated that popular cyber opinion can potentially attract public attention and instantly trigger national attention and debate. The equalizing platform of social media has empowered average Chinese citizens with an unprecedented opportunity to expose misconduct.

DISCOURSE STRATEGY

In discussions of sensitive topics, netizens rely on lexicons and discourse strategies to avoid censorship and scrutiny from the authorities. Their dynamic and creative discourses reflect the fluid sociopolitical environment in China.[34] The party-state can no longer monopolize the distribution of social resources and has to allow greater civic and political speech freedom for its own legitimacy and survival. Disgruntled citizens are no longer howling in the wilderness—the government now listens on social media. To be sure, digital empowerment is not tantamount to democratization but nevertheless is an important ingredient in helping move the Chinese society from authoritarian rule to a more democratic form. As such, the Chinese authoritarian rule appears to become more stable by allowing people to vent their frustration.

The Chinese Internet users employ various discourse strategies to organize subtle online petitions/campaigns and to defy censorship. These discourses are often in response to the official discourse.[35] Netizens have created new words or have changed the meanings of existing words to express an idea on a censored subject. For example, they use "zf" to indicate "zhengfu" (政府) or government when criticizing it. This simple technique helps bypass state censorship because there is no way that the automated censorship detectors can censor such an abbreviation, which could mean many different things. However, netizens know exactly what it means in that subtle context.

These linguistic and discourse strategies help establish, maintain, and sustain online interactions and defiantly avoid censorship. These coded discourses enable the Chinese public to interact right under the radar screen of the state. For expressing their views through coded language, neologisms, and satire to evade censorship and avoid repression,[36] citizen-turned amateur journalists creatively and successfully use flexible Chinese characters to evade and confuse the automated keyword censorship systems. Before being erased or blocked, many posts have already gone viral.[37]

Alternative and disguised expressions help bypass censorship. For example, breaking up the name of a former Chinese premier Li Peng (李鹏) into separate Chinese characters (李月月鸟) while mentioning him negatively can dodge censorship. Other sophisticated strategies to evade censorship include using coded phrases, metaphors, and satire in veiled and hidden criticism.[38] For example, using hama or toad (蛤蟆) to refer to the former Chinese President Jiang Zemin if mentioning him negatively is a popular tactic employed by Chinese netizens, who creatively, humorously, and playfully counter the state censorship. Such innovative language input techniques, which would have unlikely survived scrutiny in old media, thrive in cyberspace.[39] Now Chinese social media users can discuss almost any social issues to a potential mass audience, which is equivalent to having a huge rally. In this sense, citizens have earned more freedom for themselves and set the agenda for the public.

RETHINKING CENSORSHIP

Studies have shown that not only the sheer volume of flowing information and postings on the Internet makes it impossible to track all of them[40] but the time lapse of posted information and content ambiguity of some posts and their rapid dispersion challenge the censorship scheme.[41] Furthermore, the Chinese authorities concede that citizens' creative anticensorship strategies force them toward thinking that responding to citizens is probably a better strategy than controlling information.[42] To do so, the Chinese government has promoted administrative transparency and public supervision of government agencies. This strategy has gradually led to more freedom in China's cyberspace, which allows Chinese citizens to exchange, share, distribute information and opinions, and debate a wide array of social and political issues.

Research has shown that the weaning of direct financial subsidies since the 1990s from the state has forced the state media to be creative in attracting readers and advertising revenue.[43] As a result of commercialization, Chinese media have become less politically driven and more socially motivated organizations despite their continuous ideological and political obligation or loyalty to the CCP.[44]

The Chinese authorities understand that censorship in the digital age only make it harder for the public to find certain sensitive or censored information, but it cannot entirely block them especially due to the availability of proxy or circumvention technology. Furthermore, as more Chinese are traveling overseas and more foreigners are traveling to China than at any time in history in 2014, over 100 million Chinese traveled overseas, the largest number in any nation[45]—Chinese citizens are already exposed to a variety of censored information. Additionally, public resistance toward censorship has also compelled the Chinese government to focus more on guiding the information flood than blocking the seeping information.

The Chinese government realized that guiding the public opinions through effective dissemination of "correct" information will more likely produce "correct" thought among netizens than the control of "wrong" information. Moreover, the Chinese government also believes that ill-informed decisions often lead to disastrous consequences, and censorship can destroy citizens' trust for the government and create suspicion on even valid and true information from the state.[46] Additionally, censorship has attracted condemnation at home and abroad and can trigger public resistance, not to mention the staggering financial costs of censorship (purchasing or developing the filtering software as well as hiring and training people to censor and implementing the censorship mechanism).[47]

CONCLUDING REMARKS

As a public space to collectively articulate and amplify public opinions, social media have reduced people's reliance on state media, or any one source of media, for information, thus diminishing the state's ability to set the agenda for the public. Social media are powerful platforms and forces that facilitate communication among the public as well as between Chinese authorities and the public. They empower the Chinese netizens with more freedom in setting public agenda with their active online participation in public and social affairs, which has, in turn, created an increasingly vibrant online environment to help force China's unilateral authoritarian control toward more transparency and pluralism.

As the Bi Fujian video incident has indicated, the Chinese citizens' active engagement in information production and dissemination through social media have enabled them to not only be able to set public agenda but also guide public opinion. The public's civic discourses have set and, occasionally, upset official agenda or media agenda by collectively raising doubts, requests, and suggestions about the nation's political, social, and public affairs. There is no doubt that Weibo, WeChat, and other Chinese social media have empowered the Chinese masses to balance the state monopoly of information and agenda setting. A consensus between the public and the state is that social media provide not only a channel to vent citizens' frustration and dissent, but they also serve as a safety valve for the CCP and the Chinese society.

NOTES

1. Guangchao Feng and Steven Zhongshi Guo, "Tracing the Route of China's Internet Censorship: An Empirical Study," *Telematics and Informatics* 30, no. 4 (2013): 335–345.

2. Wilfred Yang Wang, "Weibo, Framing, and Media Practices in China," *Journal of Chinese Political Science* 18, no. 4 (2013): 375–388.

3. Pauline Cheong and Jie Gong, "Cyber Vigilantism, Transmedia Collective Intelligence, and Civic Participation," *Chinese Journal of Communication* 3, no. 4 (2010): 471–487.

4. Elaine Yuan, Miao Feng, and James A. Danowski, "Privacy in Semantic Networks on Chinese Social Media," *Journal of Communication* (2013). doi:10.1111/jcom.12058.

5. Julie Makinen, "China's Dick Clark in Hot Water over Unscripted Mao Comments," *Los Angeles Times*, April 9, 2015, http://www.latimes.com/world/asia/la-fg-china-mao-comments-20150409-story.html.

6. Ibid.

7. Ibid.

8. Maxwell McCombs, "A Look at Agenda-setting: Past, Present and Future," *Journalism Studies* 6, no. 4 (2005): 543–557.

9. Gary King, Jennifer Pan, and Margaret Roberts, "How Censorship in China Allows Government Criticism but Silences Collective Expression," *American Political Science Review* 107, no. 2 (2013): 326–343.

10. Cindy Chiu, Chris Ip, and Ari Silverman, "Understanding Social Media in China," *McKinsey Quarterly* (April, 2012): 1–6.

11. Ashley Esarey and Qiang Xiao, "Digital Communication and Political Change in China," *International Journal of Communication* 5 (2011): 298–319.

12. Jon Sullivan, "A Tale of Two Blogs in China," *Media, Culture and Society* 34, no. 6 (August, 2012): 774–783.

13. Steven Millward, "The Rise of Social Media in China, with All-New User Numbers," May 2012, https://www.techinasia.com/rise-of-china-social-media-infographic-2012/.

14. Steven Chaffee and Miriam Metzger, "The End of Mass Communication?" *Mass Communication and Society* 4, no. 4 (November, 2001): 365–379.

15. Bethany Allen-Ebrahimian, "Drunken Chinese Celeb 'Rap Geniuses' Mao-Era Song," April 8, 2015, http://foreignpolicy.com/2015/04/08/china-mao-censorship-rap-genius/.

16. Yinchun Xu, "Understanding Netizen Discourse in China: Formation, Genres, and Values," *China Media Research* 8, no. 1 (2012).

17. Lijun Tang and Helen Sampson, "The Interaction Between Mass Media and the Internet in Non-democratic States: The Case of China," *Media, Culture and Society* 34, no. 4 (2012): 457–471.

18. Lina Yang and Juan Zhao, "Xi Jinping Summarizes the Mass Line Campaign," October 8, 2014, http://qzlx.people.com.cn/n/2014/1009/c364565-25792940.html.

19. Daniela Stockmann, *Media Commercialization and Authoritarian Rule in China* (Cambridge: Cambridge University Press, 2014).

20. Zhongdang Pan, "Articulation and Re-articulation: Agenda for Understanding Media and Communication in China," *International Journal of Communication* 4, (2010), 1932–8036/2010FEA0517: 517–530.

21. Matt Schiavenza, "Xi Jinping Eats Some Dumplings at a Restaurant," December 3, 2013, http://www.theatlantic.com/china/archive/2013/12/xi-jinping-eats-some-dumplings-at-a-restaurant/282719/.

22. Wenhong Chen, "Taking Stock, Moving Forward: The Internet, Social Networks and Civic Engagement in Chinese Societies," *Information, Communication & Society* 17, no. 1 (2014): 1–6.

23. Paul Carsten, "China's Tencent Shuts Down 133 WeChat Accounts for 'Distorting History," *Xinhua*, January 20, 2015, http://www.reuters.com/article/2015/01/20/us-tencent-censorship-idUSKBN0KT0WM20150120#jVwOsyXi7ETtJzsO.

24. Miles Yu, "Hero or Zero? Communist Party's Revolutionary Military Heros Challenged," June 4, 2015, http://www.washingtontimes.com/news/2015/jun/4/inside-china-credibility-of-communist-chinas-revol/.

25. James Leibold, "Blogging Alone: China, the Internet, and the Democratic Illusion?" *The Journal of Asian Studies* 70, no. 4 (2011): 1023–1041.

26. Qin Gu, "Sina Weibo: A Mutual Communication Apparatus between the Chinese Government and Chinese Citizens," *China Media Research* 10, no. 2, (April, 2014): 72–89.

27. Ying Li, "Anti-corruption Campagin on Weibo," *China Economic Weekly* 48, (December 11, 2012): 22–23.

28. Manya Koetse, "Weibo Is Watching—China's Corrupt Comrades," September 6, 2013, http://www.whatsonweibo.com/corruptcomrades/.

29. Jonathan Kaiman, "China's Brother Wristwatch Yang Dacai Jailed for 14 Years for Corruption," September 5, 2013, http://www.theguardian.com/world/2013/sep/05/china-brother-wristwatch-yang-dacai-sentenced.

30. Didi Tang, "Chinese against Sex Abuse: Sleep with Me, Not Kids," June 3, 2013, http://news.yahoo.com/chinese-against-sex-abuse-sleep-not-kids-063856968.html.

31. Xinhua, "Principal Sentenced 13 Years for Checking into Hotel Room in Hainan with Under-age Girls," June 20, 2013, http://www.xinhua.com.

32. Zhongshi Guo and Guangchao Feng, "Understanding Support for Internet Censorship in China: An Elaboration of the Theory of Reasoned Action," *Journal of Chinese Political Science* 17, no. 1 (2012): 33–52.

33. AP, "Chinese Teen Sparks Outcry after Writing Name on Egyptian Temple Wall," May 28, 2013, http://www.foxnews.com/world/2013/05/28/outcry-after-chinese-teen-defaces-ancient-egyptian-temple/.

34. Elain Yuan, "Language Use as Social Practice on the Chinese Internet," 2013, http://eyuan.people.uic.edu/Research_files/Yuan_InternetLanguage.pdf.

35. Ibid.

36. Ashley Esarey and Qiang Xiao, "Political Expression in the Chinese Blogosphere: Below the Radar," *Asian Survey* 48, no. 5 (September/October, 2008): 752–772.

37. Ibid.

38. Ibid.

39. Qin Gu, "Sina Weibo: A Mutual Communication Apparatus between the Chinese Government and Chinese Citizens," *China Media Research* 10, no. 2, (April, 2014): 72–89.

40. Rebecca MacKinnon, "Flatter World and Thicker Walls? Blogs, Censorship and Civic Discourse in China," *Public Choice* 134 (2008): 47–65.

41. Qin Gu, 2014.

42. Ibid.

43. Shanthi Kalathil, "Chinese Media and the Information Revolution," *Harvard Asia Quarterly* 6, no. 1 (Winter, 2002): 27–30.

44. Jason Lacharite, "Electronic Decentralisation in China: A Critical Analysis of Internet Filtering Policies in the People's Republic of China," *Australian Journal of Political Science* 37, no. 2 (2002): 333–346.

45. Christina Larson, "Chinese Tourists Make More than 100 Million Overseas Trips in 2014," December 5, 2014, http://www.bloomberg.com/bw/articles/2014-12-05/theyre-coming-chinese-tourists-will-make-100-million-trips-abroad-this-year.

46. Gary King, Jennifer Pan, and Margaret Roberts, "How Censorship in China Allows Government Criticism but Silences Collective Expression," *American Political Science Review* 107, no. 2 (2013): 326–343.

47. Haiping Zheng, "Regulating the Internet: China's Law and Practice," *Beijing Law Review* 4, no. 1 (2013): 37–41.

Chapter 14

The Global Impact: Using Social Media to Learn about World Politics

David McCoy

INTRODUCTION

The study of global social media allows a deeper view of world cultures and politics as well as a concise understanding of one's place in the world. This chapter outlines the role Web 2.0 tools play in developing learner awareness, enhancing research comprehension, and producing meaningful instructional activities that focus on the understanding of transnational social media use. Moreover, it examines the key steps required for the enactment of a course that uses social media to study Web 2.0 political engagement in other countries. The experiences of multidisciplinary students at a small liberal arts university are described within the context of accessing social media to research, design, and implement course-assigned global studies.

This chapter depicts a pedagogical approach that provides multiple beneficial outcomes. First, the study of global social media permits a way to see these mediated applications as more than just personal communication tools. Second, the active learning and discovery methods employed through research opportunities reflect current best practices of collegiate teaching and learning. Third, individual and group course assignments allow students to effectively work with new digital literacy tools, such as Facebook, Twitter, and blogs. Finally, the planning, implementation, and assessment processes required to implement a globally oriented social media course into a collegiate environment can be integrated across numerous disciplines. Therefore, the intent of this chapter is to convey both a pedagogical design method and the instructional usefulness of a globally oriented social media college course.

SOCIAL MEDIA, GLOBAL AWARENESS, AND POLITICS

This section begins with a central question. Why would the study of global social media be so important to American college students? According to a TNS Digital Life research study, global media consumers spent more than five and a half hours per month on social networking sites. This usage extends beyond physical borders. Global social media users receive detailed access to areas and events that traditional media cannot cover while revealing first person insights about native cultures.[1] The relevance of these factors cannot be dismissed, as the increased awareness and knowledge about globalization and its mediated aspects have been urged for the education of students as valued twenty-first-century skills.[2]

More critically, global awareness is a pivotal goal of modern learning as students are called to process and reflect upon information in new and more meaningful ways. This "information literacy" skill set, as described by Waycott, Bennet, Kennedy, Dalgamo, and Gray, engenders the ability to locate, evaluate, and use effectively information for global endeavors.[3] Information literacy has developed a "global recognition" that supports "everyday tasks, lifelong learning and successful engagement with the local and international community" and therefore produced an enhanced awareness in individuals.[4] Additionally, the need for cultivating globalization topics in higher education courses relates to both crucial citizenship qualities and self-growth. In her study of small private U.S. universities that feature specific courses that address international news and global issues, Lisosky stated that global efforts in American higher education have a twofold purpose that include an improvement of the knowledge and skills to function adequately in an increasingly intense global environment and to "sensitize U.S. students to variations in cultural similarities and differences, which contribute significantly to students' critical thinking abilities" and widen their appreciation of the workings of other nations' institutions, including political systems.[5]

Although mediated communication is not the prime mover in political and social change, it is a very powerful instrument for imprinting individual's outlooks on life. Social media, for many young people in most countries, plays an important role because it is the go-to source of current public opinion. Part of the change from a mass-mediated model to a social-mediated dynamic results from the openness or closeness of different societies. Open nations use the Internet and social media to both enhance political information and engage in citizen feedback. In some countries, there is little or no room for viewpoints that criticize the political order, thereby leading mass media to perform as governmental public relations vehicles. Individuals are compelled to seek out social media tools as a method to voice personal beliefs and form groups of political action. Social media, in turn, allow for a fifth estate of citizen political participation and viewpoints.

Using and mastering social media in a process of studying how others employ social media is a twenty-first-century skill that is very beneficial. Various empirical studies have shown that the need to teach and research the global influences of social media are growing due to the rapid use of digital devices and Web 2.0 applications in international business, tourism, and politics.[6] Worldview awareness and the digital devices of mediated communication are converging in ways not imagined only a few years ago. In this construct, a global attention economy has arisen. More importantly, the "culture of connectivity" promises a dynamic evolution in an "online ecosystem embedded in a larger sociocultural and a political-economic context" that begs to be researched, analyzed, and communicated.[7]

Understanding how others use new media can align with the goals of global citizenship. By viewing how nations and constituencies demonstrate civic action or practice politics, students can become informed global citizens. By learning how to use data from various global sources, students can analyze and convert this information into meaningful modes. By employing specific techniques in Internet and social media research, they can tap into networks of international groups and more fully realize the critical importance of political action.

World politics, specifically, are transformed by the use of the Internet and social media. Political uprisings, such as the Arab Spring, demonstrate both the internal and the external communicative and social power of personally mediated technology.[8] Political campaigns in other countries are increasingly using social media as practical supplements to older forms. By studying these approaches, American students can compare and contrast the political dynamic and develop a clearer awareness of citizen participation. In essence, the study of global politics through the Internet and social media helps Americans learn about our own political system and our place in the world. Social media, therefore, becomes a viable electronic connection that extends individual understanding of one's own future and the conceptualization of the lives and interests of world citizens.

SOCIAL MEDIA IN THE COLLEGE CLASSROOM

The focus of this section is to illustrate relevant studies in the literature that examine how social media are used as collegiate course instructive instruments. These studies offer descriptive details into class assignment use, research capabilities, and collaborative learning techniques.

An increasing amount of recent studies on student expectations reveal significant interest in the employment of social media as class assignments. In a Pew Internet and American Life study, Smith, Rainie, and Zickuhr found that undergraduate students reported positive experiences with new and engaging technologies when employed as tools needed for the completion of assignments.[9] While many students rate faculty knowledge and subject expertise as the most crucial elements in learning, multidisciplinary student expectation studies suggest that Web 2.0 technologies enable a stronger comprehension of subject material and provide a wider range of content that can be more concisely analyzed.[10]

A growing number of college professors are seeking innovative, meaningful, and relevant ways to both improve and enhance classroom instruction.[11] The increasing level of implementation, moreover, can result in a discovery of new methods and applications that enable both the student and the teacher to learn and grow.[12] This approach is critical to improving college teaching as conveyed by Sternadori and Littau's study that surveyed 359 university journalism and mass communication professors who featured either Twitter or blog assignments in their instruction.[13] The researchers discovered that the inclusion of social media as course tools led to "enhanced communication between faculty and students," which prompted higher semester-grade point averages and positive student evaluations. These findings follow the work of Tiryakioglu and Erzurum who asserted that the use of social networking in teaching improves student problem-solving skills and increases faculty credibility.[14]

A blending of fundamentally established instructive assignments with the focused use of Web 2.0 technologies, such as social media, can yield a fresh approach for teachers. Guy's extensive review of how college teachers implement social media within instructional practice supported this point.[15] Guy found that social media was often used to support faculty lectures and enhance student discussions in project-based collaborative online venues. Furthermore, the melding of learning actions with the increasingly familiar technology tools of today encourages an engaging environment for learners.

Many college students hold a working understanding and relationship with social media and blogs. Yet some of those students have little training regarding the myriad possibilities, such as information gathering and research collation, of the technology.[16] In particular, blogs are increasingly useful learning tools with comprehensive curricular applications.

These pedagogical blogs can effectively work in numerous disciplines, such as political science, art, history, business, and communication studies. Beyond the apparent utility of blogs within a single major curriculum, the multidisciplinary role of academic blogs has immense potential to propel discovery for collaborative teams of students from varied backgrounds.

Blogs are a growing way of communicating individual political thought. Relying on networked expression, blogs enable a diversity of reflection, knowledge, and disclosure to be voiced on political issues.[17] As with websites, individuals exchange images and accounts of events happening to others in remote locations. This action can raise global awareness in a sharing, revealing manner.

Blogs are useful tools for conducting beginning research capabilities. Kjeliberg posited that blogging for research purposes supports creativity and provides a feeling of being connected to one's work as a researcher.[18] In their study of research blog assignments used in multiple undergraduate courses, Halic, Lee, Paulus, and Spence concluded that a student's use of blogs for research purposes increased retention, supported reflection, built a sense of community, prompted collaboration, and harnessed a greater understanding of new concepts.[19] All of these attributes are prized outcomes for any collegiate course experience.

This worldview is accentuated by the mastery of communication technologies that can be used for the deep research of other cultures. For example, Beise incorporated social media blogs in a Global Information Systems Management course that focused on researching how social media are used by businesses in other nations.[20] Moreover, social media as research aids are increasingly being adopted and accepted in academia. Nackerud and Scaletta suggested that blogs are especially useful as "forms of academic production" and as "a vehicle for scholars to become public intellectuals," which is a primary goal for an advanced study.[21] Mortensen and Walker related that the process "to blog is an activity similar in many ways to the work of the researcher," where a mass of data is filtered, selected for relevance, commented upon, analyzed for significance, and connected to research themes.[22] Clearly, blogs are an effective source for the implementation and revelation of research findings.

Therefore, the body of literature suggests that the collegiate learning environment is extremely fertile for the inception of a course that uses the Internet and social media as impactful research and communication tools.

THE GLOBAL IMPACT OF SOCIAL MEDIA COURSE

Based upon the aforementioned literature review on learning and social media, this section details a case study that highlights a college course that compels students to use social media tools to discover how global citizens create, filter, and consume cultural, social, and political messages. More critically, this section displays a pedagogical approach that highlights informed inquiry, data gathering, and descriptive analysis that results in a web-based research project.

The motivation to create a course that extends the technological and worldview abilities of college students formed the rationale for the inception and design of the Global Impact of Social Media (GISM) course at a small midwestern liberal arts university. The fundamental intent of designing a course that studied the global influence of social media was to move students beyond traditional areas of research and into a new realm of knowledge generation. Another desired goal was to increase students' comprehension of the internal and external applications of Web 2.0 technology within diverse countries and cultures that could potentially both broaden and deepen perspective. A potential outcome might accent learners' abilities to communicate with others on a global scale to expand values, attitudes, and beliefs about other cultures. In this respect, the course could function as the framework of a digital bridge—one that spanned cultural awareness, political applications, and linked learners to increased and varied methods of social media use.

GISM was designed to serve all university student populations as an upper-division social science core elective. The course design called for an overview and examination of social media's history and how it changed the way society and individuals communicate on a global scale. The course's intent was to focus on relevant media and cultural theories in order to better understand how social media shapes and restructures interpersonal and mass communication on a global level.

Learning a new technology, such as computer tablets or smartphones, is not as critical as comprehending the technology's methods and impact upon individuals and groups. This concept fueled the reasoning that social media's impact could be more important than the mastery of any Web 2.0 technology and it required deeper academic inspection. As part of the course content, students actively engaged in the use of Facebook, Twitter, and blogs as part of the learning process and conducted their own textual and content analysis studies of global and cultural social media usage. The assessment phase centered on a collaborative web-based research project, an individual capstone project that ascertained social media's impact upon a specific domain, such as political knowledge, within another country, and a cumulative in-class presentation of findings.

IMPLEMENTATION OF THE COURSE

The purpose of this section is to present and to discuss the implementation of a college course designed to assist students in understanding the global influences and regional political uses of social media. It provides an overview of course design elements, teaching aspects, and student online research techniques. The section is intended to suggest a pedagogical approach that can be considered for other college courses that use and analyze social media tools to examine the impact of Web 2.0 technologies upon cultural, political, or social aspects.

During the first meeting of the class, students were asked about their uses of social media. The responses elicited further questioning on their understanding of global issues and how social media fit into the exploration of those issues. Subsequent discussion led to an initial examination of cultural, political, and media theories that helped explain how social media could both reflect and report culture. It was important to introduce historical, social, cultural, and political issues to give a context to the subjects that would be researched. During the first two weeks of the class, instructor-led lectures and online search strategies were the primary components of the course. This intent was to provide a solid foundation of rich theories and proven research techniques that students could refer to during the research and analysis phases of the course.

A detailed series of lectures revolved around the various uses of social media in the BRIC (Brazil, Russia, India, China) countries. As rising economic global powers, these nations offer excellent examples of diverse cultural, social, and political constructions. The lectures included PowerPoint presentations illustrated by statistical graphics, maps, hyperlinks, and audio and video stories. As multimedia components, the lecture PowerPoints aided the general instruction, guided the small group in-class discussion sessions, and served as learning archives for later study and reflection.

DISCUSSION POINTS ASSIGNMENT

After the grounding of cultural, media, research, and technology theories was instilled, a concerted effort was made by the instructor to enhance the analytical ability of GISM students by employing strategies tailored to active learning. This preparation was included to shift the class from domination of teacher lectures and toward more experiential learning activities.

To promote further engagement during class sessions, the required text, *The Digital Divide* by Mark Bauerlein, offered excellent articles on the pros and cons of the Internet and social media.[23] On days when a previous article reading was assigned, students were required to complete a Discussion Points handout that illustrated interpretations of key concepts and themes from the article. In the first 10–15 minutes of the class, students described their impressions. The observations were noted on the board in a circular graphic form. Students, then, were placed in small groups, usually with four members, to ascertain the links among these concepts and discuss how these interpretations fit into the global uses of social media. The final part of the class was devoted to group explanations of the findings. The intent of this technique was to deepen their learning by observation, discussion, analysis, and presentation methods.

As noted earlier, students were required to read assigned chapters and complete a brief Discussion Points analysis for in-class reflection. However, this was not the only purposeful use of the Discussion Points assignment. At the beginning of the lecture-oriented class meetings, students offered their Discussion Points observations regarding the assigned book article. This served as an effective transition to the topic lecture. In fact, it was a form of icebreaker, where the instructor could focus on a few essential concepts raised by the students' responses. Not only did this exercise birth well-constructed, insightful, and elaborated concepts, it also enabled students to learn about the interests, beliefs, and comprehension levels of classmates.

FACEBOOK ANALYSIS ASSIGNMENT

The initial graded inquiry learning experience for the students was centered on a critical review of a Facebook page. Facebook is the world's most popular social media site, and most of the GISM students had individual Facebook pages. They were, however, unfamiliar with accessing social media with the intent to ascertain the viability, strengths, and shortcomings needed for conducting a deeper and more effective research endeavor. To assist their understanding of advanced social media research techniques and assessment outcomes, each student was given a general checklist that displayed key elements from an instructor-led Facebook analysis. The in-class analysis served as a model for students' subsequent research. The pedagogical importance of modeling was to provide essential cues and create a foundation for research discovery methods that would be used on each course assignment. Students then selected a political Facebook site, used the basic checklist, modified and developed additional evaluation criteria, wrote a research report, and reported on the findings during an in-class presentation.

Overall, students produced studies that encapsulated a broader range of global understanding, such as Facebook's use for a variety of nations' government, business, religious, tourism, and political domains. In course evaluations, a majority of students cited that this project helped them find their ground on introductory social media research techniques and that they employed knowledge learned here to more efficiently research subsequent assignments.

The Facebook analysis demonstrated a clear focus on learning research outcomes rather than performing mere techniques. The identification of emerging patterns in this exercise revealed a few key qualities of social media literacy, such as changing cultural norms, the perception of mediated information, and the production of ideas. This experience permitted a stronger, and more detailed, analysis of social media's global influence. It prepared students for the next phase of the course that involved the creation of a website based on the research findings of small collaborative groups. Moreover, the Facebook research project promoted critical thinking attributes, as shown by students' in-class research presentations and course evaluation statements. Critical thinking is a central component of the pedagogical outcomes within higher education.[24] Teaching students critical thinking skills builds confidence in both individual and group endeavors. Critical thinking abilities assist the development of responsible citizenship and global awareness qualities. Essentially, it generates careful evaluation of complex issues and permits objectivity and informed reflection.[25]

GLOBAL SOCIAL MEDIA RESEARCH ASSIGNMENT

A social media research assignment was used as an introductory information-gathering element for the subsequent global social media project. This component was installed to keep students on a focused path toward information gathering and propel a discovery of unique global social media types. The project called for a full-scale evaluation of an international or regional social media application, such as Twitter, Renren, Weibo, or VK. Students selected a topic from an instructor-prepared list, or they were permitted to add an international site that was relatively new. After the selection phase, the instructor provided a model of information-gathering techniques and displayed a few regional sites for review and ascertainment. Students were given two weeks to research and write reports about the nature and applications of the sites. Specific detail was addressed as to how the social media services related to various disciplines (education, political science, communication studies, journalism, and business). Data relating to the inception, history, site intent, and intended users were collected and evaluated. This discovery of information about these social media sites provided an archive of data about the national orientation, the specific focus, and the utility of each site. The archive then could be used as a foundation in conducting further research for the small project team assignment.

PROJECT RESEARCH TEAMS

The next inquiry learning experience required the formation of small project teams that would research how social media were used in a specific country or region. The domain focus could be very specific (Political Social Media in India) or very general (Social Media Use in Europe). The teams would produce a social media blog site that would visually, aurally, and textually represent the scope of the study. The projects were evaluated on the following criteria: organization, originality, technical quality, research depth and diversity, and communication effectiveness.

Designing and implementing collaborative projects in a collegiate setting can be very problematic. Installing collaborative teams in a class constituted of diverse academic majors, who tended to be strangers, was daunting. How to form bonded teams that could effectively communicate and share workloads was a paramount question.

By listening and observing others in the early-semester Discussion Points class sessions, students vetted classmates and gravitated to peers with shared interests and abilities. This self-selection process made the task of team formation much easier and quicker than expected. They were now ready to collaborate, research, and produce global social media research blogs and websites.

GLOBAL SOCIAL MEDIA RESEARCH ASSIGNMENT

This section explores the role of websites and blogs as valuable class assignment platforms for the establishment of a global research effort. As described in the literature review, Internet-based sites allow for descriptive multimodal digital narratives complete with an archive of autobiographical writing, video, audio, still images, and hyperlinks.

The GISM collaborative research and individual global social media projects needed a digital home to serve as a repository of findings. The powerful yet versatile qualities of websites and blogs were well suited for this dynamic. A student's academic use of these digital technologies presented a valuable venue for creating, sharing, storing, and accessing course assignments and a helpful guide for student evaluation purposes. Moreover, the creation of multiple projects, both group and individual, for the course needed to be both economically efficient and easy to master. Blogs and websites were low- or no-cost alternatives to having a personal website. With Blogger, WordPress, Weebly, and Wix, no fee for a domain name was required. Moreover, the open source toolware was designed for those without advanced web design or programming skills; yet, each software company provided quick set-up, ample professional look templates, and intuitive menu displays.

Students were required to set up a site, design a professional look from provided templates, create text posts, and devise and generate multiple relevant still images and hyperlinks to sites for additive content. The projects were evaluated on content, quality, clarity, depth of research, and organization. An important feature was to stress the scholarly value of effective research and how the site could add to the body of knowledge regarding social media's global impact.

It was essential to devote class time to explaining the process of creating blogs and websites while reviewing some excellent examples. As a practice, students were asked to find a research website, review its basic components, and report on its qualities. Further class time was allocated to the reexamination of essential research components, the electronic adaptation of research findings, and the process of creating concise summaries. The remainder of in-class time was delegated to the laboratory phase of individual student experimentation with the software and the eventual planning and execution by the research teams. By using these learning sessions within many classes, the students acclimated to the software's capabilities in a swift manner while efficiently planning, designing, delegating responsibilities, and researching. The instructor offered help when solicited; however, students asked fewer questions once a mastery of the software was achieved.

The GISM course featured a structured timeframe for project deadlines. The course design called for multiple achievement mileposts during the semester. At the quarter semester mark, all students needed to form teams for the group research project. During the midterm week, students selected topics for the social media research assignment. At week 10, topics were finalized for the global research project. When the semester was at week 12, a working site with hyperlinks to one's region of study, a title, and a few posts relating to the topic served as the focal point for a student and instructor critique meeting. During the last week of classes, students presented their global research sites and findings to classmates and the instructor for additional feedback. The refined sites were then formally presented to the class during the assigned course's finals session.

COURSE SUMMARY

In this course, students employed problem-based learning attributes, as they investigated challenging issues and topics, inquired about the scope of social media's impact, and garnered understanding about global contexts. The learning experience was relevant, timely, and interesting. The experience was deemed significant in that it built knowledge through the creation of research artifacts. The artifacts for this course were the collaborative and individual research-oriented websites and blogs.

While the projects in this course featured a diversity of topics, some of the research teams chose to investigate aspects of either the Arab Spring or political activism in other countries. One group designed an impressive website that featured graphics, statistical lists, numerous hyperlinks, written narratives, and originally produced audio interviews with Arab students. Another group researched the role of social media control in Russia. Their site looked at VK, the largest Russian social media application, and the Putin government's economic and political ideological command of VK.

In course evaluations, a majority of students reported that the social media projects, both group-oriented and individual versions, greatly assisted their knowledge both about other countries and about social media research fundamentals. They felt that the sites facilitated a new way to look at research—one that was described as being "realistic" and "enjoyable" to use. Students stated that the discovery of new and unique regional forms of social media presented an opportunity to broaden their understanding that the Web 2.0 technology is much more than Twitter or Facebook. Furthermore, students expressed that the experience caused them to realize how much they did not know about other countries' use of social media and appreciate what they discovered during their research.

Responses to the politically oriented research sites drew upon both censorship controls and activism influences themes. Many students expressed that they were unaware of political structures in other countries and cited the specific experience of viewing peer sites were "eye-opening" and "shocking" to them. Others described the impact of the global political use of social media as "real, enlightening, and important" to understanding how the Internet affects everyone's life. All of the students agreed that the experience of collaborating with students from other disciplines, especially political science majors, enhanced their appreciation of the topic.

In retrospect, the use of social media tools to research the impact of global social media permitted the expansion of student learning beyond the walls of the classroom, as students planned, researched, collaborated, wrote, and learned about global activities. The selected student project sites listed below provide a cogent illustration of the effective introductory scholarly work produced in the GISM course.

The experiential education realized in these sites was a valuable additive to each student's intellectual and personal growth. The semester-long improvement, as witnessed first person by this instructor, depicted qualities such as researching, writing, information analysis, and social media technology mastery that can best be comprehended by viewing these final works. Of particular interest to faculty who wish to implement similar projects into a course is the integrated use of information graphics, videos, and web links to support student textual summaries. This multimedia approach, with its blend of verbal and visual acuity, presents a useful alternative to conventional undergraduate written research papers, and it conveys a method that can be integral to displaying modern college students' higher-level understanding of visual and new media data.

CONCLUSION

This chapter examined the key steps required for the enactment of a course that uses social media to study Web 2.0 engagement in other cultures. Examples drawn from this course served as both a foundation of pedagogy and a call to further inquiry. As the use of Web 2.0 technologies and digital devices become more and more prevalent in higher education, faculty can discover new ways to incorporate social media applications into the curriculum and ensure third millennium educational quality and relevance for students of all disciplines.

Effective scholarship is paramount to learning. The importance of inquiry and subsequent discovery cannot be overestimated as a cogent goal for students in higher education courses. The use and mastery of new technologies, such as social media, lend credence to enhanced scholarship. In the GISM course, students combined their growing research acumen with creative constructions of social media sites. They became independent learners when they developed the ability to critically judge their own work and gauge the efforts of peers. They learned about the social lives, political thoughts, and beliefs of people from other countries as they tested the communication innovations at their disposal. They chose to examine how other nations use social media for political and civic participation purposes. Here the digital devices often used for entertainment purposes became scholarly tools that constructed an informed link that increased global awareness and improved experiential understanding.

NOTES

1. TNS Digital Life, "Global Digital Life Research Project Reveals Major Changes in Online Behavior," accessed February 15, 2015, http://2010.tnsdigitallife.com/.

2. Simon Cottle, "Media and the Arab Uprisings of 2011: Research Notes," *Journalism* 12, no. 5 (2011): 647–659.

3. Yong Zhao, "Preparing Globally Competent Teachers: A New Imperative for Teacher Education," *Journal of Teacher Education* 61, no. 5 (2010): 422–431.

4. Jenny Waycott et al., "Digital Divides? Student and Staff Perceptions of Information and Communication Technologies," *Computers & Education* 54 (2010): 1202–1211.

5. Erst Carmichael and Helen Farrell, "Evaluation of Effectiveness of Online Resources in Developing Student Critical Thinking: Review of Literature and Case Study of a Critical Thinking Online Site," *Journal of University Teaching & Learning Practice* 9, no. 1 (2012). http://ro.now.edu.au/jutlp/vol9/issu1/4.

6. Joanne Lisosky, "The Global Is Local: Planting the Seeds for International Media Education," *Journal of Media Education* 2, no. 2 (2011): 19–27.

7. Rajalakshari Kanagavel and Chandrasekharen Velayutham, "Impact of Social Networking on College Students: A Comparative Study in India and the Netherlands," *International Journal of Virtual Communities and Social Networking* 2, no. 3 (2010): 55–67; Radihka Parameswaran, "The Rise of China and India: Promising New Teaching and Research Directions for Global Media Studies," *Global Media and Communication* 6, no. 3 (2010): 285–290.

8. Jose Van Dijick, *The Culture of Connectivity: A Critical History of Social Media* (New York: Oxford, 2013), 9.

   9. Gadi Wolsfeld, Elad Segev, and Tamir Sheafer, "Social Media and the Arab Spring: Politics Comes First," *The International Journal of Press/Politics* 18, no. 2 (2013): 115–137.

   10. Aaron Smith, Lee Rainie, and Kathryn Zickuhr, "College Students and Technology," *Pew Internet and American Life Project*, accessed May 23, 2015, http//www.pewinternet.org/Reports/2011/College-students-and-technology/Report/Findings.aspx.

   11. Paul Umbach and Matthew Wawrzynski, "Faculty Do Matter: The Role of College Faculty in Student Learning and Engagement," *Research in Higher Education* 44, no. 2 (2005): 153–184.

   12. Chris Jones, "A New Generation of Learners? The Net Generation and Digital Natives," *Learning, Media and Technology* 35, no. 4 (2010): 365–368; Glenn Bowen et al., "Listening to the Voices of Today's Undergraduates: Implications for Teaching and Learning," *Journal of Scholarship of Teaching and Learning* 11, no. 3 (2011): 21–33; Paul Tess, "The Role of Social Media in Higher Education Classes (Real and Virtual)—A Literature Review," *Computers in Human Behavior* 29, no. 5 (2013): 60–68.

   13. Miglena Sternadori and Jeremy Littau, "With a Little Help from My Friends: Motivations and Patterns in Social Media Use and Their Influences on Perceptions of Teaching Possibilities," *Journal of Media Education* 3, no. 2 (2012): 5–20.

   14. Filiz Tirakioglu and Funda Erzurum, "Use of Social Networks as an Educational Tool," *Contemporary Educational Technology* 2, no. 2 (2011): 135–150.

   15. Retta Guy, "The Use of Social Media for Academic Practice: A Review of Literature," *Kentucky Journal of Higher Education Policy and Practice* 1, no. 2 (2012). http://uknowledge.uky.edu/kjhepp/vol1/iss2/7.

   16. Allison Head and Michael Eisenberg, "Truth Be Told: How College Students Evaluate and Use Information for the Digital Age," *Project Information Literacy Progress Report*, accessed November 3, 2014, http://www.projectinfolit.org/; Janna Bouwma-Gearhart and James Bess, "The Transformative Potential of Blogs for Research in Higher Education," *Journal of Higher Education* 83, no. 2 (2012): 249–275.

   17. Stephan Coleman, "Blogs and the New Politics of Listening," *Political Quarterly* 76, no. 2 (2005): 272–280.

   18. Sara Kjeliberg, "I Am a Blogging Researcher; Motivations for Blogging in a Scholarly Context," *First Monday* 15, no. 8 (2010). http://firstmonday.org/ojs/index.php/fm/article/view/2962/2280.

   19. Olivia Halic et al., "To Blog or Not to Blog: Student Perceptions of Blog Effectiveness for Learning in a College-Level Course," *The Internet and Higher Education* 13, no. 4 (2010): 206–213.

   20. Catherine Beise, "Global Media: Incorporating Videocams and Blogs in a Global IS Management Course," *Information Systems Education Journal* 4, no. 74 (2006): 1–8.

   21. Shane Nackerud and Kurtis Scaletta, "Blogging in the Academy," in *Using Emerging Technologies to Enhance Student Engagement*, eds. Reynol Junco and Dianne Timm (San Francisco: Jossey-Bass, 2008), 71–88.

   22. Torill Mortensen and Jill Walker, "Blogging Thoughts: Personal Publication as an Online Research Tool," in *Researching ICTs in Context*, ed. Andrew Morrison (Oslo, Norway: Intermedia, 2002), 249–287.

   23. Mark Bauerlein, ed., *The Digital Divide: Arguments for and against Facebook, Google, Texting, and the Age of Social Networking* (New York: Tarcher, 2011).

24. Linda Behar-Horenstein and Lian Niu, "Teaching Critical Thinking Skills in Higher Education: A Review of the Literature," *Journal of College Teaching and Learning* 8, no. 2 (2011): 25–42.

25. Alison Burke, "Group Work: How to Use Groups Effectively," *The Journal of Effective Teaching* 11, no. 2 (2011): 87–95.

BIBLIOGRAPHY

Bauerlein, Mark. *The Digital Divide: Arguments for and against Facebook, Google, Texting, and the Age of Social Networking.* New York: Tarcher, 2011.

Behar-Horenstein, Linda and Lian Niu. "Teaching Critical Thinking Skills in Higher Education: A Review of the Literature." *Journal of College Teaching and Learning* 8, no. 2 (2001): 25–42.

Beise, Catherine. "Global Media: Incorporating Videocams and Blogs in a Global IS Management Class." *Information Systems Education Journal* 4, no. 74 (2006): 1–8.

Bouwma-Gearhart, Jana, and James Bess. "The Transformative Potential of Blogs for Research in Higher Education." *Journal of Higher Education* 8, no. 32 (2012): 249–275.

Bowen, Glenn, Carol Burton, Christopher Cooper, Laura Cruz, Anna McFadden, Chesney Reich, and Melissa Wargo. "Listening to the Voices of Today's Undergraduates: Implications for Teaching and Learning." *Journal of Scholarship of Teaching and Learning* 11, no. 3 (2011): 21–33.

Burke, Alison. "Group Work: How to Use Groups Effectively." *The Journal of Effective Teaching* 11, no. 2 (2011): 87–95.

Carmichael, Erst, and Helen Farrell. "Evaluation of Effectiveness of Online Resources in Developing Student Critical Thinking: Review of Literature and Case Study of a Critical Thinking Online Site." *Journal of University Teaching & Learning Practice* 9, no. 1 (2012). http://ro.now,edu.au/jutlp/vol9/issu1/4.

Coleman, Stephan. "Blogs and the New Politics of Listening." *Political Quarterly* 76, no. 2 (2005): 272–280.

Cottle, Simon. "Media and the Arab Uprisings of 2011: Research Notes." *Journalism* 12, no. 5 (2011): 647–659.

Guy, Retta. "The Use of Social Media for Academic Practice: A Review of Literature." *Kentucky Journal of Higher Education Policy and Practice* 1, no. 2 (2012). http://uknowledge.uky.edu/kjhepp/vol1/iss2/7.

Halic, Oliva, Debra Lee, Trena Paulus, and Marsha Spence. "To Blog or Not to Blog: Student Perceptions of Blog Effectiveness for Learning in a College-level Course." *The Internet and Higher Education* 13, no. 4 (2010): 206–213.

Head, Allison, and Michael Eisenberg. "Truth Be Told: How College Students Evaluate and Use Information in the Digital Age." *Project Information Literacy Progress Report*, accessed November 3, 2014, http://www.project infolit.org/.

Jones, Chris. "A New Generation of Learners? The Net Generation and Digital Natives." *Learning, Media and Technology* 35, no. 4 (2010): 365–368.

Kanagavel, Rajalakshari, and Chandrasekharen Velayutham. "Impact of Social Networking on College Students: A Comparative Study in India and the Netherlands." *International Journal of Virtual Communities and Social Networking* 2, no. 3 (2010): 55–67.

Kjeliberg, Sara. "I Am a Blogging Researcher: Motivations for Blogging in a Scholarly Context." *First Monday* 15, no. 8 (2010). http://firstmonday.org/ojs/index.php/fm/article/view/2962/2280.

Lisosky, Joanne. "The Global Is Local: Planting the Seed for International Media Education." *Journal of Media Education* 2, no. 2 (2011): 19–27.

Mortensen, Torill, and Jill Walker. "Blogging Thoughts: Personal Publication as an Online Research Tool." In *Researching ICTs in Context*, edited by Andrew Morrison, 249–287. Oslo, Norway: Intermedia, 2002.

Nackerud, Shane, and Kurtis Scaletta. "Blogging in the Academy." In *Using Emerging Technologies to Enhance Student Engagement*, edited by Reynol Junco and Dianne Timms, 71–88. San Francisco, CA: Jossey-Bass, 2008.

Parameswaran, Radihka. "The Rise of China and India: Promising New Teaching and Research Directions for Global Media Studies." *Global Media and Communication* 6, no. 3 (2010): 285–290.

Smith, Aaron, Lee Rainie, and Kathyrn Zickuhr. "College Students and Technology." *Pew Internet and American Life Project*, accessed May 23, 2015, http://www.pewinternet.org/Reports/2011/College-students-and-technology/Report/Findings.aspx.

Sternadori, Miglena, and Jeremy Littau. "With a Little Help from My Friends: Motivations and Patterns in Social Media Use and Their Influence on Perceptions of Teaching Possibilities." *Journal of Media Education* 3, no. 2 (2012): 5–20.

Tess, Paul. "The Role of Social Media in Higher Education Classes (Real and Virtual)—A Literature Review." *Computers in Human Behavior* 29, no. 5 (2012): 60–68.

Tiryakioglu, Filiz, and Funda Erzurum. "Use of Social Networks as an Educational Tool." *Contemporary Educational Technology* 2, no. 2 (2011): 135–150.

TNS Digital Life. "Global Digital Life Research Project Reveals Major Changes in Online Behavior." Accessed February 15, 2015, http://2010.tnsdigitallife.com/.

Umbach, Paul, and Matthew Wawrzynski. "Faculty Do Matter: The Role of College Faculty in Student Learning and Engagement." *Research in Higher Education* 44, no. 2 (2005): 153–184.

Van Dijick, Jose. *The Culture of Connectivity: A Critical History of Social Media*. New York: Oxford, 2013.

Waycott, Jenny, Sue Bennett, Gregor Kennedy, Barney Dalgamo, and Kathleen Gray "Digital Divides? Student and Staff Perceptions of Information and Communication Technologies." *Computers & Education* 54 (2010): 1202–1211.

Wolfsfeld, Gadi, Elad Segev, and Tamir Shaefer. "Social Media and the Arab Spring: Politics Comes First." *The International Journal of Press/Politics* 18, no. 2 (2013): 115–137.

Zhao, Yong. "Preparing Globally Competent Teachers: A New Imperative for Teacher Education." *Journal of Teacher Education* 61, no. 5 (2010): 422–431.

About the Editor and Contributors

GLENN W. RICHARDSON JR. is a professor of Political Science at Kutztown University of Pennsylvania. His research has been published in the *Harvard International Journal of Press/Politics, Journal of Communication, Political Communication, Rhetoric and Public Affairs, American Communication Journal, Political Research Quarterly, New Media and Society,* and *Poroi*. He is the author of the chapter on political advertising in *Communication in U.S. Elections: New Agendas*, and of "Visual Storytelling and the Competition for Political Meaning in Political Advertising and News in Campaign 2000" that earned the 2002 *American Communication Journal* Article of the Year Award. He is also the author of *Pulp Politics: How Political Advertising Tells the Stories of American Politics*. He is the coauthor (with G. R. Boynton) of "Re-framing Audience: Co-Motion at #SOTU" in *Political Campaigning in the Information Age* (2014), "The Language of Threat in Our Political Discourse" in the *Handbook of Research on Political Activism in the Information Age* (2014), and "Agenda Setting in the Twenty-First Century" in *New Media and Society* (2016).

BERNADETTE BARKER-PLUMMER (PhD, 1997, University of Pennsylvania) is a professor of Media Studies at the University of San Francisco where she teaches Media Theory, Gender and Media, Media and Politics, and other media courses. Her research interests are in communication, social movements, and social change, and she has published work on women's movements and media, gender and war news, social movements and new media technologies, and transgender identity in media, among other topics. Some of her work can be found in *Critical Studies in*

Media Communication, Feminist Media Studies, Journalism Quarterly, Journalism Monographs, and *Peace Review*.

DAVE BARKER-PLUMMER is a senior research scientist at Stanford University's Center for the Study of Language and Information. He holds a PhD from the Department of Artificial Intelligence at Edinburgh University. He is the author of papers on automated reasoning, reasoning with diagrams, and architectures for heterogeneous reasoning. Dave has taught computer science and logic at Stanford, Swarthmore College, and Duke University.

THOMAS BREIDEBAND is a dual PhD candidate in English and American Studies at Georgia State University in Atlanta, USA, and at Johannes Gutenberg-University in Mainz, Germany. His academic work lies at the intersection of new media, the rhetoric of discourse communities, and political communication. His research has been published in *Technoculture* and he presented at meetings of the Association of Internet Researchers. Since 2014, Mr. Breideband has been holding an innovation fellowship at Georgia State University where he is working toward the innovation of research techniques and pedagogical practice to meet the demands of a twenty-first-century academic environment.

GINA MASULLO CHEN, PhD, is an assistant professor in the School of Journalism at the University of Texas at Austin. Chen's research focuses on the online conversation and how it influences social, civic, and political engagement and the larger public discourse. She is coeditor of *Scandal in a Digital Age* (2016/Palgrave Macmillan) and author of *Online Incivility and Public Debate: Nasty Talk* (forthcoming in 2017/Palgrave Macmillan). Before becoming a professor, she spent 20 years as a print and online newspaper reporter and editor.

ANGELA M. CIRUCCI is an assistant professor of communication studies at Kutztown University. She received her PhD from Temple University's School of Media and Communication. As a researcher and theorist, Angela explores social network sites and the ways in which their structures and affordances influence identifications. She is particularly interested in the burgeoning anti-anonymous culture that normalizes visibility and the related implications for marginalized communities. For more information, visit www.angelacirucci.com and follow Angela on Twitter @angelacirucci.

AMBER DAVISSON is an assistant professor of communication at Keene State College. She is the author of *Lady Gaga and the Remaking of Celebrity*

Culture (McFarland, 2013) and the coeditor of *Controversies in Digital Rhetoric* (Bloomsbury, 2016). Her interdisciplinary scholarship on identity, politics, and digital technology has appeared in such journals as *Rhetoric & Public Affairs*, *Journal of Media & Digital Literacy*, *Journal of Visual Literacy*, and the *American Communication Journal*.

BRUCE E. DRUSHEL, PhD, is an associate professor in the Department of Media, Journalism, and Film at Miami University. He currently serves as vice-president for Programming and Area Chairs of the Popular Culture Association/American Culture Association and chairs its Gay, Lesbian & Queer Studies area. He is editor of the book *Fan Phenomenon: Star Trek*, was coeditor of the books *Queer Identities/Political Realities* and *Ethics of Emerging Media*, and is coeditor of the forthcoming book *Sontag and Beyond: New Perspectives on the Camp Aesthetic*. His work also has appeared in *Journal of Homosexuality*, *Journal of Media Economics*, *European Financial Journal*, *Techno Culture*, *Journal of American Culture*, *Reconstruction*, and *FemSpec*, and in books addressing free speech and social networks, free speech and 9/11, media in the Caribbean, C-SPAN as a pedagogical tool, LGBT persons and online media, minority sexualities and non-Western cultures, and AIDS and popular culture. He is founding coeditor of the journal *Queer Studies in Media & Popular Culture* from Intellect. He recently edited a special issue of *Journal of Homosexuality* on AIDS and Culture and coedited a special issues of *Reconstruction: Studies in Contemporary Culture* and *Journal of American Culture*.

BOBBIE FOSTER has a master's degree in journalism from the University of Arkansas, Fayetteville. Her studies focus on the visual framing of candidates in political memes. She works as the assistant director of the Center for Ethics in Journalism at the University of Arkansas, where she also acts as a journalism instructor. Foster's background is in multimedia and print journalism, including the production of an award-winning documentary short. She continues to work as a freelance writer and copy editor. While in graduate school, she owned and operated a small podcasting network in Northwest Arkansas. Other research interests include media ethics, citizen journalism, bio politics, and humor studies.

CANDICE LANIUS is a PhD candidate in the Department of Communication and Media at Rensselaer Polytechnic Institute and currently serves as a communications fellow for the Alliance of Digital Humanities Organizations. As a data sociologist, she studies how big social data and ubiquitous data collection are changing daily life. She is cochair of the Research Data Alliance's interest group on Ethics and Social Aspects of Data and a member of the Big Data, Ethics, and Society Network.

KEITH MASSIE is an assistant professor in the Department of Communication Studies at Kutztown University. He has published research in media history, media effects, media ecology, video games, and Lacanian psychoanalysis. His primary focus is on representations of various social signifiers within mediated communication.

DAVID McCOY is the chair and assistant professor of Journalism and Digital Media at Ashland University. Before his teaching career, he was an EMMY award-winning television producer-director for educational and public broadcasting in Ohio. He has published numerous scholarly articles in the *Journal of Media Education*, *Journal of Language and Social Psychology*, *Global Media Journal*, and *Mobile Media and Communication*. His areas of research specialization are social media use, digital media teaching, and television documentary production.

PAROMITA PAIN, a former journalist with *The Hindu National Newspaper* in India, researches citizen media, civic participation, and gender issues in the news. After graduating from the University of Southern California, she is now a PhD student in the Department of Journalism at the University of Texas at Austin. Her research papers have been presented at various conferences such as the Association for Education in Journalism and Mass Communication, American Association for Public Opinion Research, International Communication Association, and International Association for Media and Communication Research.

SARA STRAUB is a PhD candidate in the Department of Communication at the University of Oklahoma. Her research focuses on the intersection of sport, media, and the public with an emphasis on identity cultivation and meaning making.

CINDY S. VINCENT is an assistant professor at Salem State University in Media Studies and Public Relations. Her research focuses on the power of civic media for social change within marginalized populations. She also investigates the use of dissent in democratic participation for negotiation of political power and social change. Cindy received her PhD in communication from the University of Oklahoma, MA in communication, and BA in journalism from California State University, Sacramento.

LAURA WILLIAMS is an award-winning speech writer and political ghostwriter, running a small strategic communications firm located in Atlanta, Georgia. She holds bachelor's degrees in Political Communication and in Writing from Susquehanna University, a master's in writing from Johns Hopkins University, and is currently an Advanced Teaching Fellow and doctoral candidate in rhetoric and composition at Georgia

State University. After years of writing speeches and providing lobbying and campaign support in Washington, DC, she returned to academia to study the intersections of digital rhetoric, critical thinking, argument, and political advocacy. Her dissertation (in progress) compares the potential of crowd-funding platforms to empower "clicktivist" rhetorical activism to enact performative political change in the era of Citizens' United. When not chained to a keyboard, Laura plays team trivia, participates in lively debates (occasionally with willing opponents), volunteers for a sexual assault crisis center, and covets other people's books.

JASON ZENOR is an assistant professor of Communication Studies and pre-law advisor at State University of New York—Oswego. He teaches courses in media law, media industries, and politics and media. He has a juris doctorate and master's in public administration from the University of South Dakota. He also has an MA in media studies from Syracuse University. His research interests include government speech, employee speech, and the free flow of information. He is the editor of *Parasocial Politics: Audiences, Pop Culture & Politics* (Lexington, 2014). He has published in several journals including *Communication Law & Policy*, *Nova Law Review*, and *University of Florida Journal of Law and Public Policy*. He is also a contributor to *The Encyclopedia of Social Media and Politics* (Sage/CQ Press, 2014) and *We Are What We Sell* (Praeger, 2013).

YU ZHANG teaches Communication and English at the China program of the New York Institute of Technology. His research focus is on Chinese political communication, popular discourse, and diplomatic rhetoric.

Index